Frank Exchanges

Frank
Exchanges

Letters 1959–2005 between Frank Whitbourn, theatre
authority and enthusiast, and David Wood, 'the national
children's dramatist'.

Edited by Chris Abbott

The Book Guild Ltd

First published in Great Britain in 2023 by
The Book Guild Ltd
Unit E2 Airfield Business Park,
Harrison Road, Market Harborough,
Leicestershire. LE16 7UL
Tel: 0116 2792299
www.bookguild.co.uk
Email: info@bookguild.co.uk
Twitter: @bookguild

Typeset in 12pt Minion Pro

Printed and bound by CPI Group (UK) Ltd, Croydon, CR0 4YY

ISBN 978 1915603 876

British Library Cataloguing in Publication Data.
A catalogue record for this book is available from the British Library.

For Irving Wardle, who sadly died shortly after writing the generous Preface for this book. Thank you, Irving, for being the first theatre critic to give serious consideration to my children's plays. In recent years I have so enjoyed and valued your friendship, and will much miss our Zedel lunches and chats.

DW

Acknowledgements

From the very start of our decades of corresponding, I treasured Frank Whitbourn's letters to me. I was fifteen years old when I saved his first letter, and kept every communication until Frank died nearly fifty years later. Latterly, my letters to Frank were typed and I kept copies. It was thanks to Frank's sister, Mary Wright, that I discovered that Frank had kept all my early handwritten letters. She kindly returned them to me, enabling me to collate all our exchanges. Thank you, Mary.

Thanks are also due to Frank's family, particularly David Sommerville, who encouraged me to share this correspondence. Thanks also to Christopher Lee, one of Frank's star pupils at Collyer's School, Horsham, who, like me, kept in touch with Frank over several decades.

When researching Frank's early life, I came across the name Ralph W Kerns, a young Army officer, based in Iran (Persia) for several years during the Second World War. Frank was there, working for the British Council, directing and acting in plays. Ralph played major roles in the productions, and became a lifelong friend. I'm extremely grateful to Andy Harman and John Carlo Encarnacion from the Center for American War Letters Archives at Chapman University, Orange CA, for delving into the archives and finding biographical information about Ralph Kerns, and photographs of him with Frank both on and off stage, and for allowing the material to be used in this book.

Thanks to Jane Devonald for painstakingly typing up the manuscript. Frank's handwriting is highly decorative, but occasionally tricky to interpret. Thanks too to my daughter Katherine Wood for proof reading and double-checking with admirable care – and for coming up with the apposite title!

Sincere gratitude to Irving Wardle and Rod Mengham for the Preface and the Foreword. Irving's interest in my children's theatre work, from an early stage, is much appreciated. And Rod, as a former pupil of Frank's, at Collyer's School, Horsham, offers acute insight into this special man, from a different angle.

Finally, gratitude unlimited to Chris Abbott for so patiently and skilfully navigating his way through the correspondence and editing it so sensitively. It has been a real pleasure to work with him.

David Wood

Preface by Irving Wardle

Although countless artists have paid their respects to some particular teacher who first encouraged them, these usually amount to no more than brisk thank-you notes on page three of their memoirs, and give no idea of just what the inspiring ghosts did to ignite the sacred fire. In this, as in other matters, an exception must be made for David Wood, actor, composer, director, producer, international children's dramatist, and star student of Frank Whitbourn, director of an annual residential young people's drama course in West Sussex, whose forty-five-year correspondence with Wood survives to reach a larger public in this heart-warming book.

As a mentor, Whitbourn had immaculate credentials: stage-smitten at Oxford, he went on to lengthy spells in Iran and Mexico where he acted, directed plays for the British Council and founded a British-style international school; while, back in England, he combined teaching with working for Jean Stirling Mackinlay's children's company, and for the youth theatre productions of Harcourt Williams at the Old Vic. He cannot be credited with discovering a latent talent in David Wood, for, by the time they met, Wood was already in demand as a boy magician and had a clear idea of where his future lay. What Whitbourn did supply was a most refreshing recognition of his young student's gifts and a determination to give them unconditional support; and later to act as a trusted sounding board for Wood's adult writing. From these sources, a lifelong friendship took root.

They shared the optimistic outlook of people who love their work. Obtuse critics and the Arts Council come in for a bashing from time to time; but the prevailing tone is one of appreciation and accomplishment, in which favourite writers are appraised or the problems of Wood's latest adaptation or magical effect lucidly analysed. Whenever a problem crops up, it is always taken for granted that a solution will be found.

If that makes the relationship sound too cosy, it underwent a life-changing convulsion in 1968 when Wood and his then wife Sheila Ruskin were invited to adapt Edward Lear's *The Owl and the Pussycat* as a children's play. When it opened at the Swan Theatre, Worcester, the ecstatic response of the audience was such as to convince Wood that he could not turn his back on it and limit himself to acting. Having brought a show into the West End while still an undergraduate, his acting career was flourishing, but the revelation of writing for children converted his career into a vocation. He often directed his own plays as well, and, as I observed in 1983 in *The Times*, gave children their own 'self-respecting artform'. I also dubbed him 'the national children's dramatist'.

Britain, notoriously, is the disgrace of Europe in its disregard for children's theatre, and Wood launched a crusade for it to achieve parity of talent, funding and artistic respect with the adult stage; forming his own company, Whirligig Theatre, which toured for twenty-five years and staged several of his seventy plus plays and adaptations which immeasurably enriched the juvenile repertory. For the benefit of would-be fellow practitioners, he also co-authored (with Janet Grant) a manual, *Theatre for Children*, which lays out his techniques for awakening the imagination in steps as down-to-earth as an introduction to carpentry. This is an apt approach, for Wood's plays are so well constructed that their architecture is almost visible; and what they have to say about the world is inseparably embedded in their structure. The other key factor in his work is to make the crucial adjustment of giving fantasy and reality an equal status; so that an actor can be equally a human being and a valiant rabbit or a villainous oil slick.

Both those examples – from *The See-Saw Tree* and *The Selfish Shellfish* – were also singled out by Whitbourn in a letter of 1992 with which I cannot compete for a last word: 'These are works of a very special art aimed to give pleasure to young audiences in their own right as brilliant drama. They offer development of action, characterisation, play of relationships and language. They are visually and aurally beautiful; and that should be enough for anybody's money.'

Irving Wardle, writer and theatre critic,
notably for The Times.

Foreword by Rod Mengham

Frank Exchanges has more life, more joie de vivre, than any other collection of letters I can think of. Which is hardly surprising, given the dramatis personae involved: David Wood, with his unrivalled fertility of imagination; and Frank Whitbourn, with his lifelong passion for the theatre. Frank sustained his side of the correspondence well into his nineties, but there is no abatement of enthusiasm or of clear, focused thinking. And this comes as no surprise to those who knew him. I also exchanged letters with him over a period of thirty-two years, until shortly before his death in 2005, and it staggers me to think that while he was responding in such detail to David's observations on theatre, he was also giving detailed feedback to my own reports about reading and writing poetry.

Frank was nothing if not totally dedicated to the power of words, and during four decades of teaching and their aftermath he sustained an extraordinary commitment to the pleasures and responsibilities that came with them. I first encountered his teaching in my third year at Collyer's School, the local grammar school in Horsham. But he was already an impressive figure to me, because of the panache with which he organised the drama in school, and because of his resounding baritone voice and his eloquence. The actual teaching, when it came, was genuinely riveting. As a classroom teacher, he did not need to command attention – we were all ears, and the forty-minute-long periods were absolutely too short. He was also a shrewd and energising marker, mixing ready praise with hints for improvement. Perhaps I would never have become a writer if he had not taught me when he did.

And he was also kind and generous, noting expressions of interest and following them up. When I entered the sixth form and asked him which edition of *Piers Plowman* I should buy, he said he would check up. The following week he simply handed me a brand-new copy of the Salter edition – which I still have.

But, of course, it was the drama that was most impressive. The productions were very ambitious in terms of scale: the casts were sometimes enormous, and each member of the cast had to be coached; there was often an imaginative use of music, in ways that might be quite unexpected, but always just right; the lighting was brilliantly choreographed; and when it came to the actors, Frank was brilliant at allowing those with significant speaking parts to develop their own ideas, introducing changes gradually where he saw the need to steer people in a different direction. I remember his emphasis on the actor needing to 'make sense of' the character, in ways that can't just be said, but needed to be embodied, all the time the actor is on stage. Common sense if you are a real actor, but it made all the difference if you weren't.

Perhaps the most significant aspect of Frank's teaching was the real passion with which he engaged with poetic and dramatic writing. He was a compelling reader, and it was his skill as a reader that actually persuaded many of his pupils, I think, of the significance, the importance and the necessity of literary writing. You might think it would be impossible to rouse a set of Lower Sixth Form boys to show anything but a faint interest in the archaic intricacies of Edmund Spenser's *The Faerie Queene*. But when Frank read it aloud, and then expounded its allegorical meanings, it became riveting. I remember looking forward keenly to every next instalment.

And he wasn't in it only for the duration. By which I mean, when you finally passed your A levels and left school, he didn't just forget about you. And if you wrote to him, he always wrote back. School was just the start of a conversation that he was always ready to carry on, via the theatre, or via poetry. Frank was an exceptional human being, in fact, as I believe this volume now shows.

Rod Mengham is a poet, critic and Emeritus Professor of Modern English Literature at Jesus College, Cambridge.

Prologue: 1926

Just before Christmas 1926, a schoolteacher with theatrical interests wrote to an ex-pupil, congratulating him on his part in a school play. That teacher, Claud Gurney, went on to direct stage productions professionally in the West End and elsewhere, and films in the 1930s and 1940s.

Hurstpierpoint College, Sussex
Dec 21ˢᵗ 1926

My dear 'Franny'

I am sending you a very small book in memory of our work together in Romeo. *I can't thank you enough for the way you worked at your part; that is it, which turns all one's toil into delight and makes the way so plain. The only thing that I regret is that I was not clever enough myself to make the part even better for you. But as far as I could imagine and do, you carried out to the letter and I was very pleased. Good Boy.*

I am very sad when I remember that this is my last play at Hurst but you children made it such a glorious time for me and made such a glorious success of the play itself that the glow of your success almost drowns the other feelings.

Simms has turned out a wonderful photo of you which everyone marvels at.

My dear old Boy you were magnificent and I was very proud of you. I hope that in all the coming plays in which you will star that you will go from good to better and remember a few of the things which I have tried to show you.

But now I bid thee turn again to thy Xmas dinner and have

another helping of plum pudding to keep the cold out. But be
wary lest the Devil doe urge thee to eate too much and sicknesse
come in the morning.

> *Goodbye old Boy*
> *Good luck and good wishes*
> *Always yours affect.*
> *Claud Gurney*

The affectionate tone is evocative of the age in which it was written; the addressee, Franny, was Frank Whitbourn. Frank went on to encourage and support his own students with theatrical aspirations – including David Wood, who attended drama courses led by him.

Frank Whitbourn (1910–2005)

Frank Whitbourn was educated at Hurstpierpoint and Merton College, Oxford. He taught first at Clayesmore School in Dorset, and had stage experience with Jean Sterling Mackinlay's Children's Theatre, before serving in the RAF as a flying officer. He was stationed in the Middle East before being seconded to the British Council, where he became Assistant Director of the British Institute in Tehran. During this period, he directed and acted in plays for the British Council in Persia. After several years in Persia, Frank returned to the UK in 1946. He then went to Bogota, Colombia before a longer stay in Mexico.

For three years, he was Assistant Director of the Anglo-Mexican Cultural Institute in Mexico City, where he founded a theatre that revived interest in drama among schools and colleges in the country. He taught at the National University and the National Institute of Fine Arts. He then co-founded and was the first headmaster of Greengates School, the only school offering education in English in the city, and which is still operating today. While he was in Mexico, Frank also directed and acted at the Mexican National Theatre, including playing a part in the Latin American premiere of T S Eliot's *The Cocktail Party*. He also played Alfred Doolittle in *Pygmalion*. After six years in Mexico he returned to the UK, where he was, for many years, Head of English at Collyer's School, Horsham.

Frank Whitbourn wrote several books, including *Mr Lock of St James's Street* in 1971 (he was related to the founder of the celebrated hatter). He also wrote plays which were widely performed by schools and youth groups, and some of which were heard on BBC Radio. He had worked in theatre for young people produced by Harcourt Williams at the Old Vic and shared friendships with eminent theatre people, including Sybil Thorndike. He shared with David Wood a common respect and admiration for the plays of JM Barrie, not just *Peter Pan*.

David Wood

David Wood was born in 1944. He has explained how his ambitions to go into theatre led to him meeting Frank Whitbourn. "When I was thirteen, my headmaster at Chichester High School asked me what I wanted to do in life. I replied that he would probably laugh, because most people did, but that I wanted to go into the theatre. To his credit he didn't laugh, but suggested that before exams became too time-consuming, I should get as much experience as possible, not only by taking part in school plays, but also by attending the West Sussex County Council's annual summer residential youth drama week. As a result, I found myself at Lodge Hill, near Pulborough, welcomed, as the youngest participant, by a jovial man called Frank Whitbourn, the director of the course."

David was fourteen by then, and was surprised to find the convention was to call all the staff, including forty-seven-year-old Frank, by their first names. "I look back on that week in 1958 as the best week of my life. For the first time I was with people who shared the same interest – in theatre – as me. We worked and played hard, enjoying voice and movement sessions, making props, and building towards the presentation of three productions attended by friends and family. Frank's enthusiasm and encouragement were infectious."

David was also able to help Frank learn his lines for a production. "Our relationship wasn't a teacher/pupil one. We were both members of a team, revelling in being part of a cooperative endeavour, sharing a common purpose that gave us a sense of achievement. For me, that week provided confirmation that my dream of working in the theatre could, with serious application and a helping of good luck, become a reality."

David went on to attend Frank's courses for five years, acted in plays for him and even took part in a revue that toured Sussex village halls with Frank's Sussex Youth Theatre. Frank, who was by then an English teacher at Collyer's School, Horsham, came to Chichester to see David in school plays and as an extra in *Saint Joan* and *The Workhouse Donkey* at the recently opened Chichester Festival Theatre. "As an Oxford graduate himself, he shared my delight when I gained a place to read English at Worcester College, Oxford. He came to see me as Algernon in the OUDS production of *The Importance of Being Earnest*, and became a huge supporter of my endeavours."

During his undergraduate years, David was in three productions that transferred to London. *Hang Down Your Head and Die*, the anti-punishment revue, for which he wrote songs as well as performed, and for which he received a nomination as Best Newcomer to the West End in the Variety Critics' Poll; *A Spring Song,* transferred from the fringe of the Edinburgh Festival to the Mermaid Theatre, and the musical revue *Four Degrees Over,* played at the Fortune Theatre.

Over the next few years, Frank's support of David Wood's acting career continued. He was pleased when David became part of Watford Palace Theatre's first Theatre in Education team, and then an actor/director with the brand-new repertory company at the Swan Theatre, Worcester. He saw him in the Royal Shakespeare Company production of *After Haggerty*. He was always there to encourage and offer praise, particularly when David co-starred in Lindsay Anderson's film *If…*, played on stage opposite Mark Dignam and later Sir Michael Redgrave in *A Voyage Round my Father*, and gained television experience, including a role opposite Shelley Winters in *The Vamp*.

"I treasured his enthusiasm for my acting activities, but it was when I started writing, particularly plays for children, that Frank, as it were, came into his own as a mentor. His lifelong interest in drama for young people made him the perfect correspondent with whom to share the ups and downs I experienced as a children's theatre writer, producer and director, at a time when those of us working in the children's theatre sector were often regarded as operating in the second or even third division. There was little respect shown for this sector by the public, by the critics, by theatre managers or institutions like the Arts Council. The work became a challenge, a passion, and a mission to prove to the world how important the work was in preparing children for the delights of witnessing adult theatre. Not that we were simply attempting to provide future adult audiences; we wanted to show that children were entitled to their own kind of theatre by producing work that was entertaining, intelligent and naturally educational in the widest sense."

David sent Frank the first draft of all his plays as the letters will show, and Frank in return offered encouragement as well as criticism. "He understood what I was trying to do. And he sympathised with the problems I faced, particularly when I managed to create my own touring children's theatre company, Whirligig, which gradually managed to attain bookings in prestigious touring theatres, as well as in the West End." Many of the plays were taken up by repertory companies throughout the UK, and sometimes by companies abroad. *The Gingerbread Man* became the most popular play, Whirligig played regular seasons at Sadler's Wells in London, and eventually David adapted many well-known children's books, particularly those of Roald Dahl.

Over several decades, his correspondence with Frank confided aspects of his work that he rarely shared with others. "I knew he would be interested and would understand. Not only that, the correspondence revealed many aspects of Frank's history, much of which was new to me. Frank's wisdom, wit, knowledge and enthusiasm shone through his letters, which I treasured throughout our friendship. When he died, aged ninety-four, in 2005, I discovered that he had kept my letters just as I had carefully collected his. I hope that this volume of our edited correspondence will not only convey our warm friendship, but also provide a useful reflection on five decades during which theatre for children gained in confidence and approval as recognition of its value increased. Thanks to him, I never felt the urge to give up when disappointment came."

When Irving Wardle in *The Times* in 1976, dubbed David Wood 'the national children's dramatist', and when he was awarded the OBE in 2004 for services to literature and drama, his first instinct was to share the news with Frank, whose dedicated support of his journey had been such a valuable contribution to him achieving such recognition.

Chris Abbott

Dr Chris Abbott is a theatre reviewer and journalist with a particular interest in pantomime and puppet theatre. He is the author of books on repertory theatre pantomime and the last of the touring puppet theatres, and his next book is a history of the theatres in Salisbury. He is Emeritus Reader at King's College London and was the Founding Editor of the *Journal of Enabling Technology*.

1959

FW first wrote from his then home in Goring-by-Sea to DW in 1959. The fourteen-year-old DW had appeared in a play written by him.

5 Jan

Dear David,

I must just write a line to say 'Thank you' to you for taking part in The Glad Tidings. *It is of course always a pleasure to have you around even when I haven't to be bullied into remembering lines; but it is more than pleasure, it's a profit, to have you in a play! You did your part very well indeed, for which my warmest thanks.*

Here's to our next enterprise! Meanwhile, school looms large for the likes of us – oh, dear!

Every blessing,
Frank

The letters from DW to FW have not survived for the rest of this period but are often referred to in FW's correspondence. Later that year, he wrote again after DW played the lead at Chichester High School in Molière's *The Imaginary Invalid*.

29 Nov

Dear David,

I must just write a line to congratulate you again on your splendid performance as Argan. It was a revelation – the timing and technique were excellent and the whole spirit of the thing truly comic. It was far and away the most accomplished 'schoolboy' performance I have ever seen: you played like a veteran.

I was sorry we didn't get a chance of a chat – one never does on these backstage occasions. And I didn't settle with you for the tickets. If we don't meet at a Committee soon, we must meet during the holidays – maybe to do a show.

It was an enjoyable evening! Many, many thanks!

Blessings and more congratulations –
Frank

1961

The next surviving letter from FW (now living in Brighton) appears two years later, but the tone suggests there were others in between, and that theatre was becoming an all-consuming passion for both men. At this point, FW was fifty-one and DW was seventeen years old.

14 Sep

Dear David,

O, Hell's balls!
Never mind – bless 'em ball –
Thanks for yours –
…Incidentally, I think we've got the use of the Barn Southwick, for 11 Nov… It was unexpectedly free, so I said, 'O.K. Armistice or no Armistice!' Would you like to do Sweeney there?

No costumes for Sat next. But I think it would be well to bring the Tape Recorder.

3 cheers for Thieves' Carnival! [Another Chichester High School production] *What has overcome our Geoffrey?*

Twelfth Night has started well. Performances 22–25th

November. Let me know which night you would like tickets for and how many – Friday or Saturday, I expect.

I start work with Northbrook tomorrow evening on Tonight The Circus *and scenes from* Midsummer Night's Dream. *Never a dull moment!*

See you Sat. Hurrah,
Frank

A few weeks later, it is clear that both were still busy arranging performances of various kinds.

09 Oct

Dear David,

I've just been on the 'phone to Miles about possible replacement for Shelagh next Sat. The lady he hoped for is not available, having just signed up with Guildford Rep.

Miles suggests therefore that we should drop 'Build Up' and 'Beginners Please' and would like you to ask Heather if she has any item in her repertoire (solo and/or with some buddy) which could replace one or both. If she hasn't, can you import any other act? Miles and John will fill in if all else fails, but would much prefer that youth should have its fling!

Will you do what you can? I will leave the programme vague!

Michael has sold 53 tickets advance booking so far and I have been after my ex-Goring Hall locals who have promised to support us. So we may have a reasonable house (I call 100 very good for Ferring).

…I do hope you can find some filler-inners. Tell Heather not to worry but to go to it – this is her chance to make the Top Ten!

Ever –
Frank

1962

It is clear that the Sussex Youth Theatre in which DW took part, and which FW organised, was an important experience for both of them, and by 1962 they were jointly planning a reunion.

3 Feb

Dear David,

I'm hoping to fix up a Youth Theatre Reunion at the New Rose Wilmot Youth Centre in W. Worthing. How would the Chichester and Bognor section feel about 17th or 24th March as possible dates?

…we might offer to entertain the Portslade Approved School on the 24th.

…I have in mind a dancing and cabaret evening – rather like the one at Burwash – with members allowed to bring a guest or two – and a charge to cover expenses – food and that – of 2/6d a head. Wot say? Let me know as soon as you can, because of booking the hall…

Ever,
Frank

The party seems to have gone ahead as planned, and later that year, FW (now living at 35 Pelham Court, Bishopric, Horsham) was writing to congratulate DW on being offered a place at Worcester College, Oxford.

27 Dec

My dear David,

Heartiest congratulations! I am glad. I am quite sure Oxford will be the right setting for you – and it has been a wonderful spring-board into the theatrical world for so many. No doubt I am prejudiced, but I am sure there is no place quite like it – and you are much too good for the red-brick world.

…A repertory company is starting in Horsham on 7th January, at the Capitol. But I have a feeling that it's going to be a ropey affair. If it isn't, and they do anything worth doing, you must come over some time. I'm going on an outing with the local Dramatic Society which I have now joined, to see Scofield's Lear *at the end of next month. And on New Year's Day (not Eve) I'm going to* Blitz.

Again, three cheers for David Wood of Worcester Coll. (Oxon). When you're in residence, Miles and I will have to come and see you.

Ever and ever,
Frank

1963

FW's decision to join the local Dramatic Society soon found him very much involved, as his letters show.

19 Jul

My dear David,

…Dangerous Corner went well. I've started work on Lady Windermere *and am enjoying it very much. I think the cast are surprised to find how good a play it is – splendid opportunities in it.*

I'll certainly let you know when I'm coming to Vanya *– and I'll bring over your magic circle thing!*

School ends next Friday. Oh goody!

Excuse scrawl. Sheer exhaustion. Too many late nights this week, what with rehearsals and theatre parties!

Ever – Frank

FW continued to keep in touch, sending sympathetic messages when DW had chickenpox while an extra at Chichester Festival Theatre, and relating his latest problems with casting or prop hunting. They also managed to meet up from time to time, and FW continued to document his theatre-going.

29 Aug

Dear David,

...Saw Charles Boyer in Man and Boy *at Brighton on Tuesday – very interesting Rattigan but doesn't quite come off, I fear. Am just off now to* The Ides of March *which seem to be as unpropitious for Sir John as for Caesar!*

The Dame Sybil Concert was terrific!

...Ever, Frank

By now, DW was at Oxford and must have been keeping FW informed about life there, although his letters have not survived.

10 Nov

Dear David,

Tremendous joy to get your letter and to learn that you have taken to Oxford life like the proverbial duck. I thought you would! The drama news is splendid – since this is really your main purpose, make the most of all opportunities as far as the authorities will allow! One of the good things about Oxford is its ready recognition of all types of ability. What she really requires of her alumni is that they shall not be negligible! And you'll never be that.

Are you into Milton and Anglo-Saxon so soon? No P. Mods? 'Divvers', I know, went years ago – I was among the last candidates, I think!

Very interesting that you have Christopher Ricks as tutor. His Milton book is on my reading list – I am an admirer of the old poet and it is good that he is finding supporters again.

The improvisation sounds fascinating. By the way, I see John Wiles has a new play on Commercial TV tomorrow.

Lady Windermere's Fan *went over well, apart from some technical hitches… I crossed swords with the Adjudicator, who didn't seem sufficiently appreciative of the period and purpose of the play… The new hall is nearing completion, and I think the stage 'machinery' is due to be fitted this week. There's generous stage floor space, but certain mistakes have been made, simply because school architects will not listen when they are told what is wanted. They never stop to think how what they design is to be used. Ah well – it'll be a great improvement on the old arrangements.*

Heigh ho. I must get to bed to catch up on all the sleep lost for Lady W. *It was good of you to send your news. Make the most of every minute…*

Hope you can read this –

Ever and ever –
Frank

Over the next few years, FW must have looked on in interest and probably pride as DW became established as a writer of theatre for children. DW's acting career was developing too, and he was frustrated to discover that there follows a gap in the correspondence, just at the most important stage of his career, as he explains below.

"In 1963, before going to Oxford, I had been a bingo caller at the Theatre Royal, Bognor Regis, as well as an extra in the Chichester Festival Theatre season, an eye-opening experience. The 10th November 1963 letter from Frank came a few weeks after I had started my first term at Oxford. The frustrating thing is that the thirteen years that elapsed before the next letter in the collection were arguably the most formative in my development both as an actor and as a children's playwright/director/producer. Oxford, for me, was a wonderful three years, during which I really did very little academic work, although I did manage to scrape together a third-class degree in English. My tutor, the celebrated Christopher Ricks, seemed to respect my theatre obsession. At the end of the three years, at the usual sherry party, he said, perhaps not in jest, that he had offered me a place at Worcester College, partly because I was capable of getting a degree, but also because he thought I might be an interesting student to have around, because of my interest in magic. And indeed, he used to pay me to entertain at his children's parties. But often when essays were late or problems arose in theatre productions I was involved with, he was extremely tolerant.

"During my three years at Oxford, I acted as Algernon in *The Importance*, the Fool in *King Lear*, wrote songs for and appeared in *Hang Down Your Head and Die*, the anti-capital punishment revue that transferred to the Comedy Theatre in the West End, for which I was nominated Best Newcomer in the 'Variety' Critics' Poll. I appeared at three Edinburgh Festivals in fringe shows, toured Europe in *King Lear*, directed the musical *You Can't Do Much Without a Screwdriver*, appeared in cabaret, both in Oxford and in London, and co-wrote and appeared in *Four Degrees Over*, the revue, which we toured immediately after finals, and which transferred to the Fortune Theatre in the West End. I also appeared in *A Spring Song* at the Edinburgh Fringe, which transferred to the Mermaid Theatre. During these three years, I acquired agents for both acting and writing.

"I know that Frank saw many of my performances, and must have written to me during this time. In my last year, 1966, I was lucky enough to play Richard Burton's servant in *Dr Faustus*, when he and Elizabeth Taylor came to the Oxford Playhouse to appear in the play alongside OUDS students. An extraordinary event, which I have written about elsewhere.

"In 1967, I appeared at the Traverse Theatre, acting in *A Life in Bedrooms*, a musical I had co-written about the infamous rector of

Stiffkey. This later transferred, in a new production (retitled *The Stiffkey Scandals of 1932*) to the Queen's Theatre in the West End. It was a disaster there! Meanwhile, I had been invited by John Hole, whom I had first met when I was an extra at Chichester (he was in the accounts department), to be an actor/director in the first repertory season at the Swan Theatre, Worcester. I had met up again with John in Oxford, when he was working at the New Theatre, and also at the Mermaid Theatre. Sam Walters (later to run the Orange Tree) and I acted in and directed alternate productions at Worcester. A wonderful professional career start, which included appearing in and organising Saturday morning children's theatre. This led to John inviting me to write my first Christmas play, *The Tinder Box*, which I don't think was very good, but encouraged John to ask me to write a Christmas show for the next six years, followed by another seven years when he was at the Queen's Theatre, Hornchurch. A remarkable thing for a playwright, to have a regular commission. I never saw *The Tinder Box*, because I was giving my Wishee Washee at the Palace Theatre, Watford for Christmas 1967. Previously, I had done their first-ever TIE tour, which was another link to theatre for children.

"While I was at Worcester, I wrote lots of letters self-promoting my availability as an actor, and subsequently got cast as Malcolm McDowell's fellow rebel schoolboy in Lindsay Anderson's *If....* This opened up my career in both television and on stage.

"In 1968, when *If....* was released, I co-wrote *The Owl and the Pussycat Went to See...* for Worcester. This proved very successful. The show I was appearing in at that time, in Manchester, closed in time for me to see a week's worth of performances of *Owl and Pussycat*, which convinced me that it couldn't just end there. My Oxford friends Bob Scott and John Gould, with whom I had co-produced *Four Degrees Over*, agreed to allow our small production company to mount *Owl and Pussycat* in London for Christmas 1969 at the Jeannetta Cochrane Theatre, where it got a couple of great reviews and did well enough to return the following year. The play became a repertory theatre staple, and we mounted several more productions in London. Eddie

Kulukundis, for whom I was acting in Alan Ayckbourn's *Me Times Me Times Me* on tour, put it into the Apollo Theatre in the West End. At the same time, he took my 1970 Worcester play, *The Plotters of Cabbage Corner*, into the Shaw Theatre (its first-ever Christmas show). Julia McKenzie played Ladybird.

"In the early '70s, I met Cameron Mackintosh, who had seen and loved *Owl and Pussycat*. With him, I toured the play a couple of times. Meanwhile, I carried on writing the Worcester Christmas productions. Cameron also put me together with Tony Hatch, to write *Rock Nativity*, which played in Newcastle, then toured, but never made the West End. It was published, however, and is still done by amateurs here and in America. During this time, acting-wise, I played opposite Shelley Winters in a London Weekend play *The Vamp*, played the young John Mortimer in *A Voyage Round My Father* at Greenwich, and later, opposite Sir Michael Redgrave, in Toronto. I did lots of television, too. I also was in *After Haggerty*, the David Mercer play, for the Royal Shakespeare Company at the Aldwych, and later at the Criterion.

"The success of *The Owl and the Pussycat Went to See…* particularly in the reps, and then, having been published by Samuel French, amongst the amateur companies, made me realise that children's theatre was probably where I best belonged! Having said that, I did some lovely classic serials for the BBC as an actor, and became a children's television performer in *Jackanory* and *Play Away*. In 1975, John Hole went to the Queen's Theatre, Hornchurch, and I wrote my first 'pantomime substitute', *Old Mother Hubbard*, which went well enough for him to continue to commission a Christmas show from me for the next six years. The children's connection had also continued with me writing the screenplay for the 1974 film *Swallows and Amazons*. This came about because Neville Thompson, who had worked on *If….*, suggested me to Richard Pilbrow, the *Swallows* producer.

"During 'the missing years', my marriage to Sheila Dawson, whom I had met at Oxford, and who was Elizabeth Taylor's understudy in

Dr Faustus had come to an end. We had co-written *The Owl and the Pussycat Went to See…* and also *Larry the Lamb in Toytown* (both for Worcester). Sheila had changed her name to Sheila Ruskin. She chose the name as a kind of revenge against the Ruskin Art School in Oxford, who had asked her to leave, partly because of her association with *Dr Faustus*, which had led to her not doing much academic work! Sheila and I were divorced in 1973. I married Jacqueline Stanbury in 1975. Katherine, our first daughter, was born in 1976. Soon after, I wrote *The Gingerbread Man*, which first played at the Towngate Theatre, Basildon in 1976. Cameron Mackintosh and I took it to the Old Vic the year after, and then produced it for several years in the West End, usually at Christmas. The play took off all over the UK, and most of the repertory companies did it at least once. The play also took off abroad, and for many years was the most popular children's play in Germany.

"In my Faber book *Theatre for Children*, I write about my development as a children's playwright. Surely, during these 'missing years', Frank would have featured quite a lot. I think a file of letters must have gone missing, or never been collated. Very frustrating! *Owl and Pussycat* and *Plotters* had received very good national newspaper reviews. *The Gingerbread Man* achieved the same, particularly in 1977/8 – our Old Vic seasons. By this time, Irving Wardle had called me 'the national children's dramatist', a soubriquet I have used ever since!

"It may not be clear in the correspondence, but the formation of Whirligig Theatre, my touring children's theatre company, in 1979, was extremely important in the way things developed thereafter… Whirligig arose because the productions of *Owl and Pussycat*, initially by WSG Productions (Wood, Scott and Gould), were obviously seasonal. And in London. Similarly, *Plotters*, with its two Christmas seasons at the Shaw. I wanted the work to be seen outside London. By then, I knew that the schools' audience was arguably the most important. The public were, yes, very important too, but I realised that children who would never get the chance of being taken to the theatre by their parents, might get the chance if an interested teacher were to book and bring a party. But I realised that subsidy or sponsorship (a dirty word then) were essential, because the seat price had to be kept low. Not only that; the major regional touring theatres were really not interested in putting on children's shows.

"John Gould and I decided to experiment with a pilot tour of *Flibberty and the Penguin*, another one of my Worcester plays. This happened in 1978. Johnny Ball was in the show, which did a short tour and played a Christmas season at the Alfred Beck Theatre in Hayes. The modest success of this pilot venture convinced me that a touring children's theatre was what I wanted. Jacqui, my wife, while we were on holiday in Menorca, saw an article in the *Sunday Times* Business section (a part of the newspaper we never normally read!) talking about Bill Kallaway, an arts sponsorship arranger. He was a pioneer in this new area of arts funding. I arranged to meet him. He had two young children. Always a help when looking for support! Within a short time, he had achieved sponsorship from Clarks Shoes, which enabled us to set up the first Whirligig tour – *The Plotters of Cabbage Patch Corner* – in 1979. We opened at Sadler's Wells, which was very exciting, where we played for two weeks and got some good reviews. Then the company went off on tour. Whirligig continued for twenty-five years, some of them bumpy, some of them empty, when funding became impossible. But, as is explained in some of the Wood/ Whitbourn correspondence, I believe we transformed the landscape by showing that large numbers of tickets, albeit for a lower price than for an adult show, could be bought by schools during the week and the general public at weekends, making a touring week viable for the commercial theatres. I believe that our pioneering work led to an acceptance of the idea of children's theatre becoming a recognised integral ingredient of a touring theatre's programming. Subsequently, working with Clarion, a commercial company, on *The BFG* and *The Witches*, proved that this genre of theatre could work, particularly for shows with big titles. The encouraging thing about Whirligig was that I was able to produce unknown titles, yet still get an audience, because the schools came to trust the name 'Whirligig'.

"Meanwhile, of course, problems with Arts Council Touring persisted. We wanted to be, and I believe deserved to be, a revenue client, rather than a company that applied for project funding each year. But this was never to be. We were always existing hand to mouth."

1967 The Tinderbox –

Swan Theatre, Worcester – 26ᵗʰ December 1967

A soldier acquires a magic tinder box that summons three powerful dogs to do his bidding.

1968 The Owl and the Pussycat Went to See… –

Swan Theatre, Worcester – 26ᵗʰ December 1968

The Owl and the Pussycat's quest to find a ring and someone to marry them is helped by other Lear characters, including the Dong with a Luminous Nose, the Quangle Wangle and Professor Bosh, and hindered by the Jumblies and the villainous Plum Pudding Flea.

1969 Larry the Lamb in Toytown –

Swan Theatre, Worcester – 26ᵗʰ December 1969

Larry the Lamb and Dennis the Dachshund help Ernest the Policeman save Toytown from a fearsome dragon and a dastardly Highwayman. The Mayor suffers from the Magician's spell going wrong, and the Inventor and the bad-tempered Mr Growser get involved, but all resolves itself in time for the Mayor's special tea party.

1970 The Plotters of Cabbage Patch Corner –

Swan Theatre, Worcester – 26ᵗʰ December 1970

The 'ugly' garden insects are infuriated by the constant 'spraying' by the Big Ones (the human owners of the garden). Slug, Greenfly and Maggot call for a rebellion. But the 'pretty' insects – Red Admiral, Ladybird and Bumblebee – oppose this and war is declared.

1971 Flibberty and the Penguin –

Swan Theatre, Worcester – 26th December 1971

Young Penguin has come from Iceland to find his mother and father before the spring weather becomes too warm. He is helped by Flibberty, a genial goblin, and eventually the pair discover the parent penguins in the zoo and set them free.

1972 Tickle –

Dance Drama Theatre – Schools – Autumn 1972

A workman eats too much pepper. He complains of a tickle in his nose and sneezes violently. The 'tickle' is ejected – and arrives as a newborn baby on the stage, who is anxious to find a friend and a home.

1972 The Papertown Paperchase –

Swan Theatre, Worcester – 26th December 1972

The Salamander, a sort of dragon, is in trouble with the Fireflies, because he is unable to create a fire by breathing on a pile of sticks. To redeem himself, he is sent on a mission to burn down Papertown, whose inhabitants are all made of paper – Professor Paperback, the Postman (an envelope), Mr Quid (a banknote), Lady Carrier Bag and Tishoo. Helping to defend Papertown are Fireman Silver (made of silver paper), Spike the Pen (the Keep Papertown Tidy Man) and Litterbug.

1973 Hijack over Hygenia –

Swan Theatre, Worcester – 26th December 1973

Hygenia is the cleanest kingdom in the world and disease is unknown. But, as a result of all this cleanliness, Dr Spicknspan is always out of work, and so he arranges for Measle to enter the kingdom illegally and bring everyone out in spots!

1974 Rock Nativity –

Playhouse, Newcastle – 18th December 1974

Written with Tony Hatch, a family musical version of the Nativity and the Flight to Egypt.

1975 Old Mother Hubbard –
Queen's Theatre, Hornchurch – 16ᵗʰ December 1975
One Christmas Eve, a lonely dog arrives at Mother Hubbard's Home for Lost Children, but her cupboard is bare and worse still, she and her brood of nursery rhyme children are turned out by the Bailiff.

1976

The surviving correspondence restarts thirteen years later, in 1976, with a letter from DW asking for advice about drama teaching.

15 Jul

Dear Frank,

…Can I pick your brain? I have let myself in for the job of being a tutor on a drama course for the B.T.A. – young people – 14 – 20, I s'pose.

Two specific things I have to do are direct a ½ hour epic with a cast of, say 20 (13 F, 7 M). tackle 'scenes' as exercises in 'acting' during morning sessions.

You must have ideas!!! My mind has gone blank! And I can't even remember what we might have done at Lodge Hill or Burwash, apart from Dark of the Moon!

Any thoughts would be terribly welcome – by letter or phone! All good wishes.

Yours truly,
David

A quick reply seems to have been sent, and the letter of thanks from DW, sent while on holiday in Cornwall, also contains an update on his playwriting, now a major part of his career.

Dear Frank,

…Two new ones this year – Old Father Time *for the Queen's, Hornchurch and* The Gingerbread Man *for a tour and Basildon…! Lots to do – plus the fact I'm acting in an episode of* The [New] Avengers *for a couple of weeks starting soon – I always dislike the beginning of the Christmas build-up – I suppose it's the knowledge that theatres are already publicising something which hasn't even been thought of! The title comes first – a 'selling' one – and then a show has to be devised to fit it! Also it looks as tho' the London production of* Owl and Pussycat *will be at the Yvonne Arnaud, Guildford for Xmas, which I'll direct if I can, so sudden casting problems loom up too!! Still, I'm not really complaining – it's nice to know that whatever rubbish you churn out, somebody's actually going to perform it!*

The Tunbridge Wells Owl *is one I knew about but don't know much about if you see my meaning. It was done at Chelmsford by Newpalm a couple of years ago, and they've clearly hung on to the set and costumes. But I've no idea what the production is like.*

I love your idea of a local amateur prod – it would do very well at the Capitol as a seasonal offering. Would you like me to arrange for a reading copy to be sent to you from French's?

…All for now – must get some shut-eye before the alarm clock summons me to work! Meanwhile, poor Jacqui is up twice during the night feeding baby Katherine, who, at 3 months, is lovely though 'demanding'!…

Cheers,
David

1976 The Gingerbread Man –
Towngate Theatre, Basildon – 7th December 1976
Set on a Welsh Dresser, characters include Salt, Pepper, the Old Bag (a tea bag), Sleek the Mouse and the newly-baked Gingerbread Man, who tries to cure the sore throat of Herr Von Cuckoo, who lives in the cuckoo clock.

1976 Old Father Time –
Queen's Theatre, Hornchurch – 20th December 1976
A time-travelling tale, which begins when Big Ben stops and Old Father Time, who lives in the clock and controls time, travels to various periods in history.

1977 Nutcracker Sweet –
Redgrave Theatre, Farnham – 20th December 1977
Set in the Nutty May Fair, the play follows the struggle of the nuts against the villainous confectioner, Professor Jelly Bon Bon, who is searching for nuts from which to create a new chocolate assortment.

1977 Mother Goose's Golden Christmas –
Queen's Theatre, Hornchurch – 19th December 1977
Mother Goose gives her nursery rhyme children each 'a big moment' in her story about a lovable Goose, and the family's struggle against the Big Bad Wolf, the Bigger Badder Wolf, Giant Bossy Boots and the Monster of the Moat, who guards the Giant's castle.

1978

By 1978, FW is writing about attending more plays, some by DW, as well as an update on ex-pupils. By now, FW is showing how closely he watches the evolution of the plays, and noticing even the smallest change.

9 Jan

Dear David,

A very brief line (brief because writing is difficult on a/c of a groggy shoulder, result of buying too many secondhand books and humping them home) to say how much I enjoyed Nutcracker *and* Gingerbread Man. *One at Farnham (whither five adults escorted my great- niece!), t'other at The Old Vic. At both theatres, the kids fairly raised the rafters – esp. at the Vic. I noticed that in* GBM *you began the audience participation much earlier. Both productions were splendidly staged and choreographed – the chases superbly. I loved the arrangement of 'Come the light' at the Vic. A moment's hush was a masterly touch.*

…I was proud of S.French's window full of Gingerbread Men!

Blessings to you all for '78. Have you moved to your mansion yet? I address to the Crooked Billet and hope for onward transmisshun!

Love –
Frank

DW was quick to reply, and to give an update on other projects.

11 Jan

Dear Frank,

Many thanks for your letter and its generous remarks! So glad you saw and enjoyed both shows. I was thrilled with The Gingerbread Man, *but felt* Nutcracker Sweet *needed work! Mind you, the script gives every opportunity for participation from the audience, but somehow it got missed – and I felt in general the production lacked clarity; – still, French's have taken it, and I'm trying to mount a new production for next year.*

Have seen about 10 of my productions – very exciting! Most of them have been very good – the Brighton Gingerbread Man *is excellent (on till 21st).*

Now on to new thoughts! Am working on a tv series (writing) based on 2 Ransome books. And I have two new plays to write for '78 Christmas!! The Old Vic season proved very successful, and as a result we revive there Owl & Pussycat *for Easter – then* Gingerbread Man *will return next Xmas!…*

All good wishes as ever –

Yours truly,
David

In a precursor of many plans that were not to be, *The Owl and the Pussycat Went to See…* was, in the event, never seen at the Old Vic.

1978 Babes in the Magic Wood –
> *Queen's Theatre, Hornchurch – 11ᵗʰ December 1978*

It is Christmas Eve and worryingly, the toys are still being made. A Fairy Godmother intervenes and the toys are then magically finished – but the Fairy Godmother is not all she seems to be.

1979

By May 1979, DW has moved house and more plays are being produced. In a characteristically quirky letter, FW has a request.

29 May

Dear David,

Ave! (Greek for Bung-ho!)
I write (scribo) because it is a pleasure to write to you anywhere, anywhere, but especially at 14 Belvedere Drive, S.W.

(Have you a carriage-sweep?) but prompted hereto by request from a former Collyer's pupil now teaching Geography, Music and Drama to young ladies of the upper-muddled classes… where a New Hall (where does the money come from? I'm thankful to have an old hall) is to be opened in the week ending 8th December '79, with 2 performances of your Rock Nativity *(seen at Wimbledon). The producer, John Groves (played the Common Man for me years ago in* Man for All Seasons*), wonders if there is any chance of your gracing any of the performances with your presence. He is very sensible that this will be your busiest time of the year, but nevertheless makes so bold as to ask me to ask you. Any chance? Over to you.*

That's point one. Point Two is that John came with me to The Luck of the Bodkins *at Windsor, where we were both enchanted by it. He is wondering whether there would be any chance of your allowing it to be presented by Horsham's Theatre 48 (the lot I play around with) at the Capitol, Horsham, next year. They are a very competent company, and he is a very good producer – he has done* Salad Days, The Boy Friend *and* The Canterbury Tales *(me as Chaucer), and* 1066 and All That*) (me as compere, having a wonderful ball!) with huge success and making a profit, too. You can be sure that he (and the co.) will do you credit. Of course, I have no notion what the state of play is with this particular opus – perhaps someone is about to do it on ice with J. Curry – but again, I said yes, I would ask. So here I am asking. If there is a possibility, he would appreciate a copy of the script to show to the Committee (there's always a committee) and some indication of fees.*

And that's my good turn for to-day. Now whose good angel shall I be tomorrow…?

My love to you and the family.

Ever –
Frank

By June, DW was filming *North Sea Hijack* in Ireland, and wrote proudly to FW on the production letterhead.

7 Jun

Dear Frank,

Thought I'd show off with the flashy letterhead of my latest effort! It's a big £5,000,000 American action movie!!! …most of our time was spent on an oil rig supply vessel 50 miles off the West Coast of Ireland – for 12 hours a day!! Nice part – splendidly unheroic character who's seasick most of the time!

Now – thank you for your letter – delighted to hear your news. Re. Rock Nativity *– v. glad to hear it's being done there… I will make a very special effort to get there…* Rock Nativity *is uppermost in my mind at present since we are currently preparing a t.v. version for R.T.E. (the Irish t.v. company, based in Dublin). Tony Hatch now lives in Ireland for tax reasons!*

Re. Luck Of The Bodkins *– John and I see no objection at all to the Horsham company doing it – we'd be delighted. We are still trying to get it off the ground, because we still believe very much in it. …we have done rewrites since Windsor, but these may not be in a fit state yet – the script/score that is ready is the exact version you saw.*

What news? Well, we expect baby no 2 in Sept. Our house is smashing, with lots still to do – PLEASE come and see us…

The Gingerbread Man is on tour… it has recently opened in N. Zealand, is a big hit in Germany (6 'state theatre' productions planned for this Xmas) – and has just been announced for the National Theatre of Sweden in Stockholm. Very pleasing. Am just finishing a new opus for 6 actors and 30 schoolchildren – There Was an Old Woman… *which plays in Leicester (Haymarket) for five weeks from July 25. Most exciting really is the formation of my new company WHIRLIGIG THEATRE, which is a new national touring children's theatre, under commercial sponsorship (in this case CLARK'S shoes). We open with* Plotters of Cabbage Patch Corner…

Hope to hear from you soon.

All best wishes,
David

The formation of Whirligig Theatre was indeed an important step and would be a major force in the production of theatre for children for many years. In his reply, FW noted his inability to match up to Hollywood letter headings.

The something of something '79
Written, dictated and composed by Frank Whitbourn
by, to, with and from F.W. (Inc.)

Dear David,

I can't compete. I shall frame it. With a gilt edge! What super news – all those productions…

It's great to know that you've broken out of the Christmas season into the summer time. John is bringing me up to the 5pm matinee at Wimbledon… If we don't find you there, we'll hunt you down at Belvedere Drive afterwards unless I hear from you that this would be inconvenient. (You might be bathing the baby.) Splendid to hear that you're expecting again. I'm all in favour of a pair. …Give them all a year or two and I'll bring them to the Wood cycle in Chichester. You ought to do the lot* in repertory at Christmas. Anyway, I shall come to Sadler's Wells in October for the launching of Whirligig…

Ever –
Frank
*I mean the plays, not the babies.

The next letter from DW was on Whirligig notepaper ('another letterhead with which to wow you') and FW declared himself impressed in his reply.

The tale of Whirligig Theatre deserves a book all of its own, but it is an important parallel story to that of the playwriting which is told through the letters. In 1978, DW and John Gould (who had run WSG Productions together) met in a pub on Wimbledon Common and discussed forming a touring children's theatre company, to perform in major venues, targeting primary school audiences on weekdays and family audiences at weekends. The pilot tour took place in 1978, and good relationships developed with a number of venues like the Civic, Darlington; the Bristol Hippodrome, the Thameside, Grays; Theatre Royal, Newcastle; Palace Theatre, Newark and the Rex, Wilmslow. Sponsorship was found from Clarks Shoes and Whirligig was named (after the 1950s television programme) and launched with a tour of *The Plotters of Cabbage Patch Corner* in 1979. Always run on a shoestring, Whirligig lasted for twenty-five years, despite never getting revenue grants from the Arts Council which would have enabled them to plan ahead. It all came to an end with a party at Polka Theatre in 2003, attended by many performers past and present. But, at this stage of the correspondence, that is all in the future…

1979 There was an old woman… –
Haymarket Theatre, Leicester – 25th July 1979
Mother Shipton lives in an overcrowded shoe with her many children. But the shoe actually belongs to a giant who lost it and has been looking for it – with one bare foot – ever since. Mother Shipton's attempts to save their home are helped and hindered by The Great Boon, a not-very-good magician.

1979 Cinderella –
Queen's Theatre, Hornchurch – 10th December 1979
Some of the panto characters, but two mice instead of Buttons.

1980

By June 1980, DW was 'busy casting *Nutcracker Sweet* for Whirligig and desperately trying to get ideas for Christmas,' presumably a reference to the Christmas show for Liverpool Playhouse. DW and FW managed to meet up in Chichester in June.

1980 Chish 'n' Fips (later **The Ideal Gnome Expedition**) –

Liverpool Playhouse – 3rd December 1980

Two garden gnomes, Mr Fisher and Mr Wheeler, embark on an adventure into the concrete jungle of the city. The audience help them learn road safety, they escape from a fierce Securidog and Wacker, a ferocious tar-whacking machine, and find their ideal holiday island – a traffic island.

1980 Aladdin –

Queen's Theatre, Hornchurch – 8th December 1980

The traditional story but also featuring a monkey, a baby dragon and a different genie.

1981

Only a single letter from DW survives from this year, telling FW to look out for the tour of the now renamed *The Ideal Gnome Expedition* and hoping they could meet up afterwards.

1981 Robin Hood –

Nottingham Playhouse – 29th May 1981

A group of villagers are celebrating May Day with a variety of pastimes – singing, dancing, acrobatics and competitive sports. The villagers take on Robin Hood roles to tell the various well-known tales of Robin Hood and his Merry Men.

1981 Meg and Mog Show –

Arts Theatre, London – 10th December 1981

Meg, the inefficient witch, Mog, her cat and Owl need ingredients for a spell to rid them of a rampaging Stegosaurus. Their quest takes them to a castle, to the moon and to the zoo.

1981 Dick Whittington and Wondercat –

Queen's Theatre, Hornchurch – 17th December 1981

A crowd gather to greet Sir Richard Whittington on his installation as Lord Mayor of London. One young boy is not impressed until he learns, through the telling of how Dick Whittington came to be Lord Mayor, that this Mayor is indeed a good man.

1982

FW saw *The Ideal Gnome Expedition* at Brighton and declared himself impressed.

7 Jan

Dear David,

Just a note of congratulation on The Ideal Gnome Expedition. *…we both hugely enjoyed ourselves. The characterisation was delightful and I'm glad you employed* The Big Ones Again. *I recognised your voice, of course. Were Jacqui and Katherine also involved? If so, splendid family co-operation.*

The sets and costumes were beautiful. I'm sure the scene changes gave tremendous joy, and the lighting was particularly effective. I liked the device of having the children read the signs on the playground. They were completely absorbed. One little boy just in front of me was very sharp, and was quick to shout, "Look down the drain!" for the lost key all by himself…

Love to you all – Frank

P.S. I was especially impressed – as I have been before – by the skill of your rhyming, and the singability of your words – very deft management of vowels and consonants – the secret of Gilbert's success – and of D'Oyly Carte's diction in their palmier days.

In his reply, DW shows the extent to which he takes seriously the comments he is sent.

10 Jan

Dear Frank,

Thank you for your lovely letter! Am so glad you enjoyed Ideal Gnome *– it has certainly gone down very well nationwide as they say! We virtually filled Bristol Hippodrome with it – 1,500 children per perf.! – and although I really believe the work is best seen in medium-sized theatres, nevertheless the reaction in the biggies is tremendous! You are the first person to ever say nice things about my lyrics, rhymes, etc., and I bless you for it; I love the mathematical puzzle of lyric-writing – my crossword puzzle mind coming out!! Yes, Jacqui was Mrs Big One. But Miss Big One was actually Melody Kaye, who also played Baby Duck! Katherine's turn will doubtless come! Clarks have agreed to support us again this year – it has been touch and go (as you spotted, the recession has hit them hard!) but their support is still strong. We now await the Arts Council for their subsidy offer. Then we can decide what to do. We may revive* Owl *if we can afford to pay 12 actors! Meanwhile, my new one –* Meg and Mog Show *– is doing capacity business at the Arts. Based on popular children's books, the show has really taken off – even Puffin want to publish a version of the play for teachers to use with children. And another new one –* Dick Whittington and Wondercat *is doing very well at Hornchurch. It's a play within a play – the citizens of London await the Lord Mayor's Procession (Sir Richard W. is to be* *enthroned or whatever). A ragged urchin yells, "Rubbish – why cheer him? – he's a wealthy nob who won't help us real folk" – and the crowd explain – by acting our Sir R's story – that he is a caring man! – they inveigle the boy into 'playing' the young Dick. Works quite well.*

…Have a happy year – we must get together when the snows lift! Let me know in advance if you are planning a London trip – maybe we could do a matinee!

Love from us all, and thanks again for your lovely letter –
David

A flurry of letters follows with more updates on productions, and attempts to set up a meeting, which eventually happened on 2ⁿᵈ February, when FW passed on some of his theatre book collection.

5 Feb

Dear Frank,

It was a very happy morning – many thanks for your hospitality and conversation. I am very grateful to you… I do assure you they will be looked after, in their own section of the 'library', under 'The Frank Whitbourn Collection'! You are more than welcome to come and see them any time.

All good luck on your move. Let us know your Winchester address, and next time we call on my sister-in-law and family, will impose upon you and your sister too!

Bless you and thank you again.

All good wishes,
David

FW had indeed moved to Winchester by the time he wrote again, rather under the weather after a hospital visit but having enjoyed a meeting with DW. His next letter mentions an ex-pupil with theatrical ambitions ('he's very much interested in children's theatre… you naturally for him are The Master') and forewarns DW that his advice will be sought. In return, DW promises to do his best to help, and passes on news of further tours and planned Christmas seasons. He writes again in November and mentions some new plans.

7 Nov

My dear Frank,

Your card gave me great joy! Thank you. …quite honestly, you are the first person to actually notice any craft in my lyric-writing and I bless you for that! …Making the record was great fun, and I hope that over the years will sell enough copies to pay for it!

How are you? Well and busy, I hope – possibly seeing more shows than me at present! I've got Owl *on the road, doing great business, plus* Gingerbread *in rehearsal for London Xmas season. Also just finished* Jack and the Giant *for Hornchurch. Have also been doing Saturday perfs. of my one-man D.W. Magic and Music Show – going back to my roots entertaining children myself!...*

…Next year beckons – new plays to write for Farnham and Pitlochry, plus revival of Meg and Mog Show *to direct at the Arts for Easter. Plus WHIRLIGIG!...*

Do hope to see you soon – thanks again so much for writing –

Love and best wishes,
David

1982 Jack and the Giant –

Queen's Theatre, Hornchurch – 6ᵗʰ December 1982

Mrs Macdonald's Farm is the setting for DW's version of the traditional tale. Her children, Jack, Mac and Jeannie Mac, struggle with penury and have to sell Marigold, the cow. Instead of beans they receive tins of baked beans, which later grow into a baked bean tin tree, at the top of which lives the Silver Giant, whose henchmen are robots, Beep and Buzz.

1983

The new year began with FW seeing DW's version of *Robin Hood*, now at the Young Vic, and then going on to make a suggestion that would later bear fruit.

3 Jan

…The whole show worked wonderfully. I was particularly interested in the May Day folk setting, as years ago at Collyer's (before anybody else thought of it!) I did a version of Gawain and the Green Knight *grafted on to the Sussex Mummers' Play of St George. I was wondering what was the contribution of your collaborators? Chiefly, I imagine, in the folklore and the dancing? The finale was superb – catching the kids into the action was a splendid new twist to audience participation – more than one-up on the song sheet!…*

…Have you thought of the Children's Book market at all? The Gingerbread Man *and* Flibberty, *for example, suitably illustrated… could be first-class attractions – even foregoing the music. There'd be a place for some lyrics, though – perhaps as narrative.*

I have acquired an italic pen to improve my handwriting – at least to make me more legible. My typewriter has a touch of the temperamentals.

Love to you all and every good wish for '83!
Frank

1983 The Selfish Shellfish –

Redgrave Theatre, Farnham – 29th March 1983

Life for the rockpool dwellers is full of uncertainty. Every new tide brings fresh surprises or new problems. But they cope reasonably well, until Seagull brings them warning of a possible catastrophe – the Great (oil) Slick is coming…

16 Apr

Dear David,

…we enjoyed The Selfish Shellfish *yesterday at Farnham. I liked the single lyric and was sorry there weren't more – but perhaps your lyrics are for connoisseurs* (if that's how you spell them) rather than for the children, who may find them holding up the action. The Great Slick, 'sticky and thick', was a splendid conception and he seemed to spread himself vastly over the pool – brilliant use of parachute silk. (I did wonder initially, from the credits in the programme, where the paras were coming into it all. I shouldn't have been very surprised if you'd organised a drop through the roof!)*

I liked the opening, the actors inviting the children onto the stage – a new kind of participation. And I loved the down-beat ending – poor Seagull! – which would, I felt, mean that the children would thoughtfully take the lesson home with them. I particularly liked, too, the development of the characters – the aggressiveness they exhibited at first appearance – though not Mussel – giving way to more attractive qualities. Poor Sludge must have had a rotten time being rolled away in the tin – I began to feel sorry for him. The Slick's disappearance was tremendous – both exits were beautifully laid in waiting…

Love to all –
Frank

*Big Ones!

21 Apr

Dear Frank,

Thank you for your letter – so glad you enjoyed 'S S'. I thought the production was good for the 'first' one – we learnt a lot from it, and this was helped by the fact that the company played it straight and didn't try to be clever! We hope to tour 'S S' with WHIRLIGIG in the autumn, and I may well write a few extra songs. But I found it v. difficult with this play – songs seemed to hold things up.

French's have bought it – with the suggestion that THE GREAT SLICK should finally be 'got rid of' by the audience, rather than down the anemone (or rather after the anemone bit). I think they're wrong. It has to be a fantasy solution, and that one seems the most logical and pleasing…

Am currently planning Xmas and the autumn; and doing definitive versions of Meg and Mog Show, Jack and the Giant *and* Robin Hood *for S. French (v. boring!)…*

All good wishes, as ever,
David

31 Aug

Dear David,

Hugest possible thanks for The Selfish Shellfish – *and especiallest for the inscription which is more than generous! It's most attractively presented – much superior to French's Editions. I notice they still act as agents…*

I hope to come to your production at Sadler's Wells in November, to see the hand of the maestro at work. The Redgrave, I believe, is putting SS on again at Christmas or thereabouts. We hope to take some of our rapidly developing grandchildren/ nephews/nieces – more accessible than S.W. for us.

...I gather from the postmark that you've been – or are – in Cornwall, in recess. We're away to Scarborough shortly. (Stephen Joseph was another of my starters – before the War (1939 edition).)

Again – many thanks. Love to you and all the family,
Frank

5 Sep

Dear Frank,

...am rushing off to start rehearsing The Selfish Shellfish.

...You ask if we are into computers yet? Not really, although I am doing a show for the Lyric, Hammersmith this Christmas – commissioned by a London management, in which three children enter the world of a video game, controlled by a witch with a computer! The music is all by ABBA, who, it seems, are internationally the most successful team of singer/songwriters at the moment. So am crossing fingers...

...I did, however, manage to get quite a bit of work done while we were away – this is always the advantage of writing. Am also writing a follow-up to Robin Hood *with my collaborators last time. This one is called* Jack the Lad, *and will be seen in January up North, hopefully as a tryout for London...*

All good wishes,
As ever,
David

30 Nov

Dear Frank,

...The new one, at the Lyric, Hammersmith, has its press night on 13th December at 7pm. I have one ticket available

for this, and, should you be able to make it, would love you to be there…

All good wishes, as ever,
Yours,
David

1 Dec

Dear David,

Huge thanks for your letter and enclosures. Yes! I am free on 13th December and of course shall love to have that ticket. Many many thanks for thinking of me…

…Congratulations on The Times *notice of* The Shelfish *the other day. My only reservation about the music was that there wasn't enough of it – but perhaps the lessening of musical interruption heightened the tension and increased the drama.*

…I lift my cuppa to the 13th inst! Huge thanks again and love to you all.

Frank

8 Dec

Dear David,

Huge thanks for the ticket! I've just been trying to send you a Telegram for tonight's performance, but you can't send Telegrams any more. How do people get married then? I asked the Voice. It replied that a Telemessage could arrive on the next working morning after despatch. I didn't think much of that, so I'm sending this to come along with your dish of rice krispies (or whatever) wishing every success to you and Abbacadabra *as of this present moment. I tried to think of a Witticism à propos or anent* Abbacadabra, *but nothing very funny came up, so perhaps it's as well that Telegrams are ORF. Maybe the GPO or Telecom or whoever attends to these things never found those greetings very amusing either. So lots of luck – and I remain yours, looking forward tremendously to Tuesday 7pm. Not to worry about transport. I'll be there!*

Love – Frank

1983 Abbacadabra –

Lyric Theatre, Hammersmith – First Preview – 8th December 1983
Press Night – 13th December 1983

Three children magically enter a computer game and help Aladdin, Cinderella, Pinocchio and the Beast escape the evil Carabosse in time to attend Sleeping Beauty's wedding. Songs by ABBA, with new lyrics by Don Black.

FW's enthusiastic response to *Abbacadabra* also touched on a topic that would recur in the correspondence – productions of J M Barrie's *Peter Pan*.

15 Dec

Dear David,

I must just take a moment of your time to say how hugely I enjoyed Tuesday evening… and the exciting ambiente of the Lyric. Lovely to come upon that nostalgic, lavish theatre through the very nineteen-eighties approaches! I love the new skeleton theatres – Chichester et al – but you can't beat Victoriana and Pollocks Tuppence Coloured for the real theatrical magic.

And Magic was what it was all about (as they say) and this – pace the 'heavies' which I have just been reading, they filter through to us in the provinces a day late – was what you achieved. The audience made that quite plain, and whatever young Wardle may say, you were about something more important than a hard sell of the old enchantment against the new. I took it that the magic of technology is as valid as Grimm and Andersen provided that the imaginative faculty, not merely the calculating capacity, of the devotees is involved. The reviewers seem to have been so bedazzled by the electronic wizardry that they missed the significance of the two wonderfully poignant moments of the evening – Peter's "We all have to die, Carabosse" (and how touchingly he said it) and Carabosse's "I'm not Nobody." I'd never seen Elaine Paige 'live' before, but that last scene of hers stamped her on my mind as a real actress, not just a musical show-stopper. And again all my reviewers, except the Financial Times *man, seem not to have sufficiently appreciated the actors, who more than held their own against the scenic devices, and directed the attention where of course it should always be, even in pantomime, on the humanity of human beings and the monstrosity of breathing, un-mechanical monsters. (Incidentally, Pinocchio and Fred were beautifully paralleled.) The children alone were worth anybody's admission money. I should like to see Jenna Russell as Wendy, and Dexter Fletcher as Peter Pan. (When, oh when, is justice to be done to JMB by presenting a boy in that masterpiece, the touchstone and cause for all children's plays, because – contrary to popular belief – it is not sentimental about children but accepts all the potential cruelty they are capable of. The last stage direction at the end of Act V – the fight on the pirate ship – is the key to the essential Barrie.*

'The curtain rises to show Peter a very Napoleon on his ship. It must not rise again lest we see him on the poop in Hook's hat and cigars, and with a small iron claw.')

P.P. has endured all these years because it is an adult play, full of action which children can enjoy, not – repeat NOT – a children's play which adults can tolerate. You are on the right road because you face the fact that children must grow up and that therefore they must be treated as persons, nearly always a step or two ahead of where short-memoried adults expect them to be. Their problems are adult problems. This is the seed of lastingness in all the classic fairy tales. This is what makes them – no matter how fantastic – true to life, and a 'criticism of life'. "We must all die, Carabosse." The line outshone all the electronic wizardry with its poetry – poetry of the order of Hamlet's "Let be" to Horatio, and Miss Prism's "my few unoccupied hours" and "in younger and happier days," as she examines her famous handbag.

I can't accept John Barber's comment (he was at Merton with me and should have been retired long ago) that the 'presence of so many cooks diluted the broth'. They all enriched it. But the greatest enrichment came not even from the musicians, but from the author of the Book.
 Again, huge thanks.

 Love –
 Frank

P.S. I'm taking my sister to the matinee on 12th Jan to give her a real treat!

20 Dec

Dear Frank,

…Bless you for your lovely letter, which I read with delight!
 The critics do seem to have missed the point, exactly as you say. However, the Mail *and the* Guardian *were very good, plus the* Standard. *So we are not really complaining.*
 What surprised me was that Wardle missed the point totally. You understood what I was on about – simply that the technological age is fine, but cannot exist without the world of the imagination. I thought it was extremely clear; the fact that the little boy is into fairy stories and the older boy is into

technology, and that the story, if you like, works for both of them is the most important thing; through the technological age, the little boy's enthusiasm for fairy stories is enhanced, and through fairy stories, the older, technological boy finds true excitement. So Wardle's last paragraph really meant nothing at all.

The interesting thing has been that the audiences, even when there have been a large number of children, have listened very hard. Children don't seem to get bored. However, I am quite convinced that this is not a children's show, and have been for some time. The reaction of the audience seems to support this.

You are absolutely right about Peter Pan. *I saw the RSC version last year, with a boy playing the role – or at least a 35-year-old actor! It worked extremely well, apart from the annoying fact that the RSC decided that they knew what Mr. Barrie meant better than he did himself, and introduced a narrator figure! But the interesting thing was that the children were obviously involved in what was really an adult fantasy. And some of the lovely stuff about Peter forgetting Wendy in later years was heartrending...*

...Elaine Paige has been off for two or three days with a throat infection. This has given everyone the Heebie Jeebies. Crossing fingers she will be all right again today.

A very happy Christmas.

All good wishes,
David

1984

1984 Jack the Lad –

Library Theatre, Manchester – 23ʳᵈ March 1984

A musical celebration of Jack, the ubiquitous hero or everyman of English legend, myth and folklore – from 'Little Jack Horner', through

'Jack and the Beanstalk' to 'Spring-Heeled Jack', the terror of London. The setting is a gypsy encampment, where a series of Jack tales and songs are performed by the gypsies to celebrate the 80th birthday of their senior member – known affectionately as 'Jack the Lad'.

It is October 1984 before the letters begin again, with DW sending an update on all of his projects after appearing in his *Magic and Music Show* at the Theatre Royal, Winchester.

30 Oct

Dear Frank,

A lovely surprise to see you on Saturday – it's funny, but deep down I think I still associate you with Horsham, tho' I know you're in Winchester! So the thought of seeing you hadn't even crossed my mind! I'm sorry it had to be such a cursory chat, but all the staff at the T.R. are amateurs and I felt guilty delaying them…

…I feel guilty I didn't let you know Whirligig dates this year – The Papertown Paperchase has been very well received, I'm glad to say, even tho' Whirligig is in serious financial problems. Nearest to you might be OXFORD – in December. We are due to go down en famille for the last perf. on Dec 15th.

Meanwhile, G. Man bounces back! And I have just finished second draft of the book of a new musical, which is meant to happen next year – called Sherlock Holmes and the Case of the Missing Santa Claus. Music by Charles Strouse ('Annie', 'Bye Bye Birdie', etc., lyrics by Don Black). It's a nice idea (not mine!), tho' very tricky to get the tone right – it's not a spoof.

Sadly, Abbacadabra has fallen by the wayside, hopefully temporarily…

Yours,
David

FW was quick to reply.

5 Nov

Dear David,

Huge thanks for your most welcome newsy letter with all the fascinating bits and pieces…

…I'm very glad you're breaking into the children's book market… The right illustrator is vital – a Shepard, a Tenniel – there has been none 'right' for Barrie so far as I know. They have all sentimentalised what is actually a horror story, the central argument being the innocent – because thoughtless – cruelty of children. Barrie's anecdote of the reception of the MS of Peter by one of the five boys is a memorable demonstration of this…

It is always a joy to see you – on or off stage – however briefly… The children have been busily explaining to each other how it was all done and have come up with ingenious solutions. But one solemnly declares no solutions necessary. "It was magic," she says. And of course she's the one who is entirely right.

Love to you all,
Frank

P.S. Oh dear! I seem to have wasted this space! Can't allow that. I'll just send you more love!
  F

P.S.2 (My life is one long afterthought.) The S. Holmes (how indestructible he is) is very intriguing. But I wish you were doing the lyrics as well as the book!
  F

And that rounds off the correspondence for 1984, apart from a card from FW congratulating DW on his breakfast television appearance and reporting on a local production of *The Wind in the Willows*, which did not impress.

1985

There were no play premieres in 1985 but plenty of revivals. DW updated FW on the Christmas season.

5 Jan

Dear Frank,

Many thanks for your kind letter – how noble to rise so early to watch me… I must say the whole thing was most enjoyable – a very relaxed atmosphere in the studio coupled with apparent genuine interest in what we were doing. Also the novelty helped – they had never had the newspapers reviewed by anyone in costume before!

The critics have virtually ignored G. Man *this year, but media exposure, as they say, has been good, thanks mainly to P. Duncan. However, it has still managed to lose quite a sum! It is ironic in a way – six London seasons have all lost money, but that 'investment' on my part has in fact established the show with a reputation for unrivalled success!! We have really bought public opinion. I don't resent it – but it is discouraging for the cast when audiences are thin. At least we all don't have that sense of doom that a 'flop' has – we reek of success apart from in the building itself! The Whirligig losses will be known soon too! – Again, artistically, we have been so successful that no one can believe we are in serious financial trouble. And that, I suppose, is good – the public should not be aware of the problem. But, on the other hand, it's hard to get money bags potential sponsors to express interest if you are, on the surface, successful! HEIGH HO…*

Yours,
David

In his reply, FW mused on some biblical matters before moving on to his response to the latest publications.

27 Jan

Dear David,

…It's horrid to think of Gingerbread Man *losing money – but I realise that the costs, even of a re-staged production, with set and costumes already 'found', must be prodigiously high – overheads and running costs. And there must be a limit to ticket prices for a children's show, simply because taking even a small family adds up, what with fares (or parking) and the monstrous price of ices and lollies! I suppose, though, the London production serves as 'promotion' (the new word for 'advertising') of productions elsewhere. Do schools tackle the Wood Repertoire? Probably not – they need large, not 'economic' casts, as the Reps. do. You have to get everybody in. So the nativity triumphs in a secular society – no end to the number of shepherds and angels who can be accommodated. Our poor Lorna was demoted to an angel in '84, having been the BVM in '83. Her prize doll, which she hoped would guarantee her a second run in the star part, was adjudged 'too large'. Never mind. She wore her wings with indifference and kept her halo at a saucy slant.*

…I'm busy – did I tell you? – with a Church Pageant for the pretty village of King's Somborne, about 8 miles off. They are celebrating the church's restoration in 1885 and hope to raise a substantial sum to repair it. And Winchester Cathedral needs £3,000,000, Salisbury £6,000,000! But I haven't been summoned by either yet. Salisbury is relying on Prince Charles.

Now – my best love – and thanks – to you all,
Frank

By the end of the year, DW must have decided it was time for another update on projects in progress; and a mixed bag it was too with a number of long-running ideas still not reaching performance stage.

1 Dec

Dear Frank,

Sunday. Should be correcting proofs, but can't get down to it!...

How are you? Busy as ever? Hope so. Why don't you come up to Wimbledon soon? ...Maybe combine it with a visit to Meg and Mog Show, *which I've just done for Unicorn (at the Arts) for the third time!*

...Workwise, it's non-stop really – very pleasing, even tho' I occasionally wonder why certain projects end up in the dustbin! Abbacadabra, *for instance – nothing has happened to it. I was asked to 'toughen' it – another director was sought, but nothing developed. Similarly, after doing 3 drafts of* Sherlock Holmes and the Case of the Missing Santa Claus *for Tennents', it's still a no-no! Earlier this year, I reworked ('doctored' is the in-word!) an American musical version of* The Country Wife – *with Ned Sherrin. Received with jubilant congratulations, since when, NOTHING!! I look back to* Rock Nativity *and other shows outside my children's field – e.g.* The Luck of the Bodkins *adaptation,* The Stiffkey Scandals, Robin Hood *(at the Young Vic) etc., and I seriously wonder whether fate has decreed that I was born to do the children's stuff and not the adults'! My involvement with an adult or family project seems to be the kiss of death!*

So, what's positively happened this year? Well, I've written a 45-minute musical for young people to perform – commissioned by Howell's School in N. Wales (Jacqui's old school) – based on a lovely book by Michael Foreman called Dinosaurs and All That Rubbish. *Premiere next July.*

Whirligig is currently touring The Gingerbread Man; *in*

spite of teachers' strikes, it seems to be going well, and comes back to London (Bloomsbury) for 3 weeks from Boxing Day. And the book has come out, after 7 years trying! The show has just opened in Tokyo and in Dallas to namedrop but two places! We had a fascinating weekend in Copenhagen seeing the Danish Nutcracker Sweet – *rather good! Audience participation all worked in the same places, which was reassuring.*

Have also written another new one, and this is quite exciting – about four years ago, I got the idea of adapting The Old Man of Lochnagar, *by HRH the Prince of Wales. At first my agent was told 'no' – there was to be no exploitation. But then HRH's agent rang back, apologised for the hasty reaction of a minion (!) and that if DAVID WOOD was interested in writing a play, then it might be possible!! I ended up at Buck House with a Private Secretary, then spent 2 years not doing much. But early in '84, I did a synopsis, involving major and radical departures from the book. This was accepted and then I wrote the play, which has just been accepted too. So, Whirligig will tour it next year. Hopefully, sponsorship will be forthcoming for this one! We are insisting that the sponsor stays with us for another year or two, rather than simply jumping on the bandwagon!…*

Take care – love from us all,
David

An excited reply from FW included an update on the renovation of the Theatre Royal, Winchester.

5 Dec

Dear David,

…the Polka Theatre sounds just the job for our next visit to London with the younger children – it's never easy to find the right sort of treat – though they always enjoy trains and tubes

and buses as much as anything. But the Arts Theatre – oh yes, I'd love to come to Meg and Mog *at the Arts*…

What a year you've had! It makes a breathless but triumphant saga! I do wonder what G.B.M. sounds like in Japanese. I shouldn't be surprised if we find them exporting ginger-bread to us, or setting up biscuit factories over here very soon. There's no knowing what the consequences may be!

(As you have extravagantly used two headed sheets, I shall do the same. That's only common politeness! And I have loads of this stuff to use up anyway.)

Of course the Royal Connection is tremendously exciting, and should be a splendid boost for Whirligig. Surely there's a chance, too, of a Royal visit to the show? What a send-off if they all came! Perhaps you could do it at Windsor?

Talking of Windsor – what a disappointment that nothing came of the Bodkins. *I loved it. But I suppose Wodehouse is too whimsical and subtle for the present taste. Everything to-day seems required to be so very heavy-handed. I can quite understand your wish to get away from the confinement of being a Children's Playwright, even though you're so brilliant at it. The ability to write for children without writing down is very rare, but I don't think it should necessarily follow that you cannot also find the adult wavelength. Milne, Barrie and Lewis Carroll did it.* Peter Pan *of course is almost for Adults Only at one level – the stage directions (which normally the audience doesn't hear, though I believe the RSC contrived to bring them in) make that very clear. The close of Act V is chilling – that whole act is the most glorious send-up of Edwardian England that ever was – the 'If' of its day, though the great British Public never saw through it, as it never saw how Gilbert was taking the mickey out of it in the Savoy Operas. Which reminds – both Gilbert and Sullivan wanted to be taken as 'serious' writers – and their serious works are entirely forgotten. But the lightsome operas live on, without D'Oyly Carte and in spite of all the amateurs can do to them. You may have to settle for the immortality of* The Gingerbread Man! *But it is sad to think of any D.W. scripts lying about in Shaftesbury Ave or elsewhere unperformed – but I suppose that's 'show business' – or lack of it.*

…My Pageant! After the most incredible expenditure of blood, sweat and tears (of frustration), it was a Tremendous Success! King's Somborne is still talking about it – it involved 131 persons in all, a tenth of the village population, and made £750 plus for their tottering old Church Tower!

…I look forward to a meeting in '86, at Wimbledon, or Buck House, or the Arts, or Kensington Palace, or some old where.

Love,
Frank

1986

1986 began with DW preparing for a production of *The See-Saw Tree* as well as acting in (and writing) a schools series about computers for television. FW, meanwhile, was eager to plan a visit to see the play at Farnham, which happened while DW was away. By August, plans were well advanced for the next productions, as DW explained in one of his round-up letters.

1986 The See-Saw Tree –

Redgrave Theatre, Farnham – 18ᵗʰ March 1986

The See-Saw Tree, an ancient oak, stands on ground which is earmarked for development into a children's playground. A public meeting, involving the audience, is called to discuss this proposal, which includes cutting down the 300-year-old oak tree. The play then shows the effect this would have on the creatures who live in the tree. The audience votes on its future.

1986 Dinosaurs and all that Rubbish –

Howell's School, Denbigh, Clwyd, N. Wales – 4ᵗʰ July 1986
A modern moral fable telling how the Earth that Man has destroyed is restored to its natural beauty by dinosaurs and the animal kingdom.

31 Aug

Dear Frank,

Hope you are well and busy! Haven't been in touch for some time, so thought I would send the latest published 'oeuvre'! First time I have written for children to perform. Commissioned by Jacqui's old school in North Wales. It went very well.

Now in rehearsal with The Old Man of Lochnagar. *All seems to be going well – we open in Aberdeen 10th Sept. The royal connection has meant media interest – plus pre-publication (Amber Lane Press are doing it) and original cast album!! – at least, cassette. We record it this Friday and First Night Records say it'll be on sale 10 days later – just shows what can be done when it has to be!*

It's been busy this year – as you remember, I wrote The See-Saw Tree *for Farnham in March,* Dinosaurs, *then* Old Man. *Also doing another series of* Chish 'N' Fips *(the Gnomes) for next year...*

...Well – I must get off to rehearsal! All good wishes as ever – take care! Hope to see you before too long.

David

FW replied within a few days with a similarly news-packed missive, as well as some insightful comments on the play for children.

4 Sep

Dear David,

Huge thanks for your letter and The Dinosaurs*! Very far from rubbish! It provides not only excellent and desirable, necessary propaganda, but admirable material for a school to work on. Not only have you provided an endless elasticity of parts to play, but you have most cunningly and wisely left room for actors, directors and all concerned in production, with scope for their own individual creativity. I hope lots of schools will take it up.*

I was very glad to hear that the preparation of The Old Man of Lochnagar *goes well. My eye caught a small paragraph in* The Times *the other day mentioning that it was to open in Aberdeen – appropriately in the Theatre Royal! [His Majesty's] I'm sure The Family will want to see it, though perhaps the youngest are still too young for theatrical treats. Young William in the audience might steal the show if his participation in the Andrew wedding is anything to go by! Did you see it? Probably not – I don't imagine you have much time to sit before The Box. Even by your standards you seem to be having a busy year. We hope to catch the* Old Man *at Sadler's Wells. Matinees are just the thing for us, and we'll make ourselves as small as possible, not to be in the way. I still remember the small voice behind me at the Jeannetta Cochrane for* The Owl and the Pussycat Went to See… *– "There's a Very Large Grown-up in front of me!" I offered to move, but the offer was declined, so I made myself as much like a jack-knife as I could…*

…And love to your 'good self', as the lawyers say. And a triumph in Aberdeen. It'll soon be time, I reckon, for me to be keeping an eye on the Honours List. You would decorate splendidly and deserve it more than most!

Ever –
Frank
Good heavens – how I have run on. Always such a rattle!

DW wrote in response a few days later, filling FW in on some of the last-minute trials of putting on a play with royal connections.

8 Sep

Dear Frank

…We had our final run-throughs in London on Thursday – I am lucky enough to have a smashing company, many of them young Scottish actors. All seem to have unbounding energy and enthusiasm, which has made it a joy to work with them. Yesterday (Friday), we recorded the cast album for First Night Records! In fact, it will be a cassette, not a record. We have suddenly come up against a few hurdles – all to do with the Royal protocol – permission has to be granted for everything by a group of Trustees, who only seem to meet once every six months! Ah well, I suppose all will work out o.k. Meanwhile, suddenly the press and media interest has mushroomed and we are expecting a well-attended press call on Tuesday, including BBC Television News! It is quite remarkable the interest the Royals generate, which rubs off onto anything they are connected with. I'm just praying for a smooth technical rehearsal, moving all the big trucks around, etc.

Thank you for your good wishes – please accept more of mine!

Love from us all,
David

1986 The Old Man of Lochnagar –

His Majesty's Theatre, Aberdeen – September 1986

The story follows the Old Man, who lives in a cave by the loch under the mountain, Lochnagar, as he sets out to save the Gorms from the menacing Giant Gormless.

FW arranged to see the new play at Sadler's Wells in November, and in the meantime read the reviews (usually called notices in his letters) with interest, before the time came to set down his response to the piece.

17 Nov

Dear David,

…I read the Prince's book on the way home and was immediately struck by the skill which had given dramatic shape, providing a beginning, middle and end to what in the original is a series of delightful episodes that never actually get anywhere. And this is achieved with a remarkable fidelity to the book so that the selection you have extracted in no way diminishes the essence or changes the atmosphere. The use of the Old Man himself as narrator within the actor retains the company of the storyteller throughout – the book is so very much a book for reading aloud – like the Just-so Stories. *I wonder if HRH was brought up on them? Ask him, if you get the chance!*

I missed The Times *notice, but am being provided with it by a kind friend. I've seen the* Telegraph *though. And what has its Art Editor got against D. Wood that the Playwright, the Mastermind behind the whole spectacular success, is never named in the course of such splendid acclamation?*

I can understand why he was unhappy with what he called 'longeurs for over-21s', by which I suppose he meant the acrobatics; but these were not longeurs to the children, who relish them – as I did, being the World's No1 example of Arrested Development, because they did not go on too long (as acrobatics generally do) and because I could appreciate the necessity to pad the action out a bit (the playwright's perpetual problem – why else all those sub-plots in Shakespeare?) without losing sight of the storyline – as the contrivers of modern – and ancient pantomime – are too apt to do. (Comment in margin: Gosh! This

49

sentence has got itself in a right mess! Sorry!) You have contrived a play for children which combines the spectacular magic of the old-fashioned pantomime with essential, spontaneous audience participation. I do hope you've recorded that rapturous, noisy delight and excitement…

> *Love,*
> *Frank*

In response, and enclosing a collection of reviews of the play:

24 Nov

Dear Frank,

…My main worry about The Old Man *is the first 20 minutes or so – setting-up time! The first song, plus Old Man monologue, into the scene with Grouse. If I could lose four or five minutes there, I would, but it's very tricky, because it sets up the Old Man so well, and it's vital they like him because he's never off!! We changed the monologue a few weeks ago – he now talks of the Pig Eagle, not (as in the text) the Boobri, and I've cut a little too – but now I wonder whether I should cut the Highland Kelpie (who is never mentioned again!). Trouble is, he does it so well! And the kids seem held by it. Heigh ho – any ideas!! Maybe I could prune the Old Man/Grouse scene, but it's nearly all plot really! Albery [Theatre] seems certain, though no contract signed yet!…*

> *Best wishes from us all,*
> *David*

FW was delighted to receive the reviews, but his letter includes a level of detail in his response which was new, suggesting specific changes to dialogue.

Dear David,

…I note your worry about the 'first 20 mins'. I can understand this – it is a longish sketch for your young audience – but if that young audience is being held (I wasn't aware of any fidgeting), I don't think you've much to worry about. Of course, some audiences will be more firmly held than others. Probably the Old Man himself, and you, if you are in the audience, are the best judges of how held any particular audience is. One generally knows when one has 'got' one's audience and when one is failing – in a classroom as well as on a stage (all the same thing really)! The Old Man may be a better judge than yourself as author and director because, in the auditorium, your anxiety that things are dragging may make you suspect inattention when actually there is none.

I wonder, though, whether some modification of the Scots accent would strengthen the grip – it might increase comprehension and quicken reaction, especially when you are playing Sassenach houses.

The substitution of the Pig Eagle for the Boobri, is, I'm sure, a real improvement. It looks forward to a character to be met later, and should arouse anticipation which will not be disappointed. Kids remember things like that and will connect backwards to him. (To instance the Bard again, Macbeth *is full of this ploy.) The Highland Kelpie is, strictly speaking, superfluous, but so long as the story is well told, it can justify its place. And, as you say, it is well told, and helps to establish character and atmosphere – and kids do like a story being told, not merely read. So I wouldn't worry about that.*

The Old Man/Grouse scene. The dialogue dances beautifully, lovely sprung rhythm, catching the ear's attention – but again is the accent perhaps obscuring some of its neater points? If you think you should cut, I'd take a look at p13. Could it be shortened by concentrating on the points essential to the future action – like this, perhaps?

GROUSE: Get away! A rest? And who'll cook your egg for you if I rest? Why don't you take yourself off and away? Then I'd have a rest.

OLD MAN: There's no place like home, Grousy. (changing the subject) How was your cousin Ptarmigan?

GROUSE: Toffee-beaked, as ever. All posh and la-di-da.

OLD MAN: She does lay a lovely egg. All I can do is lay the table.

(And thereafter as printed.)

The enlargement of 'Toffee-beaked as ever' with They're all the same… higher up' seems to me to be of adult rather than kid-appeal. 'Toffee-beaked' itself is probably of adult-appeal chiefly, too. But it sounds well, even if kids don't get the nice play of idea. The explanation, if they don't, isn't really necessary, and may be labouring the joke – too long.

I offer these rash suggestions with humble temerity! But if you are worried, they may help. The beginning – especially for a young audience – is always difficult. Attention must be grabbed immediately, or all is lost*. (Classroom experience again!) But just remember how W.S. began with a bang whenever he could, and how, directing him, in, say The Merchant *or* As You Like It *one wishes he'd never forgotten it! Caesar, Macbeth, Hamlet, R&J present no problem, but one keeps one's directorial fingers crossed at the opening of* Lear…

Thanks, and thanks again –

Love to you all,
Frank

* What cheek! As if you didn't know this! Oh, I am a right old pedagogue!

DW sent more reviews towards the end of the year, and responded to some of the suggestions made by FW.

Dear Frank,

…I thought I would let you know that I have now instrumented – if that is the right word – various cuts, which have tightened up the production really well.

    First of all, I did cut the Highland Kelpie. Iain did it very well, but it really was a red herring, so it went… I also cut a bit of the first song. Then, in Old Man/Grouse scene, I managed to cut even more than you suggested. This has helped no end. In the second half, I cut the pantomimic Spider episode, which really, although it was intended to show how the Old Man had shrunk and emphasise the scale we were now in, in honesty became an excuse to get the audience going! I also cut the Gorm Games in their entirety. These were not especially well done, and did not add anything, and only meant cutting two extra references to them earlier in the play. The Gorms' main attribute is heather spraying and energetic activity, which makes Giant Gormless want to catch them. The Gorm Games are really not relevant. So, all in all, I managed to cut about 10 minutes and am very pleased.

    We look forward to opening at the Albery next week!…

Yours, David

The year ended with FW's good wishes for the London opening of *The Old Man* at the Albery.

53

1987

DW's first round-up of the year contained disappointing news about *The Old Man* but also more positive developments.

24 Oct

Dear Frank,

…This is really to let you know that The Old Man *did pretty awful business at the Albery – losing a lot of money for the West End producers (Whirligig, thank heaven, were not involved financially). Time was against us – they announced it only 2 weeks before opening. Meanwhile, the production of* The Hobbit *at the Fortune packed 'em in, in spite of some of the worst reviews I have ever seen for a children's play!! However, after many problems, fights and panics, we did manage to preserve the production for posterity (for tv – Channel 4). We recorded it last week at the Albery and it looked v. good. I have adapted it for t.v. – one hour only; but we recorded all of it, with audience (twice), and will edit it later. SO – the irony is that the show has really achieved quite a lot – tour, cassette, playscript published, West End, tv – and it has done consistently badly at the box office! At least the reviews have been consistently good!*

Last weekend, I nipped over to Brussels for 30 hours! To see an English-speaking company doing my Hijack Over Hygenia, *a rather neglected work over here!! – nice to see it again, and nice people who entertained me royally…*

Hope to see you soon – and a happy New Year (delayed …)

David

February saw discussions about *The See-Saw Tree* coming to Winchester for Christmas, with FW enlisted as a trusted go-between since he was such a supporter of the Theatre Royal. He also took the opportunity to be a little more forthright in his reaction to the play than had been the case previously.

20 Feb

Dear David,

…How much are you re-vamping The See-Saw Tree? *When our lot saw it at Farnham they found the opening not very arresting. The committee meeting was beyond their comprehension, I think. They aren't into Social Studies yet – and I felt the medium as being subordinated to the Message. How about a couple of protesters with banners storming the stage?… We missed participation in that particular production, too, and we would have welcomed more music, I remember, to excite us before we reached the very real suspense of the approach of the tree-fellers.*

You've probably considered all these points – but I mention them because I did detect a note of disappointment among the children after the expectation aroused by G.B.M. and the S.S-F which had enthralled them. In the latter they were especially grabbed by the actors who introduced them to the set while they were waiting for the play to begin. I hope these comments aren't impertinent – they're meant to be useful…

Love to you all –
Frank

Meanwhile, FW was still trying to persuade the new manager of his local theatre to put on a DW play at Christmas.

13 Mar

Dear David,

I saw John Crow at the meeting of the Theatre Royal Supporters' Club last night, and had the chance of a fairly extended word

*with him. He improves on acquaintance and seems to have quite
a sense of humour to temper his somewhat bureaucratic air of
efficiency. (He's recently married – perhaps this has loosened him
up!) His problem with his choice of Christmas show seems to be
that he feels committed to the Horseshoe Company of Basingstoke
which has provided Christmas fare at the T.R. for a number of
years now, and proved very popular. I ventured to suggest that
term time might anyway be better for a visit from Whirligig,
so that the junior schools could bring parties during school
hours. (If the teachers aren't on strike, or the schools closed.)
As you know, Winchester has a number of private schools in its
catchment area. The Horseshoe shows –* Wind in the Willows
and Alice *have been among them – aim at a fairly extended
family age range, covering juniors and middles in a two-hours
plus performance. Whirligig's length aimed at the juniors more
specifically would be matinees (a.m. & p.m.) only, wouldn't it, as
at Sadler's Wells and the Albery?*

*Anyway, that's the gist of the meeting. I think he'd be an
agreeable character to work with and straightforward...*

*Love to you all –
Frank*

By July, DW was able to report that, despite all the efforts on their
behalf, Winchester did not want the show for Christmas, although
The Gingerbread Man would be going to Chichester. By August, the
Play Theatres were at prototype stage, and in the following month
there was more to send to FW.

14 Sep

Dear Frank,

...Am enclosing a teachers' information pack for The See-Saw
Tree *which has been produced for us by WATCH, the national*

environmental club for young people, associated with the Royal Society for Nature Conservation.

…[Thinking about productions in general] Once a production has opened, I often feel it no longer really belongs to me. The actors know the play and the way it works with an audience far better than me, having done it repeatedly, so it is sometimes arrogant to assume that one can criticise on the strength of seeing one show four weeks into the run!

We start rehearsals today. Rather looking forward to it!

Take care.

Love,
David

1988

1988 was another busy year, as was clear from a letter sent in October.

28 Oct

My dear Frank,

…Both shows have opened well – Dinosaurs, with 100 children, has been a bit of a nightmare, but opened in triumph last week!!

Am now directing Meg and Mog Show *for Unicorn again (4th time!). In fact, Wood groupies (inc. my mother and John) are making Nov. 19th a pilgrimage!!!*

10.30 AM DINOSAURS (S. Wells)

2.30 PM MEG AND MOG (Arts)

5.00 PM SHELLFISH (S. Wells)

Also, my new Pied Piper *opens in Nov. On tour in West Country, plus Xmas at Plymouth Theatre Royal.*

Do hope you are well.

Love and best wishes from us all,
David

FW was quick to confirm he would join the group visit to the plays, and had some news of his own to pass on.

2 Nov

Dear David,

...Congrats on successful launch of Dinosaurs *– I'm sure the kids had a wonderful time whatever the Author and the Animals may have thought about them! And all the best for* The Pied Piper *– more children? Are you linking up with YTS [Youth Training Scheme]?*

You will be anguished to hear that I am working on a play! I've been asked by the Friends of Ockenden (the Refugee home) to provide a piece of performance in Horsham Parish Church – my old stomping ground – as they want to 'raise a substantial sum' for the Ockenden Funds. I used to be on the Horsham Committee when I lived there. It's to be a picture of Horsham history – provisional title Horsham through a Looking-Glass, *a sort of kaleidoscope because I've found it impossibly dull to follow a conventional chronology, and it's booked in to the Parish Church for late October '89. It's keeping me very occupied and I'm enjoying it – but what the upshot, outcome or end product will be, Gawd alone knows!*

So, à bientôt – the 19th inst at 5pm. And here's wishing a triple crown for all the London prods!

Love to you all –
Frank

Plans advanced well, with *Meg and Mog* rehearsals continuing and high hopes that a screenplay based on Michelle Magorian's *Back Home* would be filmed. FW duly announced himself as 'fascinated by the current projects. How do you manage them all?'

1988 The Pied Piper –

Octagon Theatre, Yeovil – 16th November 1988

Set in modern times, it seems that the Pied Piper has returned to claim the fee denied him all those years ago, and once more spirits away the children, but this time all ends happily.

1989

The introduction of the Education Reform Act was making life difficult for many companies.

13 Jul

Dear Frank,

…Many thanks indeed for your invitation to come to your production. (I realise you haven't produced it, but you know what I mean!) I am putting it in the diary, in the hope that I can come down. I will have opened the Whirligig production by then, and am not sure exactly what will be going on. So let's hope I can make it!

Whirligig is reviving The Ideal Gnome Expedition *this year, in spite of all sorts of problems thrown up by the Education Reform Act. No doubt you've read about this. Parents now have to be asked for voluntary contributions rather than being simply told/asked to pay the money for school trips. This is legally no different from before, but is leading to all sorts of problems, schools cancelling bookings, etc., etc. Could be the beginning of the end!*

However, we will see.

…On Sunday we went to the Festival of Voices at Wembley Conference Centre, during which a choir of 1,200 (yes 1,200) primary school children sang 'When Will We Learn?' from The Selfish Shellfish. *Not a dry eye in the house!*

… I had a meeting with a company interested in doing a stop/

go animation series for television based on The Gingerbread
Man *– something I have always thought a possibility.*

*…Various projects bubbling. Waiting for confirmation of
two or three writing jobs. Trying to think of an idea for a new
children's play, but so far without much success.*

Love,
David

In return, FW once more mused on how so much could be done by
one person, and signed off in hope that DW would come to the play
in Horsham. The reply suggested that he would, and was followed by
a second indicating that all had enjoyed it.

5 Oct

Dear Frank,

*It looks as though we can all come to your play on the Saturday.
I'm presuming that the girls (now 10 and 13) would be permitted
to come…? They are theatrically quite experienced, and I'm sure
would enjoy it.*

…Have just got back from opening The Ideal Gnome
Expedition *at the University of Warwick Arts Centre. It all went
very smoothly and well, I'm glad to say!*

*…The Education Reform Act has successfully decimated our
audiences. There are some places in the country where it is impossible
to get any state school parties at all, even places where we used to
do well. Darlington Civic Theatre, where we have played for ten
successive years to capacity for ten performances, this year has gone
down to 58%. It's a crazy situation, and the Government really opened
a can of worms without knowing what was going to come out!*

*We battle on. But we have curtailed any thoughts of London
Christmas seasons of* The Gingerbread Man *or* Meg and Mog
Show.

Meanwhile, I'm working on two possible television ideas – ten-minute animated cartoon stories based on Orlando, the Marmalade Cat; *and a stop-go animation series (cf* The Wombles*) based on* The Gingerbread Man. *And I've got to write a new children's play for Cambridge Theatre Company too.*

Looking forward very much to seeing you soon. Hope you and Mary are both well.

All good wishes.

Yours,
David

30 Oct

My dear Frank,

…Jacqui and I would very much like to read your play. I could quite understand your sitting there wanting to oomph them up! But very few performances of that ilk ever really do justice to the pen, let alone the wordsmith!

Having said that, there were a couple of good, solid perfs, and the information you had so cleverly included, without it seeming like a history lesson, did come through. And lighting and sound were v. impressive. We just wanted them to get on with it! Nevertheless, a very considerable achievement – but we'd like to see it on the page now! Any chance?

…Love, congratulations and best wishes from us all,
David

After being sent further information about the Education Reform Act effects, FW was reminded of similar obstacles encountered in his early years.

17 Nov

Dear David,

Many thanks for …the very interesting and distressing news-cuttings. I shall study them in detail presently – a quick glance suggests that lobbying by parent-power (how many PTAs is Jacqui on?) and pressure on LEAs is the only answer. Whirligig, catering for the pre-examination ages, is at a disadvantage compared with companies offering set-books forming part of the very demanding GCSE and A Level Drama Courses. During the summer our Theatre Royal has been offering shows for 4–8 years, and until the onset of her back-trouble, Mary was much occupied in ushering at morning performances, mostly well attended. But we are in an area of many independent prep. and pre-prep. schools, so we are probably untypical. Local councils do – still – need a lot of persuasion to accept that children can get as much benefit from time spent outside the classroom as in it. I remember Harcourt Williams telling me – before the war – that when he suggested to the then LCC that children might be brought to see Shakespeare at the Old Vic, the reply was, "But wouldn't that be too much like letting them enjoy themselves?" There are twilight areas still where such an attitude prevails, quite apart from the problems of funding. But it should not – by patient persistence – be impossible to persuade parents (though not perhaps in Inner City areas) that play-going is worth paying for. They seem to find money easily enough for expensive electronic toys. Perhaps they see the benefit of those in keeping children occupied at home, whereas during school time they are occupied anyway and shouldn't involve further expenditure on peace and quiet!…

Love to you all – Frank

1990

1990 Save the Human –

Arts Theatre, Cambridge – 15ᵗʰ February 1990

Long ago, human beings ruled the world, but they made a terrible mess of it, and now the animals are in charge. When Becky Bear's pet human, Norman, is kidnapped by Professor Rhino's Securiboars, to be used in medical experimentation, she and her friends start a campaign to 'save the human'.

With *Save the Human* opened, DW sent a brief update on that, his *Magic and Music Show* and a forthcoming TV appearance. Later in the year, he wrote again about a forthcoming trip and some possible new ventures.

6 Jul

My dear Frank,

…Meanwhile, the Save the Human *tour is all going ahead – dates enc.! Arts Council Touring came up with the cash about 6 weeks ago. We have lost half our original cast, sadly, but have hopefully found good replacements. It also seems that Hamish Hamilton have agreed to publish a book version (as originally intended!).*

Latest good news is that Unicorn at the Arts have asked me, with my 'team', to mount The Gingerbread Man *there for Xmas season, opening Nov 17th and running till Jan 13th. The idea of it in that small auditorium is very appealing! The play is 15 years old this year, and still alive and kicking, which is very pleasing!*

Love and best wishes from us all,
David

The reply from FW contained some thoughts on masks on stage in *Save the Human*, as well as further theatrical reminiscence.

10 Jul

Dear David,

...It must have been a very difficult work to script. Did you in fact create it by improvisation of the action on the very original theme and then put it down on paper only when you'd got it all worked out? The limitation of cast must have been an additional complication, but it adds to the tightness of the form. Without it, there would have been danger of diffuseness; and as we have seen from your actual production it worked splendidly. The masks, too, are an inspired innovation for creating audience participation, not by the traditional 'Did you see him?' gag, or catching up a chorus, but by taking a real part in the action. The cartoon 'scenery' is a most happy idea because, apart from its flexibility, it is an aspect with which children are familiar from their comics. And it still fills a gap.

...And The Gingerbread Man *to have a Christmas run at the Arts for a two-month season! Just the home for it. It would be wonderful if it could be established there as a permanent successor to* The Windmill Man, *which used to occupy the afternoons in pre-war days at the Victoria Palace with Bert Coote (father of Robert, whom I was at school with as the Mad Gardner), and was in annual competition with* Where the Rainbow Ends *at the Fortune. Mercifully that did end at last – it was the most appalling patriotic drip...*

Frank

A reply quickly followed.

4 Aug

Dear Frank,

...The original script as used in the rehearsal room was very similar, except that it didn't suggest who should narrate at any point – in rehearsal we found the best way to use the troops etc., but the division of roles had been previously worked out.

The U.S. was... interesting and exhausting! ...We did Disney, Universal Studios, Graumann's Theatre, etc. Lunch with S. French man on Sunset Boulevard, purchase from magic shop on Hollywood Boulevard, visit to Jonathan Lynn (Yes Minister – original director of Plotters *and G. Man), who lives in L.A. – etc., etc. – very enjoyable – but the place itself didn't really inspire us or make us feel we wanted to emigrate!! Really rather ugly and sprawled out...*

Interesting to read about The Windmill Man *– I'd never heard of that one – what was it about?? I have read – and rejected(!) –* Where the Rainbow Ends *as yucky jingoism!...*

Love and best wishes to you and Mary, from all of us,
David

FW sent further practical comments on the next play to be published.

15 Aug

Dear David,

...So, huge thanks for Tide Race. *And for* Dinosaurs. *It's another great script. I do hope lots of schools will attempt it, especially if they can't take parties to the 'real' theatre. It's fine for enterprising drama departments, involving music, dance and song with parts for all ages. The picture on p5 for 'Build me a rocket' is great. And the mime will be hugely enjoyed. Young Lorna, who has an urge towards drama, begins at a local school with a good*

reputation for proper attention to the arts next term. I think I'll get her – when she's settled there – to bring it to the notice of her teacher. Then we'd have a chance to see it!...

    Frank

DW's next letter and FW's reply returned to the ongoing discussion of children's literature and times past.

31 Aug

Dear Frank,

*...Just read Seymour Hicks' autobiography. I find that era – Edwardian theatre – rather interesting, tho' I don't think it was a 'great' era at all – (Oscar Wilde apart?) – but Barrie and others, of course, interest me. And the way Hicks acted, wrote, directed and built theatres – the Aldwych and the Strand – fascinated me! Also just finished biog of A.A. Milne (much enjoyed) and excellent Sheila Hancock auto-biog (*Ramblings of an Actress*) – highly recommended!*

    A.A. Milne clearly resented the success of the 4 children's books because, in spite of (maybe because of) the wealth and fame, from then on no one took his adult plays seriously again, or, really, his journalism. It is ironic that the only play of his which is still regularly performed is Toad of Toad Hall!...

    Love to you both,
    David

2 Sep

Dear David,

...I was most interested in your recent reading. ...Barrie has been my lifelong love since I first saw Quality Street *at Croydon Grand*

in – let me see – 1918, I should guess. I became an addict at once, not of course appreciating what JMB owed in that work to Mrs. Gaskell. He has always been underestimated – the whimsy and the sentiment, icing applied to the cake for the benefit of the box office, have too much obscured the iron and irony which is at the heart of his work. The stage direction at the close of Act V of Peter Pan *is a revelation. However did a boy brought up in a Scots village acquire such a gift for stage-craft? Do you know Hardy's poem about him?*

I read the extracts from the Milne biog in the public prints. He does seem to have been odd! But so was Lewis Carroll. Is there a link between mathematicians and writing for children? Were you good at sums? I knew Lesley de Selincourt as a precocious child (L de S, not me) before she married Christopher Robin. Her father Aubrey was Headmaster of Clayesmore when I taught there. He was a classicist and much else besides. He wrote some splendid books for children – A Family Afloat *was one – and translated Herodotus for Penguin Classics; but as a Head he was hopeless!…*

Frank

The mention of a possible link between mathematicians and writers for children seemed to strike a chord.

17 Sep

Dear Frank,

…Interested in your love of Barrie – I haven't read all the plays, but lots of his letters, plus various biographies. It is true that many so-called 'children's writers' were odd! Lear is another and, in their ways, B. Potter, E. Nesbit and E. Blyton – but many of them were only 'made' into children's writers because of their huge success in that area when really they thought they should

be known for their other, more lofty work. Yet it's arguable, as Roald Dahl says, that writing for children is more 'difficult' than writing for adults. Maybe Maths is an essential (I took O level and enjoyed it, incidentally!) because of the need for logic within the fantasy. Children are logical to the point of the prosaic, even though their imaginations have more power than adults'. They like a pattern, a structure. You can't get away with freewheeling.

Terry Jones (ex-Python – at Oxford with me) has written a couple of very good children's novels – e.g., Nicobobinus, which he says flowed freely – he didn't know where the story was going or how it was going to end; personally, I wonder if this is strictly true! – it contains evidence of detailed planning to me! I certainly can't start to write until the synopsis is complete, with highs, lows, 'suddenlies' all plotted. Mathematically perhaps! Did I ever tell you my 'motto', incidentally? Years ago in Canada, I was on breakfast tv with the female editor of the equivalent of Puffin Books – when asked 'what children liked', she told of her own daughter (8 years old) who finished a book, saying, "I really enjoyed that" – Mother, being a good publisher, wanted to know WHY. Daughter thought, then said – "Lots of suddenlies" – now I aim at at least three suddenlies every page! – a new character, a sound effect, a plot development, a lighting effect, a sharp movement, a musical sting, a song, a revelation etc., etc. One of the faults of plays other people – agents and new writers – send me is that often two characters are on for six pages talking – nothing happens – no action, no development – just talk – and the children would not find it very interesting – no suddenlies!

Have just been asked to adapt Roald Dahl's The BFG for the stage – have you read it? If not, maybe you could – maybe you'd have some idea as to how the hell one could make it work in large theatres – I'm temporarily defeated! Yet I know it would be very popular…

Love to you and Mary…
David

22 Sep

Dear David,

How good of you to write at such interesting length all in your own hand! The time-consuming exercise is warmly appreciated by yours truly. I am a reluctant penman though inclined to run on once I get started. I can't think on to a typewriter. Can you?

Your account of your working practice of course is especially interesting to me. Before you begin to plot your highs, lows, and 'suddenlies'* though, I take it you must have a conception of the final product in mind – that is, you know where you want to get to, and the careful scenario maps the route. It has always seemed to me that all successful art must be carefully structured. A work of art, in whatever medium, is the satisfactory achievement of an intention that may give pleasure by being beautiful. Shaw used to say that he never knew what any play was going to develop into when he sat down to begin it. That was just a Shavian tease. His best plays – Candida, Heartbreak House *and* Saint Joan, *for instance – are beautifully structured. His last efforts are not. The dear old man just couldn't get out of the habit of spouting and scribbling.*

What puzzles me about GBS is what also puzzles me about Barrie. How did either of them, with his untheatrical background, acquire such a grasp of dramatic technique? I'm delighted to learn of your interest in Barrie. His stagecraft is a joy for any director – you discover his skill as soon as you begin to work on a production. Have you come upon Granville Barker's preface to The Boy David? *He pinpoints some of JMB's masterstrokes, though he tantalizingly leaves the most magical of all [un]disclosed. The respect of a lesser craftsman for the secrets of another more masterly conjuror, perhaps? He says of* Mary Rose: *"Upon the magic island she must disappear before our eyes. This is matter for a single risky moment, which is, moreover led up to with extraordinary dramatic skill, and a sympathetic producer may compass it"; that is all. He does not indicate how Barrie has done the producer's job for him.*

I read somewhere of an admirer of JMB who was so determined to discover how Mary Rose was made to vanish that he watched several successive performances determined to keep his attention exclusively on the fey heroine (Fay Compton). It was not until his third visit that he failed to be caught by Barrie's cunning. Until then, his attention was distracted, as Barrie intended it should be, from the stillness of Mary Rose, enrapt by the 'call' on one side of the stage, to the heavy action of Simon on the other stamping out the fire which had just rekindled itself. Nothing so distracting on stage as the possibility of the whole theatre becoming engulfed in flames! The scene of the making of the fire by Cameron the ghillie to demonstrate the proper way of baking a trout, absorbing in itself of course, had been carefully contrived so that the fire would have to be stamped out at the critical moment of Mary Rose's disappearance. There was no scenic trickery. She simply 'vanished' by walking into the wings while nobody was looking at her.

Frank

*What a promising critic was that child! I recall another criticising a yellow door in a production of Twelfth Night *at Worthing "because Olivia doesn't like yellow." Child logic can be devastating.*

The discussion was continued when the pair met up in Wimbledon in October, and the forthcoming production of *The BFG* must have been a topic of interest too, with its opening now set for February 1991 at Wimbledon Theatre.

Fascinating story of Mary Rose 'vanish' – I bet some producers have employed magic advisors to create an illusion when, as you say, JMB has done it all for them!

David

1991

The year began with FW making plans to catch up with the tour of *The BFG* when it reached Southampton, and DW replied with news of the production.

24 Jan

Dear Frank,

…BFG rehearsals start on Monday. We have a nice cast, but not really enough time to do it! The usual problem. Things are well advanced with the set, however, and I understand most of the extraordinary props will be available from the first day of rehearsal, which is a nice change!

Am also up to my eyes in the possible television 13-part animation series, based on The Gingerbread Man, *which has suddenly got serious, following two years of interest, storyline development, nothingness, vague interest, etc., etc. Suddenly it's all guns firing. But I'm trying to cut myself off from it as much as possible while BFG takes shape.*

Unicorn have definitely said they want me to do Meg and Mog Show *there again this Christmas, for the fifth time! And Whirligig has decided to tour* The Gingerbread Man, *following its success at Unicorn. So at least I don't have to write a new play this year!…*

…Love and best wishes to you and Mary,
David

1991 The BFG –

The play faithfully follows Dahl's story in which the Big Friendly Giant and young orphan Sophie team up to save the children of England from child-eating giants.

4 Mar

Dear Frank,

...Believe it or not, we sold every seat at Wimbledon – ten performances. I suddenly find I have a big commercial success on my hands! Theatres are doing huge business. It is ironic that the show in all but name is a Whirligig show – Whirligig personnel and Whirligig expertise – yet Whirligig will not benefit, of course, this being a commercial production inspired by another management!

Not only that, in the same week that The BFG *opened, Arts Council Touring decided, in their infinite wisdom, not to support Whirligig this year... So our tour of* The Gingerbread Man *is in jeopardy unless we can raise investment and do it as a commercial tour. This we are now attempting.*

The BFG *has been great fun to do. Very hard work in some ways, but most enjoyable and satisfying. It had a lovely review in* The Times, *a copy of which I enclose. The odd niggle in the review doesn't worry me. At least the implication is that the adaptation and the production worked.*

All good wishes, as ever, to you and Mary,
David

22 Mar

Dear David,

…At the risk of breaking your concentration (like a tea-tray dropped in the stalls during a matinee – those were the days!), I must drop you a line to say a huge thank-you for your latest letter and enclosure. The notices are splendid. I can't wait to get down to the Mayflower. I shall expect to find it packed. Rather a shame, though, that the lady from the Croydon Advertiser *should give the game away about your solution of the problem of giant-size. A brilliant solution though, and I don't suppose many eager anticipators of whizzpopping wonders will have read it, so their eager expectation of how the Giant is to be managed will not have been blunted. Pat has not given it away.*

We (that's Mary and me, not the Lady with the corgis) do hope the Whirligig tours will materialise after all. And Australia! Oh, how exciting! But do be careful when you're upside down. It was her trip to Oz that started Mary's ozteoporosis!…

Love to all,
Frank

28 Mar

Dear Frank,

…Thanks for yours of 22nd. Next week, the Mayflower calls! I hope you enjoy it – the build-up may lead you to expect too much! But BFG *continues to do extraordinary business everywhere (so far), virtually selling out at Bristol Hippo. last week and Belfast Grand Opera House this. I can't get used to being a commercial success!! (Thanks in no small measure to Mr Dahl) – strange jobs are being offered to me – e.g., a new stage version of Rupert Bear – this doesn't thrill me, except that years ago I actually researched Rupert in the Reading Room of the British Museum,*

and found the original Mary Tourtel stories, which were really rather good. So, who knows?

Meanwhile, the struggle to keep Whirligig afloat continues – fingers crossed a West End producer sympathetic to the cause… may put some money up.

All good wishes as ever,
David

Although his letter has not survived, FW must have approved, and the discussion of stagecraft continued.

13 Apr

Dear Frank,

…Delighted to receive your long letter on return from Cornwall – thank you, and thank you for kind words on BFG. What pleased me was the amount of theatricality we managed to employ – puppetry (big and small and shadow), scale – giant heads, etc., the gradual development of the 'play within a play' to 'reality' (Queen going from cardboard crown to coronation rig; toy corgi going to real corgi, etc.), lighting and sound opportunities – all seem to justifiably help tell the story, and – hopefully – introduce a brand-new audience to the excitement of live theatre – not just 'new' meaning children, but others as well; we have found that this play (thanks to Mr Dahl) is encouraging all 'classes' and conditions of men, women and children – many of whom might never visit a theatre normally except to see a Christmas panto (of the more commercial variety!). This is all very encouraging.

A few days after your visit, the Queen (Mary-Ann, whom you saw as Grouse in Old Man*) had a nasty accident, falling in a car park and bashing her face and breaking a tooth or two… So since then the understudy has been on (I think she's done well). Dramas, dramas! Next week is the holiday week. The week* *after, Oxford – I shall take the opportunity to go and see them then, partly because members of the Dahl family visit it there, and, on their yeah or nay (neigh, neah, né…?) lies the future of the show. You see, our producers only have the rights on the book till Feb. '92 – they want them extended, naturally. If permission is not granted, all rights revert, and my play becomes a version of* The BFG, *not the version, which is what we all want!…*

Rupert Bear is still a possible. The producer is finding out what sort of storylines were used for the forthcoming t.v. series (cartoons) – and whether a stage version would have to reflect the t.v. films… all to do with the Daily Express… *it may end up too much of a burden trying to please everyone!*

Whirligig still in dire straits – decision delayed till mid-May, tho' publicity needs to start then… no one wants to invest in The Gingerbread Man, *which is a shame, but, in the current climate, understandable…*

Love and best wishes – as ever,
David

17 Apr

Dear David,

… I thought the way in which the party children were metamorphosed was very clever. And the Queen's maid made a memorable character out of moments. Quite the best maid I can remember since Una O'Connor in – I think – The Barretts of Wimpole Street, *or was it* Cavalcade? *Can't be sure – but she glided across the floor on invisible feet for all the world as though she was fitted with castors. (Casters? No – that's for sugar.)*

Theatricality! Oh yes, again. This is what is lacking to-day. The photographic actuality of the large and small screens is so unexciting in itself. I suspect that's why it has to offer so much violent action to hold its audience, and why actors accustomed to acting within

75

the restrictions imposed by the camera cannot project when they come on a real stage. I remember noticing years ago the difference between a scene in Cavalcade *in the stage and the film versions. In the theatre, the arrival of the troop train at the station was tremendous. We gasped in amazement, then cheered and cheered. How was it done? Sheer magic! The same scene in the cinema had none of it. We knew it was just a photograph. Easy. Boring – even though in early films a train could always provide a highlight, not because it was dramatic but simply because a train – even a Wessex Electric thundering into Winchester – is always impressive for itself. But a train coming towards you from the depth of the stage at Drury Lane – WOW! It was much the same with the scene of the departing troopship drawing away from the quay. And the silent scene in Hyde Park after Q. Victoria's death. And the Brighton Beach episode! Oh my, oh my, what a magnificent exploitation of theatre that show was! They did it differently but well at Chichester…*

…Love to you all – Mary calls, "Are you writing to David? Send him my love!!" Here it is, from

Frank

18.4.91.

Ultimate Afterthought!

I have just remembered – oh, I am so forgetiferous in old age – that I meant to say how masterly was the 'suddenly' that climaxed the first half. It was so good to see scenery being made actively to work, not just fill space.

And I meant to say, I'm sure you need have no doubts about the verdict of the darling Dahls. How could the adaptation be more faithfully and effectively done? The reaction of the kids must surely convince them of that!

Love again –
F

29 Apr

Dear Frank,

...You will be glad to know that Mrs Roald Dahl saw the show at Oxford last week and left a note with the sound engineer at the back of the auditorium, saying 'How wondercrump! Thank you. With love. Liccy Dahl.' This naturally spread smiles among the ranks, and we are hoping that it may lead to an extension of the rights on the book, and therefore a much longer tour, with perhaps the possibility of other countries as well.

Yours, David

May saw a visit to Wimbledon by FW to give a talk to the Friends of Wimbledon Theatre, and catch up with DW and his current projects, including ongoing tours of *The Gingerbread Man* and *The BFG*. A gift of the book version of *Save the Human* was much appreciated, as was the appreciation itself.

3 Sep

Dear David,

Save The Human *has just arrived. I have read it straight through twice with increasing admiration for its unobtrusive and appropriate art. It should become a classic. It is much more satisfying than Orwell's* Animal Farm *(which I have always felt to be over-rated because its fable is so obvious) because – quite apart from its message – its characters and situations are more convincing. And the narrative is conducted with masterly art, particularly in its brevity and its skilful transitions from scene to scene. The prose style is entirely economical and right for its intended readers, but more than that it is right for the book as a whole, and there is no condescension in its vocabulary. Words like 'bashing and biffing', 'sploshing', which children might choose themselves, come quite unself-consciously, and those which they might find difficult – 'evacuate', 'reconciliation', explain themselves from their context.*

You establish each character with equally sure lightning touches: 'Ben's face crumpled...' 'growled Mr Bear, then went back to his newspaper' ... 'Becky found it frightening, but kept watching', and at moments revelation becomes universal: "'That's different," smiled her father, "Norman's our pet human."' This is poetry in Auden's definition – 'language charged with meaning'.

Tony Husband's cartoons perfectly complement the text as they did the play.

I could go on enumerating beauties for page after page, but I won't waste your time. I'll just sum up my reaction. You've written a masterpiece, a work of art. Congratulations! Thank you!

Love to you all,
Frank

4 *Sep*

Phew! Phew!
What a review!
Hope you meant it!
Glad I sent it!
Thank you
Frank you
Made my day
Thanks for everything you say.

D x

Rehearsals for *Meg and Mog Show* followed, with the show opening in November, and plans for meeting up in Winchester at Christmas.

Dear Frank,

…Have just returned from a rather fraught Dress Rehearsal of Meg and Mog Show. *A lot of stage management problems in the scene changes, which I think will rectify. But the odd thing is the show is much longer than it's ever been before! I can't quite put my finger on it, but hope that we'll lose a few minutes at the public Dress today. A live, volatile, children's audience often makes everybody pick up pace!…*

> *Yours,*
> *David*

Fri pm.

Update! Just got back from public d.r. – seven whole minutes shorter! Phew! Technical problems mainly sorted out, but still 'technology' ones like a rogue radio mike and a non-budging space buggy! Fingers crossed for opening tomorrow pm.

> *D*

The London premiere of *The BFG* followed, very positively reviewed by all but *The Times*.

3 Dec

Dear David,

The cheers are still ringing for the arrival of your supergaloptious text this morning with the news of its successful launch at the Aldwych. Who does The Times *critic think he is? Now you'll have three shows running simultaneously, two in London! What else? (As if that wasn't enough – what am I thinking of?)…*

> *Love –*
> *Frank*

A happy Boxing Day tea followed with DW and family in Winchester for a break, rounding off another busy year.

1992

The year began with FW making a trip to London to see *Meg and Mog Show*, an outing he enjoyed and was quick to analyse.

16 Jan

Dear David,

…thank you very much for Meg and Mog *yesterday and for our little chat therebefore. (If you can say 'herebefore', 'hereafter' and 'thereafter', why not 'therebefore'? A word in the earbefore of the Oxford Syndics is yndicated.) I enjoyed it all enormously – and surely never ever anywherebefore was there such immediate audience participation. As you were saying, they were very young, average age about six, I should say. What an energetic show! The choreography was fantastic! How you began to direct it I cannot imagine – so much precise timing made me think of those amazing gymnastics that are performed at the Albert Hall by the Navy for the Remembrance 'do', I can well understand that the technical side could have presented problems, but the lighting and effects were beautiful. I hadn't realised that so much 'magic' was involved – not knowing the books which you worked from. I loved the 'Which witch' number especially and the tournament. Maureen Lipman must have been a superb witch. I found this successor a little on the shrill side and inclined to lose her words – but it may be that my ageing ears were at fault. Lots of 'suddenlys' and the scene changes, especially the 'transformation' scene in the garden, a nice link with traditional pantomime, a delight to the eye…*

Love to all –
Frank

DW's reply returned to their discussion of J M Barrie.

26 Jan

Dear Frank,

*…Have been reading the Cynthia Asquith book on J.M.B.;
amused to find he went to Brighton (Royal Albion Hotel) to
write* Farewell Miss Julie Logan *– my favourite place to write
is Brighton!! C.A. has interesting things to say about Barrie –
rather than having never grown up, she feels he was made to
grow up too fast, looking after his mother, etc.*

*Seeing the enclosed review and its mention of Barrie
alongside Dahl reminds one how J.M.B. has become generally
thought of as a children's writer – on the strength of one book/
play!! Just like Milne saddled with the success of* Pooh *eclipsing
his huge success in adult work previously. Dahl, it seems to me,
is far happier with his 'children's' tag than either Milne or Barrie.*

*Have just got to the bit about J.M.B. meeting Hardy. This
took me by surprise, but I'm terrible at setting people within
their periods, working out who was writing at the same time as
someone else, who was on the rise as someone else was on the
way out, etc. Maybe I need charts!*

*I wonder if there are any recordings of JMB talking…? One
of the Friends (of Wimbledon Theatre) works in the BBC record
library – I'll get him onto it! And I think there's a national sound
archive, isn't there? It would be fascinating to hear the magnetic
tones – and the cough!*

Now I have to work out how on earth to adapt Dahl's The
Witches *– due to open in the autumn – maybe you should read
the book and share the agony!*

*With love to you and Mary – from all of us,
David*

The reply took up the discussion of Barrie but also broached the topic of adapting *The Witches*.

29 Jan

Dear David,

...Do you know Hardy's little poem on him at rehearsal? It goes – if I can remember – thus:

> *If any day a promised play*
> *Should be in preparation,*
> *You never see friend JMB*
> *Depressed, or in elation.*
> *But with a stick, rough, crooked and thick,*
> *You may sometime discern him,*
> *Standing as though a mummery show*
> *Did not at all concern him.*

I fancy 'as though' is significant. I remember an actor who had once been in a production when Barrie was at a rehearsal, telling me that he had been very much concerned and the company found him rather trying!

Cynthia Asquith is right, I think. He did grow up prematurely in his effort to replace his dead brother in his mother's affection. Because of this, his fun and games with the Davies boys were an attempt to recover his missing childhood. Because he had by that time grown up, he was able to see quite unsentimentally into the nature of children – their self-centredness (necessary for their survival) and their talent for exploitation of adults. I do wish somebody could be persuaded to stage The Boy David *at Chichester with a real boy as David and without the encumbrance of all that overpainted scenery which filled the original production. The over-star-studded cast didn't help, either. The parts were too much for the whole. You could do it superbly – you could make the visions work, too!...*

I went into the city yesterday and acquired a copy of The Witches. *What a superb book! It's beautifully crafted, isn't it? And the suspense is terrific. When I've finished it and had a chance to think about it – I have to keep grabbing it back from Mary every time I put it down for a moment – I'll let you know of any ideas I may have in case they may come in useful. The central problem, the simultaneous presentation of mouse scale and human scale, is a right corker. But you have already exploited a number of devices which might perhaps be amalgamated to resolve it.*

I feel, though, that it would be well if you could avoid repeating past effects. Not a very specific suggestion, I'm afraid! But perhaps Woody the conjuror may come up with something. It does strike me immediately that to use R.D. as a narrator could be useful as he is telling the story about himself. He would provide a thread of unity to the episodes, in league with Grandma, who is a wonderful creation, and tie in the 'suddenlies'. Plenty of those, aren't there?…

Frank

News came back of further projects that were underway, and DW's suggestion that Roald Dahl himself cannot be the narrator of *The Witches* – a proposition that did not convince FW.

4 Feb

Dear David,

…Re. your reaction to RD as Narrator. On that last page, he is clearly speaking as a narrating mouse. Grandma picks him off the table to kiss him on the nose. But he is speaking, telling his story, not writing it on paper. On p.12 of my Penguin edition he also hints – but here only hints, he wants to keep his fate in suspense – at his being mousified:

'The fact that I am still here and able to speak* to you (however

peculiar I may look) is due entirely to my wonderful grandmother.'

So the boy, never named, is hero, mouse and narrator, and RD is all three. Moreover, he seems to be stressing, since he is 'able to speak', that this is a story not to be read by a reader silently to himself, but to be listened to as it is unfolded aloud. Now I can visualise the play beginning with action heard, not seen: that devastating car crash shattering the silence of a dark, empty stage until a light comes up to reveal Grandma, smoking her 'foul cigar' in her Norwegian parlour. Very intriguing! And RD appears on a downstage corner and in propria persona (I love these Latin tags) to explain what has happened and begin his story with its awful warning: witches don't look like witches! The salvaged boy is brought to the care of his Grandma – what a superb character she is – and off we go. RD would retain his human shape as his real-life self until after his metamorphosis by the Delayed Action Mouse-maker. That operation would be the climax and curtain of Part One. We should not see him as Mouse until Part Two, both as narrator and participant in the action. The outcome of the operation would remain in suspense to carry expectation over to Part Two…

And there's still the problem of mouse-scale and human-scale. For a scene such as that between Bruno and RD alone, you might adopt the method of The Gingerbread Man *– the large-scale dresser reducing the size of the actors. For other scenes, how about an imaginary mouse – where RD is circus training William and Mary, for example? And a clever Grandma could make us see him as she pets him and talks to him. But we should need to hear his voice – on stage this time, not off, like those of the Big Ones in GBM. The Cooks could have a lovely time, suitably choreographed, chasing an imaginary mouse, with lots of melodramatic music! (I'm thinking of* Save The Human*)…*

Love –
Frank

* my italics, as they say

84

Meanwhile, DW was catching up on his reading of some of the more obscure plays by J M Barrie, but also found time to take issue with the mouse narrator problem.

10 Feb

Dear Frank,

… Thank you for your Witches *thoughts. I am intrigued by your 'triple-narrator' analysis; I can see exactly what you mean, but am rather worried about the logic of starting with Dahl talking about himself as a little boy, and then turning into a mouse – FOR EVER – how come Dahl is still around to tell the tale? And it would worry me if he narrated (or started off) Act 1 and wasn't there at all in Act 2 (except as a mouse!) – you are dead right about the mouse being able to talk – loudly! – that's made quite clear in the book, to enable him to talk to Grandma. Am still pondering! Am indeed thinking of illusionist aid for the set pieces. And variable scale will probably be necessary, though the confusion of styles worries me – for instance, if the mouse is, say, a little puppet (operated by Grandma), will it be odd to then see it as a boy in a costume? It would be OK if set up, as in BFG – i.e., we are to use our imaginations – but in some ways the whole point of* The Witches *is that Dahl wants us to see it as REAL! Heigh ho – I must THINK POSITIVE! Thank you for chipping in your ideas! Always welcome.*

All for now –
Much love to you and Mary from all of us,
David

The discussion continued and FW caught up with *The BFG* on tour ("for your private ear, the first act seemed to not really grab the audience"), while DW considered a request to write a stage version of *Rupert Bear* – and sent a first draft of *The Witches*.

Dear Frank,

...Another dilemma has reared its ugly head – I've been asked to do a new Rupert Bear *play for 'major tour' – am not sure... maybe a green 'Rupert saves Nutwood Forest' ...? The Rupert characters always seem so bland, that's the worry. And I am concerned about being perceived by others as 'selling out'! – 'others' including the Arts Council, who have said 'no' to* The See-Saw Tree. *But they want us to discuss plans for '93 – as long as D.W. has a lower profile – and doesn't write/direct all the plays...*

Love to you both,
David

3 Mar

Dear David,

...The Arts Council should be given a severe talking-to, but I suspect the more they are subjected to instruction, the more stubborn they become. Somehow, children's theatre should be given theatrical importance as well as educational. BFG *may help to establish this – better than* Rupert Bear! *He's a survivor certainly, and we've had one or two versions here, but he does need gingering up – or salting down...*

Love to all,
F

13 Apr

Dear David,

Hugissimus thanks for the draft of Witches! *You have done a magnificent job. I am particularly impressed by your selection of the essential actions and by such devices as the picture of a witch which Grandmama shows to the Boy. The pace is terrific! The S.M. is going to have a busy time, but I take it Susie Caulcutt will be doing the designs, so that everything will not only look right but more right. Smoke and sparks should take care of the metamorphoses and the climax of the first act will be a devastating 'suddenly'. The slap-stick chase in the kitchen will provide an opportunity for audience participation, I imagine. It also provides the perfect prologue to the quiet close, which is unexpected and very beautiful.*

The dialogue is especially impressive. I do hope it won't get lost in malfunctioning amplification. The moments of direct address to the audience emerge entirely naturally and help considerably to carry conviction that the surprising things are really happening. I don't think the switch from Boy-Mouse to Puppet-Mouse should create any dis-belief, because you have established the connection in the scene with Bruno beforehand. I'm not quite clear about the scene of circus-training William and Mary. Have you some cunning Magic Circle device up your sleeve for that, or some kind of remote control of the technique that is applied to model cars and aircraft? Or is the Boy simply going to make us believe that we see what he sees – like Laughton with Banquo's Ghost? Children have great powers of imagination, but they can also be sticklers for fact!

I'm sure Mrs R.D. will be pleased and proud. You have not only made the book workable in theatrical terms but you have superbly recreated the quintessence of its ethos while remaining absolutely faithful to its action. It's a masterpiece.

More thanks for the unexpected privilege of this preview…

Frank

DW was quick to thank FW for his analysis and to clarify in places; and he also passed on the news he was finally reading the original script of the play of *Peter Pan*, having found a first edition.

15 Apr

Dear Frank,

Many thanks for your very encouraging response to The Witches *– you are the first person to react to it – even Jacqui hasn't read it yet! Mrs Dahl has her copy and hopefully will respond soon! I think I'm pleased with it! As usual, it was done at speed – 40 hours this time! In the same Hastings hotel room as I wrote* The BFG! *It will be a nightmare technically, but I will have a magic consultant and, hopefully, lots of mouse puppets! William and Mary will be seen, but quite how sophisticated will be their tight-rope walking I know not… the important thing is to establish (in the scene with Bruno and Bruno's Ma, and in the tight-rope scene) that 'in this production, LIVE MOUSE EQUALS PUPPET MOUSE'. Having established that, we can break the rules and scale up at the start of Act 2. Thanks for your lovely comments!…*

…love to you and Mary from all of us – and Happy Easter!
David

25 Apr

Dear David,

…I'm glad you found that first edition of Peter Pan, *1928. My copy, in a uniform leatherbound set with dates ranging from 1928 to '32, and of course not including* The Boy David, *1938, which I have in the ordinary blue cloth and white label, first, records 3 subsequent printings in October 1928! They are called 'editions' but of course they are only 'impressions' – an 'edition'*

in bibliographical terms means re-setting. I think I'd better make the lot over to you next time you come this way – it includes the novels Sentimental Tommy *and* Tommy and Grizel, *which were published by Cassell. Look out for a gem which I don't have – The Entrancing Life, his Rectoral Address at Edinburgh. This didn't enjoy such a large printing. It must have come out in about 1928, when I suppose his star was waning a little, though there is a newspaper picture of him with Ellen Terry at some degree ceremony or other about the same time. His address* Courage *at St Andrews in 1922 was widely distributed, and one sees that from time to time; but the later – and I think better one – seems to have sunk without trace. It was shorter – and perhaps the public felt it wasn't getting enough for its money!* When Wendy Grew Up, *as you say, is the one and only edition. I was pleased to see the other day that Daisy Ashford's* Young Visiters *with JMB's introduction has just been re-issued…*

If Mrs D. doesn't like your treatment of The Witches, *she should be considered a case for treatment.*

Frank

Meanwhile, *The BFG* was on tour, and the book was translated in Xhosa in South Africa, where DW had recently travelled. He was also busy acting in a children's television series, and dealing with yet more disappointing lack of support from the Arts Council. FW was particularly peeved that they had not recognised the worth of *The See-Saw Tree* and *The Selfish Shellfish*, while DW was struggling by now with casting for *The Witches*.

12 Jun

Dear David,

The decision-makers of the Arts Council should have their scruffy heads examined. But they are probably too far gone to be susceptible to any attempt of recovery, shrunk beyond any sort of shrinkage. Surely there is no time more apt for The See-Saw Tree *or* The Selfish Shellfish *than the present, with so much hot air being exerted in Rio and elsewhere. Or do they suppose that the present awareness in print and on the air waves renders further propaganda superfluous?*

If so, they are missing the point of both plays. They are good plays designed for a specific purpose of which encouragement of environmental sensitivity is only a part. Their chief claim to support, as I see it, is that they are good plays: that is, they are works of a very special art aimed to give pleasure to young audiences in their own right as brilliant drama. They offer plot, that is, development of action, characterisation, play of relationships and language. They are visually and aurally beautiful; and that should be enough for anybody's money. Though The GBM *probably has the widest appeal, I'm coming to think that the* Tree *and the* Shellfish *are the high water marks of your very particular art so far. The death of Rabbit in the former and the concept of* The Great Slick *in the latter are elements of fine drama. It's a comfort to hear that Whirligig is devising something special for '93…*

Love from M too, to you all,
Frank

9 Jul

Dear Frank,

…In the process of casting The Witches. *Waiting to hear from one or two offers. The main difficulty is that the tour is 40 weeks long, and a lot of people don't fancy that! Margaret Tyzack, for instance, loved the script, and would have loved to have had a crack at Grandmother, but just couldn't face the 40 weeks. Also, I have decided not to go for 16-year-old boys to play the Boy*

and Bruno. Somehow, 16-year-old boys lack the strength and consistency performance-wise of 16-year-old girls! More to the point, their broken voices are still adjusting and very often they are too tall! So I'm now looking for stunted 25-year-olds!

Yours,
David

Dear David,

...Oh, what a pity Margaret Tyzack can't face 40 weeks as Grandmother on tour. She'd be splendid. I think you're wise to opt for girls rather than boys as the Boy and Bruno. Besides presenting no vocal shifts, they do have more consistency than boys – but both sexes seem to grow taller than their years these days, and you may find your initially stunted ones shooting up like gum trees over 40 weeks on the road. I take it BFG in S.A. is on 'hold' in view of the difficult situation in that unhappy continent.

    Mary calls "Tea" and "Send them all my love."
    Which I do, with mine, of course.

Frank

By now, plans for the *Rupert Bear* play were gaining pace, and FW had been sent the synopsis of *Rupert and the Green Dragon*. ('Have you taken the Dragon adventure from an old series, or is it your "own make-up"? I like the tale, anyway, and find the second act tighter than the first.')

Dear Frank,

Many thanks indeed for your letter of 18th July, which arrived at just the right moment. I was in Cornwall, as you know, and getting rather depressed with the Rupert *script. I was getting it written bit by bit, but it all seemed a bit boring and flat... You then said something in your letter which gave me the confidence to proceed! You intimated that the blandness of the characters would not matter on stage any more than it appears to matter in print. That got me going and now, thank goodness, the first draft is ready (apart from one song lyric, which I keep putting off!).*

Here it is! Your comments would be welcomed. You are quite right in saying that the first half is less tight than the second half. Having said that, I think it establishes the characters, such as they are, plus the situation, plus introduces small children into the whole idea of a story being told on stage... You asked to whom it is aimed; well, the production company reckon that this is a pre-school audience, anything from 2 upwards!...

...The Witches. Well, apart from the Boy, we're all cast, thank goodness. Janet Whiteside (RSC actress of considerable repute) is going to play Grandmother, which is cheering. And we have a very special Grand High Witch. Her name is Dorothy Ann Gould, who, for the last eighteen years or so, has been quite a name in South Africa. Quite a coincidence! She has worked many times at the Baxter Theatre, where I am meant to be doing The BFG. *I have some of my regulars in the cast, too. Lots of meetings happening at the moment concerning magic, puppetry, music, set design, etc. I have suddenly realised it's rather a big show! Certainly a lot of suddenlies... I think it might be a bit of a nightmare technically. Fingers crossed. Rehearsals start September 14th.*

... Have decided to use boys, rather than girls, for the Boy and Bruno. But they will be played by slightly older actors. Various reasons for this. First of all, a girl playing Bruno didn't seem right. And once that decision had been made, it seemed wrong to have a girl playing the Boy! The best contender at the moment is, believe it or not, 31 years old! But I'm having some open auditions this Sunday at the Lyric, Hammersmith, and we'll see what comes along.

Yours,
David

As usual, FW sent detailed notes on the draft of the new *Rupert Bear* play – and his approval was matched by the owners of the character at the *Daily Express*. And among all the news of scripts and productions, there was an announcement of some exam results for DW's daughter – leading to an outburst of verse in response.

28 Aug

Congratulations, Katherine!

Faced by questions dire and dread
Katherine has kept her head.
None will dare to sniff or sneeze
At her nine G.C.S.E.s:
ALL Wimbledon will be elated –
Katherine is certificated!
'O frabjous day! Callooh! Callay!'
Let all the bands in Britain play!
Toot the trumpets, biff the brasses
At this Tuttissimo of passes!
Ring the bells in every steeple,
Spread the joy to all the people!
Someone run and tell the Queen

The glorious news of Katherine:
Then the spokesman from the Palace
Will cry "She is as smart as Alice!
Let the voice of celebration
Sound throughout the British Nation!
Hip, hip, Hurrah! Likewise Hurray!
Make Monday Next a Holiday!"

(The rhymes may be a trifle hairy
But come
With love
From
Frank and Mary.)

9 Sep

Dear Frank,

…Am in the final run-up to The Witches *rehearsals, which start on 14th. Did I tell you that we have now decided to have a girl playing the Boy? I think it will work well. Certainly, I didn't find a boy suitable. It would be o.k. as a one-off, with just a few performances – one could even use a 10-year-old! But to get the consistency over a long period, you really must go for experience. Karen Briffett has been around for some time. She played Daisy in the first national tour of* Daisy Pulls It Off *– 9 months in No. 1 theatres and she's only 5 feet tall!…*

Yours,
David

6 Oct

Dear Frank,

...we managed two good run-throughs of The Witches *on Friday and now I'm about to depart to Sheffield to get the play on, hopefully!*

The casting has worked out very well. I don't think there's a weak link and all seem very committed to the piece. The running time seems to have worked out well. First half about 45 minutes, the second half about 40 minutes... We have just heard that it is coming into the Duke of York's Theatre, London for Christmas which, of course, gives me tremendous pleasure, because that is where Peter Pan *started off.*

Love and best wishes from us all.

Yours,
David

The casting was eventually resolved by casting a girl as Boy, and a young actor played Bruno.

7 Oct

All the very best for you and your Witches
To bring you fame and honest riches!
Fame to the Boy, fame to the Mouse,
And every show a crowded house,
With more and more the public avid
To WATCH the magic works of Woody (David)!
(The metre limps a bit I find,
But get the message – never mind!)

Frank & Mary

1992 The Witches –

Lyceum Theatre, Sheffield – 8th October 1992
Boy and his Grandmother defeat the Grand High Witch and her followers, who are holding a conference in an English seaside hotel, but, during the struggle, Boy is turned into a mouse.

12 Oct

Dear Frank and Mary,

… Am now home, having seen five public performances and given lots of notes. Hopefully, it will all tighten up a bit before I next see it. But the cast have been splendid and I think we have the makings of a very good show.
All for now – more soon!

Love and best wishes,
David

The reviews came in, all were pleased, and FW booked tickets for the London run at the Duke of York's. *Rupert*, meanwhile, was running into problems and delays, and Whirligig had further difficulties to contend with.

27 Nov

Dear Frank,

…Meanwhile, The Witches *opens at the Duke of York's next week. Hopefully, all will go well! The advance box office seems to be good.*
Janet Whiteside has had her minor op. And goes back into the show today, as far as I know. They are in Woking at a brand-new and rather splendid theatre called The New Victoria, built within a massive shopping complex, and indeed subsidised by same, I understand.
Next Friday, we have a crisis Whirligig meeting to decide

whether or not we can continue with the company. The Arts Council are still playing extremely silly buggers with us and there is just no money to do anything we want to do. We are getting all our Artistic Associates to come and discuss the matter...

Also, I have now been asked to look at, would you believe, Noddy. Clarion (my Dahl producers) have the rights. He has just come back with a vengeance on tv and in the politically correct 'revised' books. All 24 of them! Am trying to read them all to make a decision on whether to adapt or not. I have to admit I find it rather sad that the market forces-led nature of the country over the last few years has led me into a market-forces form of children's theatre. Nobody has asked me to write an original play for three years. All the reps are returning to pantomime or well-known classic titles...

> *Yours,*
> *David*

          29 Nov

Dear David,

...Your association with commercial production companies should eventually add to the general appeal of your claims for the importance of Children's Theatre to be taken seriously in the market place as well as in the school-room...

> *Ever –*
> *Frank*

          2 Dec

Dear Frank,

I'm dictating this at 5.40am! Last night, we had the first Preview at the Duke of York's, and it seemed to go very well. The stage is much smaller than any we have played before, and there were quite a lot of problems getting the show in and managing to work out what lived where in the very limited wing space!

…The main reason for writing this is to let you know that Rupert seems to be pulling itself together a bit, but has decided it doesn't like the look of Liverpool and would rather open in the leafy glades of Leatherhead – the Thorndike. January 22nd.

I realise this might be a venue which you and Mary could get to rather than having to wait till a later date!…

Yours,
David

Dear Frank,

Another letter in the same envelope! It has been rather hectic here and my letter of 2nd December got delayed!

The Witches opened successfully. Enclose four excellent reviews.

Since then, we've had a major problem in which one member of the cast was injured during the First Night party. Coping with the 11.00am performance the next day was a nightmarish situation, which we managed to resolve in the nick of time…

Best wishes,
David

16 Dec

Dear Frank,

…I hope to come and meet you at or after the performance you are scheduled to attend in January. If you have time, I would love to take you backstage. I very often stand there imagining how on earth they managed to get Peter Pan on. I think they *used a lot of cloths, but even so it must have been a nightmare. Certainly, according to the book you kindly gave me* – 50 Years of Peter Pan – *the First Night never took place! That is to say it was postponed…*

> *All best wishes,*
> *David*

FW replied that he would, of course, be delighted to go backstage and '*see those hallowed boards where PP first flew into immortality*'.

1993

The *Rupert* play finally opened early in 1993, and FW saw it when it got to Wimbledon.

1993 Rupert and the Green Dragon –
Thorndike Theatre, Leatherhead – 22ⁿᵈ January 1993
Rupert's Nutwood friends join him in this adventure. Algy Pug, Tiger Lily, Pong Ping, Bill Badger, Ottoline and Podgy Pig all help Edward Trunk have a sunny day for his birthday, assisted by the Green Dragon.

11 Feb

Dear Frank,

… Enc. Stage *review of* Rupert – *after all the problems, it seems to have worked for one critic anyway! Am rehearsing the cast next Monday before opening at Wimbledon on Tuesday – hopefully it will be O.K.*

> *Love and best wishes,*
> *David*

21 Feb

Dear David,

I must just say a huge 'Thank you' for a most enjoyable visit to the Wimbledon Theatre, and to Jacqui for a very comfortable tea. Croissants, scones, and jam – all favorite things – and such animated talk!...

...Rupert and The Green Dragon is as near a perfect specimen of its kind as anyone could hope for – and Friday's audience proved it with their concentration of approval...

More thanks and love to both you and Jacqui – Frank

Projects under discussion by DW included a trip to Japan to discuss adapting a Japanese production for a British audience, and the possibility of writing a musical of Dahl's *Matilda*; but first he had to make a decision: '*have to say yes or no to adapting* Noddy *for the autumn. Oh dear, I don't know – the* Noddy *books really do seem even emptier than* Rupert!' A series of updates was sent to FW in April.

5 Apr

Dear Frank,

...It was pouring with rain in London, too. I got very wet travelling no more than a couple of hundred yards from tube station to rehearsal room to see a run-through of The Gingerbread Man, which, as I may have told you, is being mounted for two weeks only by Theatre Royal, Norwich. I must admit I thought it was a crazy idea, because they have to sell a lot of seats to make it pay for itself, but they seem happy with the product, which is being presented as an Easter treat, so who am I to argue!

...the Rupert *tour is not doing the greatest business, and the Producer is thinking of 'pulling the plug' on the whole thing. Sadly, it appears that Rupert, as a character, doesn't have the*

pulling power of Postman Pat *or* Fireman Sam, *the two other current offerings of the self-same producer. In fact, I saw the show in a strange all-purpose venue in St Albans the other day and thought it was pretty good! I was very pleasantly surprised. I think, in my hyper-sensitive state, I had been able to see nothing but the bad aspects of the production, some of which weren't really bad at all, but, because of the production problems, had been tarred with an unfairly dismissive brush by its adaptor/ director.*

Other news. The Witches *continues fairly triumphantly. Sadly, although the business is really remarkably good, the production company will end up losing money – mainly because the Duke of York's was really too small, and costs far outweighed revenue for those eight weeks.*

I am trying to do a synopsis of Noddy, *having decided I should have a go, and having met Enid Blyton's daughter, who enthused over some of my ideas! I'm always a sucker for flattery!*

I've also done a bit of work on Matilda, *knocking together a synopsis, while Anthony and George [writers of musical theatre Stiles & Drewe], the two young men I'm working with, are doing a couple of songs. I may have told you, they are the clever duo who wrote* Just So *(from Kipling), which Cameron Mackintosh nurtured and put on at the Tricycle Theatre in London, but decided it wasn't quite right for the West End…*

Yours,
David

In the same month, FW sent one of his poems of thanks for a Wimbledon tea, and then followed up with a thoughtful appraisal of the draft of the *Noddy* adaptation.

No other tea-time half so good is
As one that's spent among the Woodies:
Such a choice of jam and scone
For happy guests to champ upon,
Choccy bikkies, doughnuts yummy,
All so welcome to one's tummy!
O! In such happy companee
What a treat is nursery tea!
These rough lines are sent to thank'ee
With love to all from faithful Frankie.

15 Apr

Dear David,

...thanks for the privileged preview of the Noddy *adaptation which I have much enjoyed... I don't think you have to worry about 'blandness'. [The characters] are admirably defined for their expected audience and are humanised by their display of emotion – the fallings-out and makings-up, Big Ears' distress for his lost cat, PC Plod's attention to duty, etc. And Noddy's dilemma in the sacrifice of his car is very real and moving.*

On my first reading (in the train), I was struck by what seemed a dichotomy (what a word! but critics love it) between Acts I and II. It seemed that what was on offer was a sequence of two self-contained one-act plays, rather than one continuous two-acter. On further reflection, I was aware that of course the two are linked by Whiskers' early appearance, and also of course the car. But it still seemed to me that the end of Act I was quite final, The End of the play. There was nothing to arouse curiosity or expectation of what might or might not occur after the interval. Would it help, perhaps, if as Noddy drives off his car in triumph we could be made aware of one or other, or both, Goblins lusting after it, so that we are left asking, "What will happen next? Will they steal it after all?" More emphasis on the struggle between the Evil goblins and the Good (but very human Noddy) would perhaps provide a more continuous plot, so that it was not just a series of incidents. I wondered, too, whether it might further help to create 'unity of action' if we saw a Goblin stealing Whiskers while Big Ears and his guests are fully occupied in his birthday celebrations. The theft might be shown to be motivated by the desire for revenge because attempts to steal the car had been frustrated.

I offer these suggestions not without trepidation! It's clear that you are giving new life to Noddy and Co as you have given new life to Rupert…

Ever –
Frank

DW's reply included a reminder that it was not just the needs of the story that should be considered, but also the practicalities of managing a cast who might be playing more than one role.

22 Apr

Dear Frank,

…One of the problems I have is that I only have six actors, doubling up like mad. This means that I can't have the two Goblins working as a double act all the way through the play.

What your suggestions have led me to do, which I think may work well, is to strengthen the two Goblins in their very first scene, just in a couple of lines or so, making it clear that they don't like newcomers and that Noddy looks pretty green, so he will be an easy target, etc., and then seeing them getting their come-uppance, one in each act!…

In other words, Sly has a go on the market stall, but manages to escape from Mr. Plod. Then Gobbo takes over, trying to steal the car at the Garage…

In Act II, it is Sly who has a go – he tries to steal the car, he steals Whiskers, he sells Whiskers to the Witch...

Then, what I propose to do, is, right at the end of the play... Sly... tries to steal the car. The audience alert everyone to the fact and Mr. Plod enters and arrests Sly.

...Enid Blyton's daughter, Gillian Baverstock, has now reacted favourably to the synopsis, suggesting one or two things. So I think I'd better try and write it...

Yours,
David

The first draft of the script followed, and by now FW was ready to respond in detail and did so, in a lengthy and detailed letter.

10 May

Dear David,

Hugissimus thanks! I am honoured and privileged to be given the first bite of the cherry. And what a splendid cherry!

You have made a beautiful job of this latest adaptation. It works as a play in its own right. This is what any adaptation or translation ought to do, but that's easier said than done... In Noddy, I take it your invention has been constrained by E. Blyton's original stories which, as I remember not too clearly, appeared in small books of independent adventures. You have triumphantly fused your selection into a coherent whole, greater than the sum of its parts. You explain Noddy's origin (shades of Pinocchio! I'm all for our seeing through gauze the carver at work) and progress fluently to a dramatic climax in which all the incidents are unified and to which all the characters contribute. I wonder whether the skittles might not be made less accidental and more incidental, as it were, by having them impede more effectively the activities of the Goblins, so that they seem less a mere speciality act?...

...your dialogue abounds in similar happy moments. They constantly illumine character. I'm thinking particularly of the exchange between Tessie and Noddy on pages 53 and 54, and on page 55 of Noddy's reluctant acceptance of Bumpy Dog as a participant in the hunt for Whiskers. Big Ears' line on p45 after Noddy's outburst of temper is another lovely revelation: 'I think that was rather unfair, my friend.' Noddy's reaction is equally enlightening. Tessie's reply to Noddy's query 'Where's Bumpy Dog?' (p.34) which shows his fear of being bounced over again (an ever-present anxiety for a Woodentop, surely), 'I had to leave him at home. We couldn't have him bouncing around in Big Ears' Toadstool House. Besides, he might chase Whiskers,' has a touch of Shakespearean 'dramatic irony'. I am reminded of Lady Macbeth's 'A little water clears us of this deed. How easy is it then?'...

...Thank you for another beautiful opus. Mary has shared my privilege and is equally enthusiastic.

> *She sends her congratulations and love with mine –*
> *Frank*

11 May

Dear Frank,

You've no idea how chuffed I was to receive your Noddy *reaction – it's not just that you flatter me with your kind comments... You always latch on to the salient points like a homing pigeon!.. Gillian Baverstock (E.B.'s daughter) will see the script tomorrow, I'm told. Fingers crossed she will feel it works, is faithful, and echoes her mother's belief that Noddy represents the young fledgling child emerging into the 'real world', where there are dangers...*

I value your Skittles thoughts – you're quite right, they are a little cabaret incursion, mainly devised to give work to the ASMs and increase the citizenship of what is (for financial reasons) a rather depleted Toytown!...

Yes, there are 24 Noddy *books, all precisely the same length, but of varying quality story-wise, in my opinion. Noddy's arrival in Book 1 is, in its Pinocchio-like charm, really rather good, as is the story much later of the lost Whiskers... I used the most emotionally involving bits, I think – always the best route...*

Much love to you both from all of us,
David

By June, DW was sending a draft synopsis of his proposed adaptation of *Kuroemon*, the Japanese play.

28 Jun

Dear David,

...you are absolutely right to discourage all attempts by Shiki to seek to win approval from a British audience by exhibiting its efficiency in adopting Western techniques in the presentation of Kuroemon. *It's a charming – and powerful – story. It might have been invented by Oscar Wilde. It should not be exploited as a 'musical', but seen, as you suggest, as a 'musical play', or a 'play with music' – that is in the D.W. tradition – as authentically Japanese as possible, with no indulgence on the part of its promoters to show just how cleverly they have assimilated Western (that is, American or British) theatrical techniques. To appeal here it must, I am sure, be 100% Japanese...*

...One last thought. The title. 'Kuroemon' is a most memorable word, and Japanese. 'Elephant' is English (Middle Eng. in fact!) and memorable also. Might the two stand together: 'Kuroemon the Elephant', with perhaps a subtitle, 'A Tale of Old Japan'?

Forgive the impertinences of all these remarks – they're meant to be helpful! And thanks again.

Love to you all –
Frank

The next news was welcome: Arts Council support for Whirligig to mount a tour of the Polka Theatre production of *Dreams of Anne Frank* by Bernard Kops.

15 Jul

Dear Frank,

The good news is that… the Arts Council have finally relented and come up with something like £20,000 for the Anne Frank *tour. This is good news indeed. Quite honestly, we were embarking on a tour without being properly financed. Arts Council Touring obviously (as I suspected) had some money left over, and thank goodness it has come our way. Hopefully, this bodes well for the future.*

…Meanwhile, I have got my cast for Noddy, *although I still haven't found my ASM/Understudies. Noddy and Big-Ears will be played by Karen Briffett and Eric Potts, both of whom you saw in* The Witches.

…Clarion are also hoping to revive The BFG *this autumn, and there is also a possibility of me going to Dublin to direct* The Witches *there for a Christmas season.*

…Went to Birmingham last week to see the Channel Theatre production of The Plotters Of Cabbage Patch Corner. *I really rather enjoyed it! What was gratifying was that the play, now 23 years old, was played without any textual change at all. It doesn't seem to have dated at all…*

Yours,
David

22 Jul

Dear David,

…I'm glad you were able to 'really enjoy' the revival of The Plotters *in Birmingham. Did you find you were watching it as*

something quite apart from yourself, as though it belonged to some other person? This is usually my experience when I turn out some ancient script. I have no recollection of having ever had anything to do with it. This enables one to make an entirely objective assessment. Very salutary. I don't think your plays should date at all, except perhaps in very minor aspects. Though you do make use of contemporary specialties – the environment, for instance – you are usually concerned with (what E. Blunden once indicated in writing me a testimonial) 'general beauties and truths'. The idiom may shift a little, but the themes remain cogent...

> *Ever,*
> *Frank*

One of DW's regular updates followed.

29 Jul

Dear Frank,

This week has been business as usual, looking for Noddy *understudies, meetings re. the set, etc. And on Saturday we have the last performance of* The Witches *tour – in Canterbury, so we're all off there in the morning...*

If I haven't said it before, thanks for your Elephant *thoughts and views, which were so fascinating I sent the letter to my producer, Andrew Fell, who was delighted to read your comments and agreed with your agreement of our aims, etc! Now all I've got to do is write the wretched thing...*

Anne Frank *play is v. good for, say, 8 upwards – especially young teenagers. Kops has done a lovely job on it. French's publishing it soon.*

Noddy *casting complete and sets and costumes designed – all O.K. touch wood.*

Witches *in Dublin still not confirmed – yes – Irish cast!*

Viewing Plotters *in B'ham wasn't quite as objective as your description of seeing one of your old works! Mainly because I have seen two other prods. of play in last year or so. But I remember seeing the British Community in Brussels doing* Hijack Over Hygenia *(a little-known Woodwork!) and honestly not knowing what came next! Rather nice feeling. And I certainly 'enjoyed' it more than watching (or worrying over) one of my own productions!…*

All for now – take care – love to you both – hope to see you soon…
    David

The first draft of *Kuroemon* followed, with FW's lengthy response winging its way within days.

2 Sep

Dear David,

…I have always felt that foreign plays need to be adapted, not merely translated.

   *…*Kuroemon *does not call for such complete metamorphosis; it is a Japanese play being offered as a Japanese play to a non-Japanese audience. Therefore, it must remain essentially Japanese in action and style, but must avoid 'translatorese', that hybrid tongue which results from literal translation…*

   The Elder's 'Haven't a clue, my lord. It's a new one on me,' struck me as slangish rather than just idiomatic, and therefore off-key, and 'dating', less timeless than I feel the language of a play with a universal message ought to be. And Tarobo's 'Kuroemon, that was brilliant!' similarly jarred because that use of 'brilliant' as a successor to 'fab' seemed too temporary. Grandfather's 'Nothing to forgive' struck me as a cliché too much beloved of the Barbara Cartland, Mills and Boon, school of novelists. And 'Don't panic', in the Narration, top of p.55, immediately called up Corporal Jones in Dad's Army! It probably wouldn't have this effect on a present-day child, but it might spoil Omiyo's thinking for a parent.

However, these reactions are really only personal nit-picking. Don't take them too seriously! The Elder's line, though, seems also misplaced because it is uttered on a ceremonial occasion. I feel he shouldn't be so chatty in the presence of a Lord who has to be prostrated to.

The Narrations are splendid. The rhythm and build-up of pace and tension, the repetition by the chorus of the solo narrator's line, is very effective, as is the use of characters as narrators. Much better than a story-teller outside the action. Having the children tell their own story directly to the audience is a form of audience participation, isn't it? It will prepare for the climax (wonderfully delayed and prepared) when they are asked to do something themselves. They will have been 'softened up' and not be shy, through their having been intimately involved as listeners.

I very much like the idea of the company appearing at first simply as actors and subsequently assuming their characters and appropriate props and costumes…

…Western-style music and choreography would be a sad mistake. The Japanese puppetry, mime and movement should be exploited to the full. The whole play must scrupulously avoid trying to imitate a Western musical, no matter how clever the Japanese are – as they always have been – at imitation…

…I like the word 'elephant' being avoided, and the Elder's being at a loss to interpret the Chinese. This keeps the audience guessing! What is behind the drawn curtain! Once the curtains are parted, they will of course know what Kuroemon is, even if the Japanese have no word for him…

Love to the whole Wood Family Show!
Frank (and Mary)

P.P.S. 5

Oh! I forgot!

p.30 The Narration, line 14:

*If you substituted 'hear as we plead' for 'hear our prayer, we beg',
you would achieve an assonance if not a full rhyme which seems to
be called for to correspond to the three following rhymes of 'skies',
'goodbyes', and 'spies'. The lack of that third rhyme previously does
seem to me to lessen the impact of the Narrator's line.*

DW's reply suggested that errant props and political disputes were
putting *Kuroemon* on the back burner, however.

19 Sep

Dear Frank,

Two weeks' hard rehearsal of Noddy *led to two good run-
throughs yesterday (Sat.), I'm glad to say. 'Get-in' tomorrow,
tech. rehearsals and dress Tues/Wed, open Thurs. Fingers crossed.
Usual panics over things not arriving in time, but hopefully they
will be resolved. Noddy's Car, when it first arrived in chassis form,
raced round the marked-up rehearsal space knocking over every
(imaginary) flat or backcloth, plus invading the orchestra pit. 48
hours later, the 'turning circle' had been radically improved and
now Noddy can turn a full circle on stage!! Rehearsals have been
enjoyable if relentless, controlled though hectic.*

You may have read of the controversy caused by Noddy *in
your area!... The Hampshire Ed. Authority is refusing to mail the
schools with* Noddy *info! Meridian sent a film crew to rehearsal*

and drove me mad for a morning! The reporter wanted to do a 'politically correct' version of a scene to please Hampshire – I pointed out that, as far as I was concerned, there was nothing politically incorrect with my version! Ah well, a bit of controversy might be no bad thing...

Re. your splendid Kuroemon *letter – points noted – I agree with most of them – modern expressions jar, it is true. Thanks for spotting them.*

Glad you liked it – believe it or not, as I write, I have had no reaction whatsoever from my producer! I don't mind specially, but I would have liked some response...

*...*The Witches *in Dublin will be directed (my production) by Adam Stafford, Bruno in the production you saw. I will, in lordly fashion, visit (three flights back and forth) at the beginning of rehearsals, in the middle and at the end (opening!). Before then,* The BFG *reopens – I start rehearsing that Nov. 1st. Albery Theatre now, not Piccadilly as first thought – followed by 6-month tour.*

Anne Frank *opened well in Swindon – I couldn't get there, but apparently it has been warmly received.*

Love and best wishes from us all,
D

1993 Noddy –

Wimbledon Theatre – 23rd September 1993
Noddy, carved from wood, escapes his creator, arrives in Toytown, meets the friendly Big Ears, acquires his car and helps foil the unpleasant actions of two naughty Goblins.

A card from DW suggested that all went well with the opening of *Noddy*, and a following letter contained more good news.

Dear Frank,

THE BFG *is cast at last! Sophie is to be a 20-year-old who has recently left drama school – wonderful name of RUBY EVANS! She's 4'9" and a splendid actress, so fingers crossed!*

At last, my producer of the Japanese epic has made contact! I'm pleased to say he is thrilled, saying I have 'got it in one' and have 'fulfilled the brief impeccably'. So now we wait and see if the Japanese lot like it!

…The Witches *has been nominated for an award! The Theatre Managers' Association Martini Award for best regional/ touring production for young people! Jacqui and I go to the ceremony in Cardiff next weekend. Fingers crossed!*

Am doing a toy theatre version of Cinderella *with my illustrator partner Richard Fowler (Baby Bear, etc.) – will probably do it in rhyme.*

Rehearsals for BFG *start Nov 1st – open Nov 22nd (Albery).*

Love to both from all of us –
David

FW eventually saw the production of *Noddy* in November, and enjoyed it despite the cast being depleted by illness.

Dear Frank,

…We opened The BFG *o.k. and business seems to be good, I'm glad to say.*

…On Monday I go to Dublin for the day to get The Witches *going. Then on Thursday I go to Glasgow for two days to work with the* Noddy *company, returning to Dublin for a bit of work on* The Witches! *And so on. And so on. Can't complain.*

…Dreams Of Anne Frank *finishes on Saturday. It has lost a lot of money, and puts Whirligig's position in a very precarious state. However, there have been a couple of good reviews, which I enclose, plus a couple of not so good ones, which I also enclose!*

We heard today that the Enid Blyton Estate are allowing Noddy, *the play, to be published by Samuel French. This also means they will eventually allow amateur performances. That is a real breakthrough. They were adamantly against that before the production opened. So I'm pleased…*

Yours,
David

Meanwhile, *The Witches* opened in Dublin, and the year ended with an update.

20 Dec

Dear Frank,

…Got back from Dublin last Thursday. The Witches opened successfully and the Irish cast are giving a very good account of it. Adam, my assistant, directed them very well, and I made three visits to 'supervise'.

…Thank you for your letter of 27th November with various thoughts on Anne Frank. *We still haven't finally counted the cost of the tour, but it will be considerable. The business was simply dreadful in many places!*

Meanwhile, The BFG *continues to do reasonable business at the Albery and* Noddy *is o.k. at Hammersmith, although I haven't seen it there yet…*

Yours,
David

1994

The year began with *The BFG* and *Noddy* still running, and the publication by Samuel French of *The Witches*.

10 Mar

Dear David,

Hugissimus thanks for the copy of The Witches *so generously inscribed. I'm glad that old Sam has brightened up his ideas of packaging. It would be a tremendous challenge for any amateur group, but I can think of one nearby which might attempt it with success – the Dramatic Society in Romsey. It has converted the former Plaza Cinema into its own theatre where it recently put on notable productions of* A Man For All Seasons *and* Nicholas Nickleby *in the R.S.C. version...*

Love to you all –
Frank

The revival of *The Gingerbread Man* by Unicorn at the Arts Theatre opened later that month, but the difficulty of attracting school audiences meant that there were no new projects on the horizon, at least for the moment. FW saw a performance of *The Gingerbread Man* in May.

12 May

Dear David,

I must write to thank you for My Most Memorable Day in Years! I can't tell you how much I enjoyed it all – and the performance of The G.B *was outstanding in that cosy little theatre...*

It's a pity that The Selfish Giant *and the* Elephant *play have not resulted in anything... ...though you find yourself at a loose end just now, the wheel will no doubt turn and produce a project to stir your imagination. I was recalling the Wodehouse adaptation you staged at Windsor. Something should have come of that. Might it not be given a second airing?...*

Maybe it will not ultimately be unproductive if your creativity lies fallow for a while – though I don't expect the hush to last very long...

Ever –
Frank

Casting around for a new project, DW asked FW to look at a story called *Froggy's Little Brother*.

13 May

Dear David,

Hurrah for Froggy! *I will give it my immediate attention this weekend... I thought when you told me of it yesterday that the name rang a bell, and I now think that I heard of it years ago from a chum of mine at school. My suspicion is that he had seen a film of that name – silent of course. At first glance, I suspect there are possibilities – the pietistic preaching can easily be omitted (like the fall of the rupee, too sensational)...*

Love to you all –
Frank

More advice was soon requested, this time on the topic of strolling players.

27 May

Dear Frank,

... The main thrust of this missive is to seek out your knowledge of strolling players in Elizabethan England! ... if you have any memories of particularly good bits of information, I'd be very grateful.

The reason for this is that a television producer I have known on and off for some years has sent me a novel by Rosemary Sutcliff called Brother Dusty-Feet. *Published in 1952, it is about an orphan boy who escapes from his unpleasant aunt and joins a band of strolling players. It's not the most wonderful book in terms of adventure, excitement, sense of climax, etc., but it is very endearing and also touches on various other people 'of the road' of the day. There is a Palmer, for instance, a Quack doctor and a 'Tom-o'Bedlam'.*

The thought is to make a television series (rather than serial) from the basic material. The boy would be constantly on the run from the pursuing aunt, and we would experience his life on the road, performing at inns, etc. He also has a lovable dog, which would work well.

Nothing definite yet. And even if I do some work on it, there's no guarantee that interest in the series would be taken up. But it has started me thinking a little – there is definitely the germ of an idea there! ...

Yours,
David

No reply has survived and the project is not mentioned again. Meanwhile, a paper pop-up theatre book was published (and given to FW) and *Noddy* appeared on video. Further updates followed in October.

21 Oct

Dear Frank,

...I did my first Magic and Music Show *at the Wilde Theatre, Bracknell the other day, and luckily seem to have remembered most of it! This Saturday, I am at the Tricycle Theatre in Kilburn, followed almost immediately by two days in Swindon and three days at the Oxford Playhouse. So I am quite busy, really!*

However, apart from Noddy Two *(!), which I have now been told to go ahead and think about, in preparation for a September 1995 production, there is not much going on theatrewise. Various meetings are taking place to try to relaunch Whirligig next year or the year after. And Unicorn have expressed an interest in reviving* Meg and Mog Show *for Christmas 1995. So I can't complain ...*

Love and best wishes,
David

The lull between projects led to thoughts about school theatre productions and young actors who later entered the profession.

2 Nov

Dear Frank,

..Yes – Chi High did produce a few theatricals – [Howard] Brenton, [David] Horlock, [Peter] Baldwin – Adrian Noble no less – plus Chris Parr, who has just produced the – in my view – excellent BBC series Taking Over the Asylum. *It is true Geoffrey Marwood and Bill Wake, who used to produce the school plays, took it all very seriously, though I don't think – even in those days – it was a particularly theatre-orientated establishment. But I shall never forget when KD Anderson, our headmaster, summoned me to his study at the age of 13 and asked what I*

wanted to do – I said, "you'll probably laugh, sir, but I want to go into the theatre." He didn't laugh, but suggested I apply to join a course at somewhere called Lodge Hill!... That led to my first meeting with you in 1958! I've been forever grateful for that. Another Chi Hi actor was Piers Stephens, who used to do a lot of radio...

You remind me of my disgraceful perf. in The Broken Jug *– what indulgence... I remember dear Gerard Young, the theatre-mad journalist, who used to help us with make-up, telling me off for my selfish performance!*

Last week, I did the Magic and Music Show *in Swindon and at the Oxford Playhouse (3 perfs) – I suddenly realised that it was 30 years since I first trod the boards there (Hang Down Your Head and Die) – where does the time go?!...*

David

1995

Noddy was published in early 1995, but apart from that, not a lot was progressing.

6 Feb

My dear Frank,

... All well here, though I seem to be in limbo work-wise – can't get 'into' anything. No money to do any children's plays – Whirligig unable to get going again, Clarion (BFG, Witches, Noddy) went into liquidation recently... heigh-ho, lots of irons in the fire, as they say, but nothing definite – and I do find writing 'on spec' very hard!

However, later this week, I fly to Minneapolis, US of A! to observe the splendid Children's Theater(!) there – purpose-built theatre doing work on my sort of scale. I've always wanted to see it and find out how it's funded, etc. Maybe it will kick me out of my lethargy!...

Love from us all,
David

Things were not much busier by April.

Dear Frank,

...I'm still trying to do the synopsis for a new Noddy *play, due to open in September. This is proving problematic, because in many ways I feel I have 'done' Noddy! Hopefully, something will click into place soon.*

I was asked recently to do a storyline for an ice-ballet! For the Russian All Stars, a company of 26 Russian skaters. They recently appeared at the Mayflower, Southampton in a version of Cinderella. *I have done a storyline based on* Beauty *and the* Beast. *Have sent in the second draft but have so far had no reaction to it!...*

...Later in the week, we go to Paris via the Tunnel! Four of us making the trip for fun really, but while over there (just for the day), we are going on a tour of the Paris Opera House (of Phantom *fame!), which will be interesting. This is partly because I have been asked to do a text for a children's book called* The Phantom Cat of the Opera. *The illustrator is an American who happens to live in Paris! Hence the combination of a private and business visit to Paris!*

Yours,
David

30 Apr

Dear David,

... Oh good for Noddy! *I'm sure you'll hit on a coherent adventure. The 'spark from heaven' will surely fall. It would be jolly to see the little car again. But did he ever take to the air? We kids would love to see him taking off (if no further) in an aeroplane. After all, there's no reason why you shouldn't follow the practice of the TV script writers who invent new fictions for established characters – e.g. Morse and Poirot – though I don't care for Morse without Colin Dexter's scenery. I hope the ballet gets the go-ahead.* Beauty and the Beast *is a lovely story. I believe there have been one or two stage (other than pantomime) versions. Could you use your storyline also sans ice?...*

Frank

FW was soon enlisted to comment on the ice-dance storyline as it was developing, in addition to the latest thoughts on *Noddy*.

2 May

Dear Frank,

...I thought I would send you the storyline I have done for Beauty and the Beast. *The Russian lady (the choreographer who trained most of the Russian Olympic skating champions) seems to like it. I'm meeting her next week to discuss it further.*

I have taken a few liberties with the original French version, incorporating one or two ideas from other versions, and trying to make it clear to an audience, without the use of words! It was quite an interesting experience. I hope it all happens...

...I have now taken the decision to split Noddy *into two (not literally, though I sometimes feel I would like to!). You will remember that last time you pointed out with great insight that*

I had written two one-act plays. Then I managed to link them through the activities of the Goblins.

I think the reason why two one-act plays were forthcoming rather than one with a glorious plotline, was quite simply that the material lends itself to slightly shorter bursts than some of my other work. All the Noddy stories are very short, and, of course, the television series appeals to such a young audience, that they're even shorter! Also, I have been thinking about the fact that the audiences that came to the first Noddy show were so much younger than I expected.

I have therefore decided to give them even more audience participation of a jolly nature, and to think a little younger. We'll see how it turns out. But I have done the synopsis of what I imagine will be Act 1. This is a perfectly straightforward Noddy story, using the same characters as the first play, involving theft by the Goblin and various events surrounding Noah's Ark. I have dragged in all my old tricks and devices, in the hope that only my closest associates will notice that I am repeating myself! But after doing this for so long, I feel it is inevitable that if something works, it's worth revamping it!

You mention the possibility of Noddy taking to the air. Indeed, I have been thinking that for some time, but I don't think the budget will run to it! Also, the Blyton Estate people are rather tricky about straying too far from the original parameters of the Blyton canon. I don't think, for instance, they want Noddy to go to the moon! I suppose they would see that as too fantasy-orientated, and away from the concept of a town peopled with toys. On the other hand, I don't see why there shouldn't be a toy space station, just as there's a toy Noah's Ark and a toy fort! Certainly, if Blyton was writing today, she would use it, I'm sure. So maybe I'll be bold!...

...any comments on Beauty and the Beast would be gratefully received.

Love and best wishes from us all,
David

5 May

Dear David,

The ice-ballet scenario is quite lovely! What I especially appreciate is that I can easily visualise the silent dialogue (shades of the Silent Movies) from the danced action. It should be easy enough to follow without mugging and only a minimum of mime. It would be a very satisfactory ballet even without the ice! It's spectacular, too! But I take it the scenery will be chiefly painted cloth and not cumbersomely realistic, so that each scene change will be in the manner of a transformation. The opportunities presented to the designers and to the choreographer are splendid. And who does the music? Is this to be original? I hope so. Anything borrowed – especially if it's from ballet – will bring too many associations with it. It's a prodigious and prestigious undertaking. What sort of backing do Tatiana and her company have?

My only misgiving on my first reading was that Beauty and her two sisters – especially if she was sweeping the floor – were reminiscent of Cinderella. But Mary brightly pointed out these are not Ugly Sisters – quite the reverse. And Beauty presumably will not be in rags like Cinderella, but on terms of equality with her siblings, though dominated by them, not so much by their cruelty as by her own good nature. Moreover, Cinderella did not have brothers. And Father is different from pantomime's Baron de Broke!

I can't wait to see it realised. I do hope it goes rapidly and confidently into production.

You're right to assess Noddy as designed for a younger audience. I see no reason why you shouldn't use all the same characters. The children who accept one book after another do just that. And your 'old tricks and devices' will be quite in order, because the younger audience will be a new audience, enjoying them for the first time from square one! The short story structure should work for them, too, because their length of concentration is short. But it would be a bonus if each could be an episode, complete in itself (leaving a possibility for separate use in schools) but nevertheless pointing towards its successor, so that at the end of each the kids want to know "What happened then?" Can a coda become a cliff-hanger? I'm in favour of cliff-hangers – with each being a link in a chain leading to an up-beat 'chord' for a finale...

...Love – congratulations and huge thanks for another privileged pre-view. I take it I may keep it with my DW Archive?

More love –
Frank

6 May

Dear David,

A hasty Postcriptum!
I meant to say yesterday (when I had my eye on the clock and the Postman) how very much I delighted in the Rose symbol – Red certainly the better, because more emphatic – and its significance throughout the action. A superb touch of poetry it seemed to me...

...Again – I do rejoice in that Rose!

Love –
Frank

11 May

Dear Frank,

First of all, I'm enclosing the latest Noddy synopsis for your perusal. I challenge you to find a link between Acts I and II!

Now on to Beauty and the Beast.

Thank you for your splendid letter and postscript! I'm glad you think the storyline works. You are quite right about the sisters – there is a danger of them making us think we are in the wrong story! But, interestingly, in the original French version by Madame de Villeneuve, the resemblance to Perrault's Cinderella is remarkable. Three sisters, one good, the others not so good; weak father; prince, who can eventually effect a rags-to-riches ending...

Research led me to various other versions of the story, and hopefully I have come up with something reasonably original.

I think it will be quite spectacular, although the expanse of ice cannot have too much scenery on it, in case it gets in the way of the jumps!

The music is to be written by the pop singer David Essex. This at first glance seems rather an odd choice, although he has written the odd musical. But the management are trying to bridge several areas of creativity to widen the audience base, as it were. The idea of having music with a slightly wider appeal has been decided upon. I'm keeping my fingers crossed that this will not dilute the classical flavour of the piece and diminish the power of the story. But, quite honestly, that is all beyond my control.

There seems to be quite a lot of money being lavished on it. I met the costume designer yesterday. He will have about 150 costumes to design! He is very good and experienced – in fact I last worked with him many years ago on Robin Hood at Nottingham Playhouse.

Yesterday, I had a meeting with Tatiana, the Russian choreographer, who greeted me warmly with kisses on both cheeks! I knew from that that she liked the storyline!

She made one or two suggestions which I now have to incorporate, but nothing radical. She now wants to have lots of white roses, with just one large, beautiful scarlet rose bush, which is the symbolic one, as well as the 'real' one. I'll try to weave that into the storyline to please her...

Yours,
David

Dear David,

...What a splendid letter! Huge thanks! First things first: The Beauty and the Beast.

I hope you weren't utterly submerged in Russian lipstick. White roses? Oh yes. They'll emphasize the red rose. But I should like that to be more dominant than just one bush among other bushes – a great big rose suspended as a backdrop so that its falling petal would make an immediate impact – something Chekovian. However, no doubt that's Tatiana's and the designer's problem, outside your brief, I suppose. David Essex for the music? That should certainly broaden the appeal and he may well make a good job of it. He has always seemed to me one of the more sympatico members of the Pop Parade. Was it he who played the Elephant Man? I hope the storyline and characterisation won't be lost in unnecessary displays of irrelevant acrobatics – pretty and even exciting to watch skating per se (I love these Latin reminiscences) but obscuring the thread of plot. I'm glad the management seems to be well funded. Might the show come to our Mayflower in Southampton? If it does, we shall be there.

And Noddy *– new adventures of! We – that's self and sister – love it. We think your decision to offer the show as two separate adventures should work well for the younger audience. They might easily lose the thread of the plot if it had to be sustained overlong for their limited powers of concentration – though those following the first piece appeared to keep up with the extended line. With so much exhilarating action, will there be time for a song or two as well as 'chase' music?...*

Frank

18 May

Dear Frank,

…I was very happy to receive reassurance on Noddy *from you and Mary! It may not be the most original thing I have ever come up with, but I think it will work both artistically and commercially. Sadly, the latter is what matters these days. We had another Whirligig meeting last night, and it really is clear that we cannot produce anything without a commercial title, and even then we need funding of some sort. I suppose 'twas ever thus – in the past, we have always managed to find some financial support. But the difference now is that the theatres themselves are reluctant to take the work, because they fear the schools' lack of support. Tricky…*

…David undoubtedly writes good tunes, and will be employing an excellent arranger. So it will be interesting to see whether it does indeed broaden the appeal of the entire Beauty and the Beast *production.*

I'm enclosing a couple of pages from the third (and I hope final!) draft of the storyline, in which I emphasise how important the 'scarlet rose bush' is. It says (though not so eloquently!) virtually what you said – and indeed what Tatiana said. Hopefully, the designer will heed it!…

Yours,
David

22 May

Dear David,

The detailed draft for the symbolic rose is masterly. I do hope Tatiana and her designer will appreciate how central and beautiful it is, and that the technicians will have the ingenuity to make it work…

Love to you all –
Frank

8 Jun

Dear Frank,

...In haste – managed to finish Noddy 2 *first draft last week...
Am now casting, etc.*

Russian Beauty and the Beast *seems O.K. – storyline agreed.
Rehearsals starting soon – in Moscow – I don't think I'll be
invited!*

*But I have been asked about going to Japan to direct/
supervise a production of* Owl and Pussycat *– next year – might
be a challenge...*

*Love and best wishes to you both –
David x*

Some work on children's books followed until the next version of
Noddy was sent to FW.

15 Jun

Dear David,

*...I think you've hit just the right note for the younger age group
by providing plenty of action and audience involvement. Will
they already know 'Old MacDonald Had a Farm'? Anyway,*
Noddy *will easily initiate them. The song makes a splendid
finale to Act One. And the dancing to Act Two. But will the
fabric of the theatre survive it? Tessie Bear's problems and Sly's
machinations provide nice suspense throughout the act, and Mr
Noah's disappointment affords a pleasing touch of pathos.*

*How will the puppet Whiskers be operated? The creature has
quite a lot to do independently of Big Ears. The Skittles get a fair
slice of the action, too. I hope neither of them will go sick when
we come to the show as one did last time!*

The children – I approve, by the way, their being addressed as 'young ladies and gentlemen', not from any snobbism, but because it shows them respect and puts them in the same league as their parents. It's a relief to get away from 'kids' and 'mums and dads'. The children, as I was saying, will love the chaos of the washing and the knockabout of the Skittles. I love the dialogue, both that between the characters and between characters and audience, and especially the cross-talk on p19 between Noddy and Tessie, and on pp 27–28 between Tessie and Mr Noah. It seems to me that you've managed to sharpen the characterisation with the lines you've given to each. I felt this notably with PC Plod and Sly. Monkey's looking offended is a charming touch, and his song should be a hit with its movements. The 'Funky Monkey' might become a dance – like the Hokey-Cokey, or even the Lambeth Walk! I love PC Plod in the Dark Wood too. I'm still chuckling as I turn over the script in front of me right now...

.... I like the neat way in which the picnic prepares for the flying sequences. I suppose the model for the aeroplane will be in the original illustrations? It shouldn't be such a costly prop as the car, which I'm delighted to see is being used again to justify the investment.

In your introduction, you say that the second story introduces new characters. Does that mean simply others than those in the first story or the earlier play, or are they Woody originals? If they are, they seem quite authentic, and the fantasy orientation is quite in keeping...

Love to you all –
Frank

16 Jun

Dear Frank,

...I use 'Old Macdonald Had a Farm' in my Magic and Music Show – in fact I open the show with it. All the children, of all *ages, seem to know it. I can always tell from the enthusiasm with which they sing the EE I EE I O section how well the rest of the show is going to go!*

The puppet Whiskers will be a glove puppet, but I'm hoping the puppeteer can make a sort of extension on a rod, with which it can appear over the top of Big-Ears' house, through the door, etc.

…'The Funky Monkey' is a bit of a cheat in that I wrote it for my version of Cinderella *twenty-odd years ago! Since then, I have recorded it on my* David Wood Songbook *album, and used it for the last fifteen years as the finale to the* Magic and Music Show. *So at least I know it works! The content seemed to fit the bill so well that I couldn't be bothered to write another song! I agree, it would be rather nice if it turned into a dance craze!*

…The aeroplane is featured in book 24 of the Noddy *series – the last* Noddy *book Enid Blyton wrote. The cover illustration, on which we'll base our aeroplane, is a nice fantasy version of an open-cockpit aircraft.*

Re. the new characters. In fact, Tubby Bear is an existing character, but new to me in terms of including him in a play. The Great Tootle is really invented by me but I cannot take the full credit by any means. In one of the books, Noody and the Tootles, *Enid Blyton introduces a gypsy family who live in a caravan. Mother, father and lots of children. The father has a tootle, which indeed makes people dance and feel happy. Unfortunately, he turns out to be a bit of a rogue, who tries to swap his horse for Noddy's car and temporarily succeeds! What I did was simply take the basic name of the character and his capacity to make people dance and incorporate these into a more dashing, flamboyant entertainer figure. The part will be played by Michael Seraphim, who you saw playing Bumpy Dog, I think. He is the black actor who has worked for me many times, and is really very clever indeed. I suspect that The Great Tootle will have a slight 'rap' feel!…*

Yours,
David

By July, casting had begun for *Noddy*.

13 Jul

Dear Frank,

… Still no Big Ears, but we have made an offer for a Sly, and yesterday I saw two possible Tessie Bears. One of them is a little tall, however! Seeing them again tomorrow.

The tour date list I'm enclosing is not for Noddy, *it is for* Beauty and the Beast. *The fact that the first date is at Cardiff Ice Rink may have given it away!*

You will see that Beauty and the Beast *is scheduled to come to the Mayflower, Southampton in March. I will put this in my diary, in the hope that we might be able to meet up…*

Yours,
David

As plans for *Noddy* developed, DW was travelling and saw the Greek National Theatre perform.

20 Aug

Dear David,

…I once went to the Greek Play at Bradfield College in its reduced-scale Greek Theatre. I was tremendously impressed. Of course, I didn't understand any of the words. Neither, I was told, did most of the actors! But they spoke them as though they did, and the movement of the chorus was quite superb. I do wish I knew Greek – Ancient Greek, that is. I find the drama even in translation tremendously exciting. In my young days, we revelled in the versions by Gilbert Murray. I am told these are not approved by modern authorities, but they had a splendid Swinburnian swing and were very actable…

…We saw and greatly enjoyed The School for Scandal *[at*

Chichester] in which Ian Carmichael gave a very, very well-thought [-through] performance of Sir Peter. I was rather apprehensive as we tottered to our seats because the stage was littered with 'blow-ups' of tabloid newspaper headlines, intended, I suppose, to emphasise 'relevance', a parallel between the 'sleaze' of Sheridan's day and our own. I needn't have worried. The actors completely ignored this unnecessary effort and let the play speak and make the parallel by itself.

We've just acquired a video machine, and are gradually learning how to press the right buttons in the appropriate order. We've been given a 'video' of Uncle Vanya – Olivier's superb production from the very first years of Chichester. Do you remember it? Were you there? I saw it twice – it was given two years in succession with an unrepeatable cast – Thorndike, Casson, Redgrave et al.

Talking of casts – how are you progressing with your line-up for Noddy?...

Love to you all –
Frank

30 Aug

Dear Frank,

...The performance of The Persians went ahead as scheduled. About eight thousand of us witnessed a Cypriot company giving a modern Greek version. I must say I found it more interesting from the point of view of the extraordinary acoustics of the theatre and also the movement of the Chorus, which was rather clever. The plot of that particular play is not the most exciting of the Greek tragedies, although, of course, the content is. But (and this displays my children's theatre persona, I suppose), all the exciting things happen off stage! I don't think, in a children's play, I could ever have a messenger come on and do five or six pages of graphic description, however wonderfully delivered – I would have to find some way of portraying the amazing happenings he is describing! But the overall experience was very special, and we all much enjoyed it...

We returned to Wimbledon... I had to prepare my Edinburgh Festival performances ...All went well in Edinburgh. I always enjoy that city, and the Festival in particular. There is such an atmosphere of optimism and enthusiasm, bright-eyed and bushy-tailed students excited and eager to try things out. It took me back, of course, and, when I went to see the Oxford Revue, I suddenly realised it was thirty years since I had been in it myself...

I start rehearsals for More Adventures of Noddy... on Monday.

Casting it was not easy – actors just don't want to do long tours any more, unless they are paid the earth. Several people turned down offers, having agreed in principle beforehand that they would like to do it. Several auditionees, having taken the trouble to come along and see us twice or even three times, then dropped out of the running. However, before going to Greece, the final offer was made, and accepted two days later... All was well until the end of my first week in Cornwall, when the news came through that I had lost Bumpy Dog! Michael Seraphim, the actor I have employed for years, and who does a wonderful job, particularly as an animal!, and for whom I had created the role of The Great Tootle, had decided to take the risk on a possible recording contract in Greece, and wanted out... This rather put a shadow on the rest of the holiday, I must say. Michael is really rather special. Anyway, to cut a long story short, we auditioned some more people yesterday and found somebody very good, who has, thank heavens, accepted the offer...

The Chichester Uncle Vanya I remember minutely, because, when it played the second time, in 1963, I was doing my stint as an extra in the other two plays – Saint Joan and The Workhouse Donkey. I used to be allowed to stand at the back *of the auditorium to watch performances of* Uncle Vanya, *and saw it about ten times! It was always splendid. Not only that, I once asked to see an understudy run-through, and this proved to be just as good! Derek Jacobi was playing for Redgrave; Robert Lang for Olivier; Rowena Cooper was understudying Rosemary Harris and Jeanne Hepple was Plowright. The performances were superb. All in rehearsal clothes with no stage lighting whatsoever! Fascinated to hear that it is on video, although I did know it had been made into a sort of feature film, and I saw it once on television. It was that same season that I had the excitement of talking to Sybil Thorndike and Fay Compton. The latter, puffing away at a cigarette before the first preview performance of* The Workhouse Donkey, *said to me, watching the audience arrive from the stage door, "Did I think they would enjoy it?" I said, "I hope so." She said, "No, they won't, they haven't paid!"…*

Love and best wishes,
David

2 Sep

Dear David,

I envy you the Greek experience. I have always been fascinated by those legendary acoustics and the power of off-stage reported action. What appears to be so static – those long speeches and the stycomathia (if that's how you spell it – it's how I'm spelling it to-day, because the dictionary's out of reach!) can be very gripping if properly delivered and projected. I once saw Ben Jonson's Sejanus *at the theatre at Sussex University (where I also saw* The Ideal Gnome Expedition*) and was surprised to find it quite gripping.*

This makes me think of my concern for the Globe and its groundlings. When Hamlet accuses them of 'being capable of nothing but inexplicable dumb shows and noise', I suspect he was referring to audiences encountered on tour in the provinces. London audiences, even the groundlings, who always went to 'hear' not to 'see' a play, must have been quick on the up-take to follow not only such close-packed, immediate exposition, without an understanding of which they would have been completely lost, but also to keep pace with the continual punning and other word-play which filled out the action…

The academics have at last come to realise that this is what matters in evaluating his achievement. The philosophy and politics are interesting, of course, but his primary concern was not uplift but entertainment, the carrying of conviction by the creation of characters whose reality could make believable the unlikeliest of events and convenient chances – and so put bums on seats or feet in the pit! I must not get carried away by this present hobby-horse! But a pilgrimage to the Globe? Oh, YES!…

P.S. …I'm allergic to Lloyd Webber. That alleged music just drools on and on without ever achieving a tune except on the cash register. The only entertainment I experienced at a matinée… was when the mechanism for raising the chandelier refused to work and we sat for twenty minutes or more while perspiring stage-hands tried to coax it into action. It was eventually raised to thunderous applause.

F

Arrangements were made for FW to see *More Adventures of Noddy* when it opened at Wimbledon, and which turned out to be another successful excursion.

1995 More Adventures of Noddy –
Wimbledon Theatre – 27th September 1995
Two new *Noddy* stories, using ingredients from the books, which were presented as two one-act plays, with an interval.

1 Oct

Dear David,

This is just to thank you for a most memorable Friday. ...the great joy of the occasion was to be with you and Jacqui, and to see Noddy's New Adventures *realised in performance. It is very illuminating to see what happens to the script when it is actually developed on stage. This leads me to reflect on how little we can know of what the immortal Bard must have done in filling out his pieces in the theatre, pillars or no pillars.*

The name I was trying to remember in connection with the reconstruction of the Globe is C. Walter Hodges. ...he demonstrates, as an architect, how the 'Heavens' could have been supported without pillars – as Henslowe wanted for his rival theatre. For the first Globe, he visualises pillars not much wider than an average human body – about 18" – standing on slightly more substantial plinths. The Swan drawing shows pillars set about half-way between the extreme front and rear of the stage, providing a considerable 'apron'. His suggestions for groupings in the Introductions to the New Cambridge Shakespeare editions of the plays are ingenious and practical. Certainly, some members of the audience would have suffered a 'restricted view' at particular moments – but so they did (and still do) in certain Victorian playhouses – and at Glyndebourne!...

Thank you again! And my love to you all,
Frank

9 Oct

Dear Frank,

...Last week, I went to Belfast for two days, to see Noddy *into the Grand Opera House, a wonderful Matcham theatre built exactly one hundred years ago. In spite of occasional bombs damaging*

its exterior, the theatre has remained remarkably intact and beautiful. Noddy *looked very nice on its stage.*

It was good to find Belfast relaxed and soldier-less. Last time I was there, I remember feeling I would be rather happy to leave. This time, I would have been quite content to stay on!...

Yours,
David

As the *Noddy* tour continued, news emerged of *Beauty and the Beast*, by then about to open.

4 Dec

Dear Frank,

... Am enclosing a leaflet for Beauty and the Beast *at the Albert Hall. Plus a new date list showing the Southampton dates in March. I will hope to come down possibly to a matinee mid-week. Rehearsals have been proceeding for a couple of months or more in Moscow. The Company are now in London, and tomorrow, Tuesday, they are giving a charity premiere at the Albert Hall in aid of the Elton John Aids Foundation. We are all going, naturally. It will be very odd watching the first performance having had nothing whatsoever to do with the rehearsals!*

Meanwhile, More Adventures of Noddy *is in the final week of its first batch of dates. Everyone has a few weeks off for Christmas, before starting again in January. Business has been mixed, but the reception has been warm.*

Things have been bittily busy (or busily bitty), mainly trying to plan a few things for next year. We are hoping that Meg and Mog Show *might tour again...*

Yours,
David

The next letter from DW arrived at the same time as FW's copy of *The Times* with a less-than-enthusiastic review of *Beauty and the Beast*.

7 Dec

Dear David,

…I hope this particular verdict won't depress the prospects of the extensive tour. I'm glad you were able to assist (as the French say) at the performance although you haven't assisted (as the British put it) at the rehearsals. I do hope Tatiana hadn't mucked about with your admirable storyline. The David Essex contribution sounds (again as the French say) un peu formidable! I'm glad to see that a fine rose features on the leaflet. We are already looking forward to the laying down of the necessary ice at the Mayflower and if you can attend the matinee, that will heighten our expectation, Tatiana or no Tatiana.

I found myself wondering about the Albert Hall presentation on Tuesday – I presume the ice is spread in the arena – keeping the £15 seaters a little chilled – How do the skaters skate to it? Does the ice have to reach into those tunnels for them to get on and off? I can't suppose they squat beside the rink to put their skates on, or totter on their blades down the steps.

Never mind. It'll be easier at the Mayflower – but I can't see them having much room to manoeuvre at the dear old Bournemouth Pavilion…

Ever,
Frank

11 Dec

Dear Frank,

…The skating itself was remarkable and most impressive. But I didn't feel that the design helped the storyline. …For some

reason, the potted storyline I had written for the programme was not available on this Gala evening. Presumably, the programmes hadn't been printed on time. So the audience had nothing to prepare them for what was about to happen. And in most ballets, and operas, I suppose, it is important to be able to refer to something which tells you what's going on! This proved the case at the Albert Hall. I certainly wouldn't have understood why Father set off for the Port with a trunk. There had been nothing much to suggest that he was poverty-stricken, or that he was selling off his antiques!

Anyway, I'm not too bothered. I think this production is very much for a specific, popular audience. It is probably unfair for critics of theatre or ballet to get their teeth into it!

To answer your question, the skaters skate on an area about 20' square. Behind it are various one-dimensional backcloths, rather old-fashioned in feel. This skating area can sit on a theatre stage or can be put at one end of the floor area of the Albert Hall and cut off with a false proscenium. I agree with you. I would rather see it in a theatre!...

I returned to London via Ipswich, where, at the Regent Theatre, a rather unpleasant converted cinema, More Adventures of Noddy was playing its last week before the Christmas break. The show went reasonably well, although the stage is so limited that several parts of the set had to be omitted...

Yours,
David

17 Dec

Dear David,

...The mis-management sounds typically Russian! No wonder they want to bring back the Commies! A potted storyline is a

must for both ballet and opera, though I think your plot for this piece must be more intelligible in its action than most, without words written or uttered. It's vital to opera. Whatever language the singers sing in makes no difference – they're always impossible to understand and might just as well whoop away in Esperanto.

The 20' square space doesn't seem to allow much room for the skaters to manoeuvre. Perhaps we've been misled by the vast arenas covered by Torville and Dean. As you say, Tatiana is catering for a special audience of folk who are not otherwise interested in ballet or theatre. Come to think of it, we've had almost everything on ice except Shakespeare and Noddy! *We look forward to it anyway...*

Happy Christmas to you all with lots of love –
Frank

1996

The new year began with *Beauty and the Beast* receiving better local notices and *More Adventures of Noddy* was to recommence touring. Other projects were being discussed, but it proved difficult to make progress on many of them. FW saw the ice show at Southampton and wrote enthusiastically about it.

7 Mar

Dear David,

...we enjoyed a really marvellous show. If you haven't seen it since the Albert Hall effort for Charity you must get to it again. The skating is quite superb and the whole thing exhilarating. I thought the scenery a little drab, but perhaps this was done to show off the magnificent costumes to advantage. There were so many of them! When they weren't on the ice, the skaters

must have been undressing or dressing. How they managed to whirl about the stage, a comparatively confined space, without colliding, left me breathless with admiration. David Essex' music served its purpose without being especially memorable, I thought, and one or two passages stirred recollections – at one moment of a popular tune from Hymns A & M on which I was brought up. But never mind. As Arthur Sullivan pointed out to a critic who cavilled at his borrowing from a greater composer, "You should remember we have only eight notes to play with." I could only distinguish the words of one of the lyrics – in the duet by the sisters, but that was very neat and deserved its laughs. The reception from a ¾ house – all us geriatrics downstairs, kids above – was rapturous, and the company seemed to be enjoying themselves as much as we were. A blue-rinse next to Mary exclaimed, "Pricey, but worth every penny!" Our transport strategy (how do you spell that?) worked smoothly…

Love to you all –
Frank

DW's reply indicated that all was not well with the production, however, and also included an update on many other projects.

19 Apr

Dear Frank,

Beauty and the Beast *came to the Albert Hall last week. I didn't get there in the end, but understand that it went well. However, we now have a dispute with the producer, who is pleading poverty and wants me to waive all my royalties… Typical! It seems that business has not been good and that the production is losing a lot of money. Quite why he should assume that I should give up my rightful pennies when everybody else involved will be receiving theirs, I don't know! I have decided to fight. I think it is a matter of principle. The Company is a very successful one, even though this production may be losing them money.*

The More Adventures of Noddy tour is back on the road and doing reasonably well, although some theatres are much better business-wise than others. I saw them in Croydon last week and they all seemed well and happy, I'm glad to say.

We have now started thinking about the revival of The Witches, which is due to open at Wimbledon Theatre in September. Hopefully, this will do a long tour and will do better business than the revival of The BFG, which probably went out a little too soon after its original tour. It is now four years since The Witches debut, so hopefully audiences will come!

…Have also done a synopsis for a possible musical based on Oscar Wilde's The Selfish Giant. It is not a full synopsis, by any means, but intended to be a discussion document. Don Black is the lyricist, and Barrington Pheloung (who wrote the Inspector Morse theme) is the composer. Polygram, a huge company specialising in records, films and, occasionally, stage shows, seems keen to promote it. I'd be very interested to see what you think of my tampering with the brilliance of Wilde. It's one of those wonderful stories that is so fragile when you come to take it to pieces that I almost wonder whether it should be left alone and not dramatised, yet alone musicalised (if there is such a word!).

…It seems that quite a lot has been going on, and I suppose it has! But I'm still trying to revive Whirligig. We are putting in a small application to the Lottery to pay for a feasibility study, considering the best way forward for Whirligig. This may involve looking for a building as a home base. But until they change the Lottery rules even more, to allow for revenue funding as well as funding for capital costs, I fear we would not be able to guarantee the stability of the Company for long enough to take the risk of setting it up…

Yours,
David

FW's reply encouraged resistance to not being paid for *Beauty and the Beast*, and also agreed with the timing of the revivals. The main thrust of his letter, however, was a detailed response to the possibility of the Oscar Wilde musical.

23 Apr

Dear David,

… Now for that 'possible musical' of The Selfish Giant. *…who thought up this idea? It is, as you say, such a fragile story, a delightful soap bubble, can it possibly be inflated to occupy a feature-length performance without bursting in smithereens?*

…You're right in your Further Thought 1 to clarify it as a fable, but I think it is allegorical rather than mythical. The Snow, Frost and Hail are representations of the forces that beat about the world considered as a garden, rather than figures in a myth who are more often presented as actual persons – the Greek and Roman gods and goddesses, for instance. The Giant is a person, of course, but he is also an allegory of self-seeking power, not necessarily an Evil Force, but a Force which may lend itself to good or evil exercises. The Boy is a sentimentalised Christ figure. (Part of Wilde's skill is that he can touch a story with sentiment so delicately that he does not make its sweetness nauseating.) He should be played for strength, I think, not pathos. This brings me to your 2.

You suggest that to personalise the characters too much will 'diminish' the story? I'm not sure that it will. Drama postulates conflict and confrontation. Because the basis of Wilde's story is allegory – as in a Medieval Morality play – the dramatis personae might not improperly be presented, if not as 'characters' at least as 'characteristics' – like Ben Jonson's 'humours'**. This would give each of the children something distinctive to personify. The slight plot has to be filled out somehow for the stage, and this would bring the other children into the same category as the central Boy. I don't think such a treatment would 'take away from the universality of the tale'. The children might even exhibit different national traits, a touch of the ethnics so much discussed today! Though Heaven forfend the piece should become a United Nations Amalgam as a tract for the times!...

Your 3 – a credible framework. You've provided that, I think, and conformed to Oscar's lay-out by presenting the garden before revealing that it is the desirable residential property of a Giant. And in your 4 you suggest a choir as narrator. Since it's Wilde's story, and an important part in all stories of his period is the presence of the author – e.g., Dickens, Austen, Trollope, Thackeray et al, all owe much of their power to the presence of the authorial voice responding to the universal appeal of 'Tell me a story' – might not you have Oscar himself to tell it? This would be a real challenge to an actor of stature. Robert Morley is unfortunately dead, but Alec Guinness still accepts modest engagements. And I'm sure there are lesser men who could attempt it with honour and success. Timothy West, for instance? The device would allow you to use some of Wilde's own words, might even suggest a parallel between the author and his creation – the power hungry are exhibitionists, and such was Oscar. He also had his genius to declare (as he memorably claimed on his arrival in New York), which was something very few others could do.

This brings me to my last Further Thought, which you have not touched on. At what sort of audience do the promoters aim their attempt?...

Ever,
Frank

**whom he distinguishes from stereotypes by individual touches

A flurry of letters followed with family news, before the next updates on tours and legal disputes.

3 Jun

Dear Frank,

Enc. a nice ice review! (Still no money, no box office returns and no response to two solicitors' letters from Mr Bush, the promoter – very vexing.)

…The Witches revival is cast – am very pleased, considering we don't start rehearsals till Sept 2nd! Good people too, I think – Katharine Barker is Grandmother – she has done a lot of good work – including the 1964 Henry IV (1 and 2) at Stratford – the famous Peter Hall one with Eric Porter, Ian Holm, Roy Dotrice as Shallow, etc., and played Lady Mortimer and a Lady, I think, but she must have been fresh out of drama school at the time!

Last week, did the Magic and Music Show at the Harlequin Theatre, Redhill and the Epsom Playhouse, both rather nice medium-scale venues set in rather boring shopping centres! Audiences not huge, but enthusiastic.

Noddy still going (reasonably) strong – last week Cardiff, this week Richmond! Tour finishes beginning of August at WHITLEY BAY!!

…Let me know if you fancy The Witches at Wimbledon Theatre in opening week (w/b Sept 23rd, opening Wed)!!

> *Lots of love to you both from all,*
> *David*

5 Jun

Dear David,

Hurrah for yours and that super-enthusiastic notice! Hurrah for Brighton and its Centre! …I'm glad that the splendid show is still on the road and the rinks. And OH YES to the opening week of Wimbledon! I refer, of course, not to the Tennis (at which I have not been invited to play) but The Witches re-opening at

145

the Theayter. Please keep a seat for me at whichever performance will be most convenient for you when you have the schedule. I'm delighted you've managed to collect a satisfactory cast prepared to take time away from the T.V. octopus. I haven't seen the Epsom Playhouse. It's well after my time in that salubrious district. It used – ie. Epsom – to have a nice little S/H Bookshop which was on my bicycle visiting list from Sutton. Redhill was off my map, though I went often to Reigate from Horsham by bus, not bike, in search of literature on the cheap, before Shopping Malls had been invented. However large or small your audiences, I'm sure they'd be enthusiastic. Will you be able to squeeze any more mileage out of Noddy, *do you think, with* Even More Adventures of Noddy?*...

...love to you all at home or abroad,
Frank

* I suppose Son of Noddy *would hardly be acceptable!*

29 Aug

Dear Frank,

... I have put down the Thursday matinée for your visit – I may well have to be giving notes before the Wednesday matinée, having only opened the day before!
    ...I was about to tell you about the bespoke production of The Gingerbread Man *Whirligig is presenting at the Birmingham Hippodrome at the beginning of November. The go-ahead director has decided to mount a major initiative to encourage up to 20,000 into the theatre in one week! His auditorium holds 2,000, which is a little bit large for the play really, but I think we will cope. Birmingham is paying for the entire production, which includes two weeks' rehearsal and only one week of performances! Ironically, if we had known about this earlier, we could have turned it into a Whirligig tour, but sadly there are not enough*

decent theatres available. But at least it will provide a focus for Whirligig once again and hopefully encourage other theatres to put on productions or join together in some sort of syndicate to guarantee enough money for such productions to tour again.

Meanwhile, More Adventures of Noddy *finished its tour earlier this month. Sadly, it has lost quite a lot of money. But the reaction everywhere was good and I'm certainly glad to have done it. The big question is whether Clarion, the producers, will ever be able to tour another one like that.* The Witches *is theirs too, but, because it plays in the evenings as well as the afternoons, the potential revenue is considerably higher and the production is not quite so risky...*

Love,
David

2 Sep

Dear David,

...Thinking it over, I believe The Gingerbread Man *will not be lost in the vastness of the Birmingham Hippodrome. If it plays to 2,000 kids per performance, it should rattle Sir Simon. And what a splendid introduction to it for a new generation. Sorry about Noddy's losses. I hope you've had your whack? Did the Russians pay up?...*

Love to all – Frank

9 Sep

Dear Frank,

... Have just finished the first week of rehearsal of The Witches. *Lovely cast. A pleasure to work with them. Fingers crossed, all is going OK so far...*

...Thank you for your comforting words re. the Birmingham Hippodrome and the scale of The Gingerbread Man. *I'm sure we will be all right. It has played in big theatres before. And I am lucky enough to have a very experienced cast.*

...I haven't received all my Noddy *royalties yet... fingers crossed. And there has been not a penny from the Russians. In fairness to them, it is the British promoter I am at odds with, not the Ruskies themselves!...*

Yours,
David

Another Blyton project was soon added to the list of possible future productions.

22 Oct

Dear Frank,

...Last week, I slipped away to the seaside again! ...The main object was to do some storylines for a possible model animation T.V. series based on Mary Mouse, *an Enid Blyton character from way back. I had already done a treatment for a series, which everyone seemed to like. However, at a subsequent meeting, certain restrictions were placed upon locations and other aspects, which has made the provision of nine storylines really rather difficult. And, in fact, I don't really think there is enough originality in the idea – and I don't seem to be able to add much, either! So it may all fall by the wayside...*

...I'm dictating this on Saturday. Rehearsals for The Gingerbread Man *start on Monday. Fingers crossed! Meanwhile,* The Witches *has been in Belfast this week. I haven't heard any news from the Company, but hope it's gone well. Sadly, the first leg of the tour is finishing earlier than anticipated – November*

16th. This means there is a two-month gap between the first leg and the second leg. I'm rather worried that I will lose some of the actors because of this…

Yours,
David

28 Oct

Dear Frank,

… First, the very welcome news that The Witches is, after all, to play a Christmas season. At the Vaudeville Theatre in the Strand, no less! We are all delighted, as you can imagine. Apparently, the owners of the Vaudeville made a very good offer to Clarion, who felt able to accept, on the basis that they were virtually guaranteed not to lose any money…

…As I dictate this, I have just finished the first week of rehearsal for The Gingerbread Man in Birmingham. We have a lovely cast, five of whom have done it before, thank heavens! We had a run-through on the Saturday which was really in very good shape. Not bad after only five days' work!

All for now. The main reason for such a speedy reply to your letter is, of course, the news about The Witches!

Yours,
David

11 Nov

Dear Frank,

Have just got back from Birmingham, which, I'm glad to report, was a tremendous success!

We reckon that about 14,000 children attended and really did seem to enjoy themselves…

...As I may have told you, The Witches *comes into the Vaudeville Theatre on December 9th. This week, I have to go to Wolverhampton for a couple of days to rehearse in a new member of the cast. It's all go!...*

Yours,
David

Dear David,

...The report from Birmingham is SUPER! (That's a dated expression, I believe, but I can summon no later equivalent.) What a pity the production can't undertake a tour, or come into town for Christmas. The interview in The Stage *is first class. My only regret is that it will be seen by a specialised and limited readership. I should like to see it repeated in* The Times *or somewhere equally influential among the thinking classes.*

...Perhaps the Lottery should fund a Trust for a Children's Theatre Movement, a sort of AA or RAC, which could make grants to managements to meet the pressure from schools to mount touring productions of plays for children. They need to be introduced to drama (which comes naturally to them) not only in the classroom but also – as you have always championed – in the Playhouse. As you say, it is not a building that you require but a bank account...

Ever –
Frank

1997

The new year began with DW touring his *Magic and Music Show* once more, and he was quick to update FW on this and other ongoing projects.

6 Jan

Dear Frank,

…Unfortunately, The Witches *has been taken off two weeks early. It has played four weeks at the Vaudeville, with very good reviews (apart from rather an unpleasant one in the* Evening Standard*) and everyone has enjoyed themselves. But, as you may remember, it was announced so late in the day that there was no time for the box office to build properly and the owners of the Vaudeville, who were underwriting the whole enterprise, decided to cut their losses.*

However, the tour resumes in two weeks' time at the Theatre Royal, Glasgow and business looks good for the first few weeks, which is pleasing.

… A couple of days ago, Katherine and I drove to Southend, to visit the Palace Theatre, Westcliff production of my version of Cinderella. This turned out to be a delightful experience. They produced it very faithfully and didn't muck about with it. And a full house listened intently to the storyline. The importance of the story can never be stressed too highly, in my view. It was interesting that in the Sunday Times *yesterday there was an article talking about some of the most successful children's films in recent months, like* Babe *and* Toy Story, *and saying how their success, amongst adults as well as children, was due quite simply to the strength of their storyline.*

… I have various projects to think about, including a possible new stage play/adaptation for the Library Theatre, Manchester, plus a possible children's opera to be commissioned by Welsh National Opera (to go into schools, I think).

...At the end of this week, I go to Birmingham to pack in three theatre visits. I'm seeing the Old Rep. production of my adaptation of The BFG, *followed by the new Rep's production of* Pinocchio *(which hasn't been very well received, I hear), and then I see the glitzy Hippodrome pantomime in the evening! Next day, I go to Cardiff to see the Sherman Theatre production of my adaptation of* The BFG, *directed by none other than Michael Bogdanov. It will be interesting to see what he has done with it!...*

Love and best wishes,
David

9 Jan

Dear David,

I say, I say! What a splendidly news-crammed letter! And all good news too, except for the cutting-back of the run at the Vaudeville. But the trouble surely was not in the play but in its late addition to the Christmas lists. Parents can only manage so many outings and these have to be arranged well in advance. The company should be able to take to the road again with renewed zest after the break.

The reviews, except for the Standard, *are all splendid. I think the trouble with that reviewer was that he knew the book and had seen the play before. The darkness was thus bound to be dissipated. No thriller can thrill on a second visit as it does on the first – unless by W. Shakespeare when other factors survive to compensate for unexpectedness. The magic in* The Witches *could serve this turn to young enquiring minds if – as is unlikely to happen – a child were given a second chance. I can imagine bright children advancing any number of bright ideas as to how it was done. Mr Nick Curtis was clearly a little disgruntled even before too much Christmas spirit. (I often wonder about that* word 'disgruntled'. If one can be 'disgruntled' surely one can be 'gruntled' autonymously? There's a word for you!)...

Love to you all as ever –
Frank

In the same month, the discussion returned to the topic of *Peter Pan*, one that fascinated both correspondents. (The young unnamed director was Matthew Warchus, now Artistic Director of the Old Vic.)

20 Jan

Dear Frank,

...*First of all, I went to see the much-lauded* Peter Pan *at the West Yorkshire Playhouse. Here is a programme for you to peruse. The production, on the whole, quite lived up to expectations. Its main attraction, for me, was the fact that it took the play seriously. It changed one or two things, but, in the main, stuck faithfully to Barrie's original text. Scenes were linked by a narrator's voice echoing through the darkness. This was done mainly to cover the scene changes, but also managed to squeeze in some good things from the story-book version, things that are not in the play. All the technical tricks were splendid. The flying was excellent. The lighting was brilliant – you could hardly ever see the wires! The crocodile, a huge puppet operated by half a dozen actors, was extraordinarily effective, and the acting was beautifully orchestrated, so that the story was told strongly and clearly, yet everything was slightly larger than life; not melodramatic, exactly, but excitingly theatrical. The young director is clearly someone to watch [out] for...*

...*You are absolutely right about* The Witches. *For an adult, let alone a critic, to expect to react in the same way second time as the first time is asking a lot!...*

...*Your P.S. about* Mary Rose *disappearing from the island*

153

is something I always quote to the actors when I'm directing The Witches. *When told that nine or ten witches are going to disappear before the eyes of the audience, the actors often express doubts as to whether the audience will really be fooled. I point out to them that if any member of the audience chooses to look in the right place at the right time, he or she will see the witches going with ease, in spite of the fact there is a goodly amount of smoke and pulsating light covering the stage! But the fact is, if you want an audience to focus on something interesting – as Barrie knew only too well – you can do it, and they will never see what you don't want them to see! In the case of* The Witches, *the sight of the Grand High Witch descending magically into the soup tureen is so riveting that even those of us on the production team, who have seen it many, many times, never actually see the other witches go!*

…In Birmingham, I saw a very good BFG, *faithfully sticking to my adaptation and breaking all box office records at the Old Rep.*

…The next day, I went to Cardiff to see another BFG, *this one directed by Michael Bogdanov, he of the English Shakespeare Company fame, who can be brilliant or can be woefully anarchic! Happily, his production was in the main very good. But I hated the music and the way in which the Queen was encouraged to play her role like a revue sketch, thus taking away from the whole point of her scenes. The English Shakespeare Company have asked to tour this production in 1998. Next week, I'm hoping to meet Mr. Bogdanov (whom I have known for thirty years or so!) to convince him to change some elements of the production…*

Yours,
David

FW's reply referred again to Barrie's stage directions in *Peter Pan*, provoking this response.

3 Feb

Dear Frank,

…I agree with you about Barrie's stage directions. In fact, there was a production of Peter Pan *at the Barbican, directed by Trevor Nunn for the RSC… In fact, I didn't like the production very much, because I thought it was very 'knowing' and rather sent up the children's side of things. But it had been decided that some of the stage directions were worth using, so an actor played Barrie, strolling through the set, almost introducing each scene. I must say I found it a bit annoying. It certainly held up the story! But the device used at West Yorkshire Playhouse, whereby this marvellous booming voice came out of the darkness, was really very exciting!*

The week before last, I went to Glasgow to 'see in' The Witches. *The Theatre Royal is beautiful and we had very good houses. Unfortunately, one of our actors didn't arrive – his parents both died within days of each other, one of a sort of heart attack and the other of a sort of stroke, plus hitting of head when falling. Dreadful business. However, the cast coped very well – two of them 'moved up one' and the show went very well. Last week, they had a bumper week in Newcastle, a virtual sell-out. But more bad luck – Bruno ricked his back, causing yet another shifting around of actors!*

A few days ago, I went to Oxford and Birmingham to discuss our proposed Whirligig tour of Babe, the Sheep-Pig…

Yours,
David

5 Feb

Dear David,

…I remember reading about Trevor Nunn's intrusion of Barrie on stage in that R.S.C. production and thinking that was not the way to do it. Barrie has to be played absolutely straight without

any attempt at disguising the sentiment. One has to believe in Tinker Bell! And he had no illusions about children and their cruelty to their own kind...

> *Love to you all,*
> *Frank*

The discussion then moved to the openings of plays, leading to FW's thoughts on comparing opera and drama, and the changes seen in his lifetime.

22 Feb

Dear David,

...Gielgud recalls in one of his books how, as late as 1923, actors came in front of the curtain to take a bow at the end of each act as opera singers do to-day. The implication of this is that the audience never thought of what was happening on stage as being 'real'. They accepted it as artificial – as the 'art of acting' and evaluated it as such. Today, the opposite approach, of taking the action for reality, results in spectators sending flowers to characters who die in the course of a TV series. They see these characters for what they pretend to be – as themselves, not as representations of a playwright's idea. I well remember how stars were once expected to 'make an entrance' to be applauded while the action of the play was suspended. And a well-contrived exit after a bravura performance elicited a similar response. And as late as the early thirties when Gielgud and Olivier alternated as Romeo and Mercutio, we went to see not Romeo or Mercutio per se, but Gielgud and Olivier performing as Romeo and Mercutio, and debated their different techniques, their distinctive art and craft. This attitude meant that the spectator/listener participated in the play, was within it as well as a witness from without. Shakespeare's use of soliloquy and direct address to the audience

(Richard's opening speech in R.III *for instance) is all part of the same attitude. All this is something which the new Globe may be able to demonstrate...*

    Frank

The announcement of J M Barrie's *The Admirable Crichton* as part of the Chichester season attracted both men, although they were unable to see the play together. DW continued his efforts to persuade the Arts Council to support a Whirligig tour of *Babe, the Sheep-Pig.* He was also engaged in writing the scripts for a proposed television series featuring Muffin the Mule.

Easter Monday

Dear David,

...I do hope Whirligig gets the backing it so well deserves, and that you enjoy writing Babe. *Tricky, admittedly, but I should think just the right cup of tea for you. Muffin the Mule? The producer who wants it Americanised should have his head examined. I remember Annette Mills very well from the old B/W days. The series appealed to adults simply because it was directed exclusively at children. Over-advanced sophistication should not be encouraged!...*

    Frank

19 Apr

Dear Frank,

...I managed to do a draft pilot episode of Muffin the Mule *for the powers-that-be to take to the big T.V. 'fair' at Cannes – and also worked on the synopsis of* Babe, the Sheep-Pig, *which is now going ahead in the autumn – no official Arts Council letter yet (typical), but assurance that we are O.K. to get going. Hooray! More of* Babe *later...*

...Now – back to Babe *– do you fancy some homework??!! Please don't feel pressured, but if you had time to look at the Synopsis and maybe read the book (the Synopsis really assumes the reader has knowledge of the book) – and if you were willing to make a few comments before I shut myself away to write the thing, I'd be most grateful...*

Take care –
David

Needless to say, FW leapt at the chance to read and comment on the synopsis of *Babe*.

22 Apr

Dear Frank,

...You're doing it proud. You've been as faithful to your original as you were with BFG *and* The Witches, *but the problems of translating narrative into stage action are, I think, even more taxing. Using the trials as a framework is a masterly idea, and so is the use of Fly as narrator, with the TV commentator taking the strain at the competition itself. I wonder, could he simply be heard over Mrs Hogget's TV in the final scene? This would avoid his taking up space on stage.*

The 'curtain' to Act One is terrific! I don't see any objection to Farmer Hogget, traditional though he is, using a mobile phone. It will be much 'cleaner' as you say, than using the phone in the farmhouse – incidentally, you call that a 'cottage'. I find myself wondering why. I picture it as an old-style farmhouse kitchen to which telephone and TV have been introduced without incongruity, because this is the natural course of development in such a setting. A small truck, certainly, for necessary mobility. Would it be extravagant to use another, opposite, for the loose-box? The first primarily Mrs Hogget's domain, the second Farmer Hogget's, where he dreams his own dreams which he does not tell her about.*

As you say in your General Thoughts, the chief problem is space. The action is going to need a lot of it. Because of this, I find myself favouring a 'cyc' with 'cut-outs' flown in to indicate particular locations. A banner announcing the Trials at the showground could be replaced by another proclaiming the Fair, and selected stall-holders, including Mrs H and her 'produce' could mount their own stalls. You'll need the back of the lorry, won't you? I notice that you've made this a night scene, and kept Farmer H at home with Mrs H in front of the TV with Fly. But would Babe have ventured up to the field by night? And would not the sheep have been penned then? I can see that it simplifies the action, but I feel that it strains credibility, though I suppose rustlers, like poachers, are more likely to work by night. Has Dick K-S cheated in order to get Babe into this action?…

…I'm sure you have a winner here. And it will be a gift to Sam French. When Whirligig has exhausted it (if ever) it will be a boon to schools looking for a few strong leads and large enthusiastic supporting casts. I can see it working well in the round, too. All my comments supra, as the learned say, are really an impertinence, but you may find 'a grain or two of truth among the chaff'. (W.S. Gilbert)…

Frank
*Making a balance and a contrast

26 Apr

Dear Frank,

…I will look at the rustlers' night scene again. Maybe it could be dusk, before the sheep are penned. Or we will take dramatic licence!! Theatricality demands night for the effect of hand torches, shadows, rough voices, etc. etc. etc.!! I'm so glad you think it could all work – it's not quite as 'obvious' as some of my plays, but I do think it has some very moving and 'big' moments and

'set pieces' which will heighten the drama of what is a charming (dreaded word) story…!!

David

The first draft of the full script reached FW at the end of May.

24 May

Dear David,

…Huge thanks for the draft of Babe. *It is tremendous!…*

I fully endorse para 3 of your notes – simple basic costume for the 'human beings playing animals'. Children will identify with this and take extra delight in the representation. And in the same way I'm sure they'll relish actors as scene-shifters. It's all part of a glorious game of Let's Pretend.

You've got over any difficulty with Hogget's mobile phone, by having him use it at the fair – to be shown by a child how to work it. That's a delightful touch which not only prepares for its introduction at the beginning of Act II but will give huge pleasure to children and adults.

The characters come over beautifully, and the build-up of suspense and 'suddenlies' is splendid. And twilight gives plausibility to the rustling. Whether or not it achieves the longevity of The Gingerbread Man, *I really do feel that this is the jewel in your crown. It is quite beautiful.*

My only worry is with the logistics. How are you going to find and manage the teams of children who, I presume, have to be recruited and rehearsed locally? They'll play their part delightfully, I know, and bring sheep, ducks and all gloriously to life. But surely they'll make a lot of work? And do they have to be 12+? And will local schools co-operate?…

Ever,
Frank

29 May

Dear Frank,

…I'm glad you think it works. Hopefully, I have managed to disguise the lack of climax made inevitable by the fact that we all know that things are going to turn out well in the final scene. And, of course, there are no through villains to vanquish! Never mind. I do think it is a splendid story and hopefully we can make it work.

You are quite right about the logistics! But we had a meeting the other day at which the plan of attack was discussed. The splendid girl [Emma Clayton] who recruits and directs all the extra ladies for The Witches *is joining us. She will be responsible for recruiting and directing the children during the tour, and (by working 7 days a week!) will also be the sheep team-leader. We will only have 7 sheep, plus the team leader and, in the early scenes, Ma. They will be recruited from dancing schools – the type that operate on Saturday mornings – rather than ordinary schools, in the hope that we get some really keen ones, who are already good at movement and used to performing. Quite honestly, we have no time for social work! We must have enthusiasts. We reckon the girls will be 11, 12 or 13 years old. Then we will have 3 boys of about 8 or 9 to be puppies, working under the team leader from the cast.*

Several weeks before the main rehearsals begin, we will be working with 'guinea-pig' children, setting everything carefully, so that we have a blueprint for everything the children do. We will hopefully put it on video, and also put the music on tape, so that we will have a little package of materials to present to the children's teacher, who will, in each place, work closely with our aforementioned lady!…

Lots of love,
David

FW's reply included his thoughts on the Chichester production of *The Admirable Crichton*.

1 Jun

Dear David,

…We had a pleasant trip over to Chichester last Thursday for The Admirable Crichton. *I thought much of it was clever – but unnecessary. The balletising of the tea party distracted from the dialogue, but I enjoyed the scene change demonstrating the wreck of the yacht, and Lord Loam was brilliant. But the director robbed him of one of his most telling moments. That "Come, Crichton" as he resumes his authority, without a second thought, as he leads the naval officer to explore 'the Island Home', should hit the audience between the eyes, not be thrown away upstage.*

But what a joy it was to hear the diction of Michael Denison and Barbara Jefford! McShane did better than I expected and was particularly good in his delivery of his "Thank you, my lord" and "Thank you, sir," but for Denison and Jefford I could switch my hearing-aid off! The final curtain was muffed, too, I suspect, because there was no curtain. I've always thought the ending the equal of Tchekov's broken string – 'She goes. He turns out the lights.' She didn't go! He didn't turn out the lights, and the moment was lost. An episode is over, but life goes on. It's like the ending of Shakespeare's Troilus & Cressida. *Nothing for it but to return to the grind…*

…I note the programme described the play as 'A Fantasy'. Fair enough, I suppose, because fantastic it certainly is, but the description is only partially true, to the method only, not to the purpose of the piece. It's a satirical comedy. And the audiences which kept it running for 328 performances at The Duke of York's in 1902 were well aware of it, and chuckled because each member thought it was getting at his neighbour, not at himself – as did those audiences which made their fortunes for G & S at

the end of the old century. They certainly didn't regard Barrie, as the programme suggested, as a Red Revolutionary…

> *Ever –*
> *Frank*

7 Jun

Dear Frank,

…I agree with your thoughts on Crichton *– the girls were rather weak (on the island), and the 'fantastical' island setting suggested, in my mind, that the whole thing was more of a dream than a satirical 'what if??' The whole question of hierarchy was somewhat softened – both in terms of below/above stairs and also in terms of the 'grades' below stairs. Anyway – it was good to see the play again (only my second production of it) – it still works extremely well…*

Next week, we start casting Babe *– early days, but hopefully we can secure the leads early. Karen Briffett (Boy in* Witches, Noddy *in* Noddy*) is hopefully to give her Babe; and Anthony (BFG) Pedley wants to play Farmer Hogget – but can we afford him??*

All for now –

> *Take care – Love and best wishes from us all –*
> *David x*

Also included with this letter was an appreciative note from *Babe* author Dick King-Smith, whose only correction related to the difference between a rifle and a shotgun.

10 Jun

Dear David,

… A gun is a gun is a gun to me, but I bet some terribly bright young swot would have picked up the point, so it's just as well you're able to get it right. Children can be surprisingly observant.

I remember going to a 'workshop', a sort of question-and-answer session at the Connaught in Worthing to which I'd taken a party from Collyer's. The director told us how at a similar gathering of primary schoolchildren one had queried the colour of two doors which formed part of the set, one representing Orsino's side, the other Olivia's. To balance the picture, I suppose, both doors were painted yellow.

"Why," asked a smart eight-year-old, "is Olivia's door yellow?"

"Oh," said the director, "no particular reason. We just thought it was a jolly colour ..."

"But," retorted the child, "Olivia doesn't like yellow. 'Tis a colour she abhors."

Why do people persist in saying that children can't take Shakespeare in the raw, but must be condescended to?...

Ever, Frank

25 Jun

Dear Frank,

...Babe, the Sheep-Pig *activity progresses. We are casting, with some auditions in early July. And later that month we have our 'guinea pig rehearsals', during which we work with a group of children on being the sheep and puppies. The idea is to establish, at this early stage, a blueprint for all the children's activity, so that we are ahead of ourselves when it comes to rehearsals proper. Also, several venues can be visited in advance and rehearsals begun with the children, as long as we all know what we are doing with them!*

The sad news is that Clarion, the production company of The Witches, *has collapsed with a major debt problem. The news came through last Friday, and by the following day, the show was off, leaving eight weeks of disappointed theatregoers...*

A consortium of six theatres, stranded in this way, is trying to get the show back on the road, in association with Equity. Fingers crossed. But one of the problems is that the set has been impounded by the transport company, who want money to compensate them for many weeks of unpaid bills…

All very sad, particularly for the people concerned, as well as the audiences. But it goes to prove, yet again, that what I have been banging on about for 25 years – ie., that you cannot do this sort of work on a regular basis without sponsorship or subsidy – is proved once more…

Yours,
David

6 Aug

Dear Frank,

Babe, the Sheep-Pig *is well on the way… We now have a cast! Anthony Pedley, ex-BFG, is Farmer Hogget. Judy Wilson, who took over very successfully as Grandmother in* The Witches, *plays his wife. Karen Briffett (Noddy and Boy) plays Babe. We have a couple more Whirligig regulars, plus five newcomers who auditioned extremely well a few weeks ago. Everybody has thankfully committed to the project at least three months ahead of rehearsals starting. This is partly due to loyalty and the feeling that the job will be fun, but also reflects the state of play in the acting profession today. There is not much work around, so, for most actors, it is not worth turning things down in the hope of something better turning up.*

Last week, we had an exciting series of workshops, during which the creative team first worked out exactly what the children in the production would be doing, followed by three days with real children to work with. In fact, they were the children who will be performing in the very first week of the tour – at the New Victoria, Woking. They are all from a dancing school, the type of school people go to on Saturday mornings. The result of this is that they are all keen, interested and cooperative. The seven girls playing sheep very quickly became an endearing unit, and the three eight-year-old boys playing puppies could well steal the show, or at least the scene they are in!

…We now have a beautiful set model, which serves the play beautifully. And, three months ahead of the main rehearsals beginning, we have a creative team – movement person, associate director, children's director and music composer, all of whom have a good idea of what is expected.

…by the time we begin the main rehearsals on October 27th, the children for all three of the opening dates will be, in fact, ahead of their professional colleagues!…

…Have you ever read the children's novel Goodnight Mister Tom *by Michelle Magorian? You may remember* Back Home, *Michelle's second novel which I adapted for the screen.* Goodnight Mister Tom *was written a couple of years earlier and won the* Guardian Children's Book *prize. I have always fancied adapting it for the stage, and have now been given permission to have a bash. No definite production plans yet, but at least I can have a go at a synopsis. It is published by Puffin if you want to have a read. I'd be interested to know what you think of it…*

Yours,
David

10 Aug

Dear David,

…the news about Babe *is very heartening. Anthony Pedley and Karen Briffett should be a reliable asset. And I'm most impressed by all the advanced work of preparation of the children. I used to think that children could not appear on stage below the age of twelve. Is this no longer so? What do you have to do to enrol eight-*

year-olds? I rejoice in the idea of your creative team supporting Susie. I gather that you go from Woking to Birmingham and Manchester. Then whither? Will you be Whirligigging down this way?…

Love to you all as ever –
Frank

P.S. Oh yes! Goodnight Mr Tom. *A splendid book. Do work on it. (You see what I mean by forgetting matters of real moment!)*

9 Sep

Dear Frank,

… Not only is Babe, the Sheep-Pig *on the slate, but also a production of* The BFG *in Newcastle. I'm pleased about this, although the production company who have taken it over from Clarion, seem to me to underestimate the scope and detail of the work required… Adam Stafford, who was in the original production, and assisted me on the last production, will direct it. He was the young man who did a great job on* The Witches *in Dublin. I'm delighted he is on board and taking a lot of the weight off my shoulders!…*

…I have been looking at Goodnight Mister Tom. *The structure of it is surprisingly rambling in a way, and I have a feeling I may have been wrong thinking it would make a play in the Whirligig style. The children really need to be played by children, and they are the core of the piece. There is also the considerable problem with the awfulness of the mother, who is so unredeemably terrible that it may be difficult to present convincingly. However, I have to produce some sort of treatment by the end of the month for the Belgrade, Coventry, so I'm hoping that suddenly I will be inspired!*

Meanwhile, there is no news of the television projects Mary

Mouse *and* Muffin the Mule, *which is probably just as well, because I certainly have no time to think about them!…*

With love,
David

Dear Frank,

…The pre-production for Babe, the Sheep-Pig *continues, of course. Susie has designed wonderful costumes to go on her excellent set. And the various other departments all seem to be busy. We have a publicity/marketing person working for us as well as an Education Officer. I will get the latter to send you a copy of the Teachers' Notes.*

Have had more discussions with Welsh National Opera about ideas for a children's opera to go into schools, involving the children. I have always wanted to do something about a feral child, and have been reading various books. By chance, I came across a children's book called The Forest Child. *This seemed ideal for adaptation, even though I had really wanted to do an original piece! Anyway, we are seeing if the rights are available.*

I did a non-treatment (for want of a better phrase) for Goodnight Mister Tom. *Then rather gave up on the idea, at least for the time being. I couldn't really find a way to do it satisfactorily…*

Yours,
David

26 Oct

Dear David,

…I hope something positive will emerge from your discussions with W.N.O. I don't know The Forest Child – *but I do know*

Kipling's Jungle Books *and the immortal Mowgli. Disney laid impious hands on him as he did on* Peter Pan, *but has anybody offered him to the admiration of the public on stage?…*

Ever – Frank

1997 Babe, the Sheep-Pig –
New Victoria Theatre, Woking – 18ᵗʰ November 1997
Farmer Hogget wins a piglet at the local fair. Babe is adopted by Fly, the sheepdog, and eventually becomes, thanks to her encouragement, and Farmer Hogget's belief in him, the world famous 'Sheep-Pig'.

9 Dec

Dear Frank,

…The good news is that Babe, the Sheep-Pig *has opened successfully. The business at Woking wasn't very good, but huge numbers of children came to Birmingham. The Christmas season in Manchester will not be as well attended as we had hoped, but it is certainly doing far better than average.*

The production wasn't the easiest, I have to admit. We had lots of problems. Indeed, I confided in one or two people that it was in many ways a copybook case of how not to do it!…

However, the company worked very hard and I think we have a good show. The children listen incredibly intently, yet join in when required.

…Am now dashing off to Newcastle where The BFG *opens shortly. Adam, my assistant, has directed it, and, in the rehearsal room, things look good! The big question now is whether it will fit on top of the other show running concurrently at the Tyne Theatre!*

Yours,
David

By now, DW had published his *Theatre for Children: Guide to Writing, Adapting, Directing and Acting*, which received an enthusiastic response in the next letter.

15/12/97

Dear David,

...I've now had time to read Theatre for Children *closely from cover to cover. It is a most satisfying job. Apart from all the good advice, the analysis of your scripts is fascinating, especially the indication of 'suddenlies' and the detail of how you set about, step by step, the creation of a play. It strikes me that a good deal of it is applicable to adult theatre as well...*

...I do hope you're surviving what must have been a stressful launch, on top of nursing the other show. We shall hope to catch Babe *at the Oxford Playhouse in May. What's next?*

Love to all the family – a Merry Christmas and even Merrier New Year,
Frank

1998

The year began with the tour of *Babe* reaching the newly opened Hall for Cornwall. DW gave an update after the tour reached Norwich.

25 Feb

Dear Frank & Mary,

...Babe, the Sheep-Pig has received great reviews, but modest houses – overall, the tour is going well, though the schools are so difficult to grab! – no money, it seems, and terror that one half-day away from the classroom, seeing something not directly

part of the National Curriculum, will jeopardise their children's chances of success in the dreaded tests!...

Am busy doing all sort of things... preparing an application for Whirligig to receive funding to revive The Owl and the Pussycat Went to See... *in the autumn. Am also booked to do the* Magic and Music Show *at the Lyric, Hammersmith April 15th to 18th. And I hope to go to Chicago in May; there is a production of* The BFG *on there...*

Love and best wishes –
David

FW was looking forward to seeing *Babe* later in the tour.

Dear Frank,

...[I] enclose a copy of a lovely letter from Dick King-Smith – author of The Sheep-Pig, *who saw* Babe *in Bath recently.*

...Have just finished first draft of my opera for Welsh National Opera Education Dept – it's called The Forest Child *– will send you a copy when it has been typed up!*

...I'm hoping to be in Oxford on May 9th when you are scheduled to see Babe *– Any chance of you arriving early enough for a bite to eat before the show?? Or staying on for a cuppa after??!*

Good News – Methuen have offered to publish collected editions of my plays! Two vols. to start with – I have to choose which plays to include...

Am scheduled to go to Chicago on May 13th for a week – The BFG *is on there, and they have organised various talks to students, etc., to pay for my trip! Should be fun.*

Babe *tour going well, though business variable – reviews still excellent, I'm glad to say!...*

All for now – love to you and Mary from all of us –
David x

17 Apr

Dear David,

...Oh, the WNO project sounds very exciting – I love the title. Have you been given a storyline to work from with stipulation for particular voices? I can't wait...

...And what splendid news from Methuen! A First Folio (sort of) David Wood! Roll over W. Shakespeare and B. Jonson! And Chicago! There you go. Does the Theatre offer concessions to gangsters and their molls?...

Enough (satis) for now (pro tem)

Mary sends love. Me too. (Moi aussi)
Frank (siempre)

20 Apr

Dear Frank,

...This letter is mainly to accompany the first draft of The Forest Child *for your perusal. Being an opera, it is quite difficult at this stage to be dogmatic! The composer will doubtless have lots of ideas and develop certain themes in various directions. However, I hope it will give you a clue as to what I am hoping will emerge. It should run for about 50 minutes, without interval, and involve lots of children singing, acting and playing instruments. Working alongside the three professional singers and three professional musicians could be a wonderful experience for the lucky children who get involved. I think Welsh National Opera intend to try it out in a couple of schools and, if it goes well, then do a few more.*

...On 13th May, I am due to go to Chicago, where the Chicago Children's Theatre is performing The BFG. *I am staying there a week, doing various talks to university students, etc. I have never been before, so it will be quite an experience.*

See you in Oxford! Yours,
David

Dear David,

Huge thanks for your letter and the draft of The Forest Child. *It's a great joy! I do hope Derek Clark (a name among many which I do not know) can match it with his music and equal the expressive simplicity of your treatment of Richard Edwards' book.*

...I take it for granted that as ever you have closely and faithfully presented the essence of your original. It's a charming story and your presentation is very moving, especially in the approach of the Boy to the Child at their first encounter. I prefer the alternative words on pp.2 and 6. I think they flow more easily and should be easier to set for audibility, though I think all your 'lyrics' should present no great difficulty because I detect no difficulty in the sequence of vowels and consonants. The opening lines for the choir with their unobtrusive rhyme reinforcing the description are beautiful, and the unexpected lengthening of the unrhymed 'beneath a million stars' is wonderfully evocative. Everywhere, I find that your ear for the line breaks is very telling and I hope the composer will observe them.

...The casting of the Child and the Boy will require WNO to look for a couple of Karen Briffetts! The Baritone for the Hunter and the Schoolmaster may be as beefy and bellyful as they please, though I should like the latter to be more quirky and acidulated. The Victorian dress for the schoolchildren will be fine, but what will today's primary kids make of scholastic cap and gown? They will never have seen anything of that sort, and I don't think they would have been worn by a teacher in a Victorian junior school, only in traditional Public Schools...

The arrangement of a School Hall for the locations of the action is splendid and if the dear little things can sit for 50 minutes without wanting to be excused, it will be a great advantage to have no interval. Maybe they will, because I'm sure they'll be spellbound with complete continence by the goings-on in front of them...

From Mary too – Love – Frank

6 May

Dear Frank,

...I was delighted to receive your appreciation of The Forest Child. *...No reaction yet from Richard Edwards, the author, but Derek Clark, the composer, is happy. He is currently Head of Music at Scottish Opera, having for some years been Head of Music at Welsh National Opera...*

...I have been faithful to the book, which is written in a very simple fable-like way. However, I have introduced the notion of the schoolroom. In the book, the Hunter takes the girl back and personally tries to civilise her. The Boy is concerned and returns to the forest to fetch the Animals to rescue her, and ends up staying with her under the million stars! The Hunter is chased by the Animals and rolls down a hill to infinity!

I introduced a schoolroom because I wanted opportunities for more children, and the strict nature of Victorian education is very theatrical! I was interested to hear your thoughts about the cap and gown. You may well be right – it may be totally alien to our audience, and it may even be historically inaccurate. On the other hand, it is, again, a theatrical device! As I won't be directing the piece, I will leave it to them to decide.

How right you are about clarity stemming from setting a single note only to each syllable. That is something I have always done, instinctively, I think. It just makes it 'posh operatic' to have people trilling away over one syllable, and often impossible to comprehend...

...Over this coming bank holiday weekend, I have to bash out a 10-page synopsis/treatment for a possible film version of

Heidi. *It has to be delivered by Tuesday, in order to be in time for consideration for possible funding from some European fund. So I had better get my skates on…*

> *Yours,*
> *David*

FW saw *Babe* in Oxford, and was quick to send his reflections on the experience.

10 May

Dear David,

…I was interested to hear that you had introduced the schoolroom to The Forest Child. *Absolutely right, from the point of view not only of staging but of plot. To have the Hunter take the child home would never do just now. It would suggest the worst!*

    I'm wondering what sort of audience and age-group the Heidi *film is aimed at. Is there a market for such a film outside TV? Mary says, "Of course!" and instances* The Secret Garden – *but that was a long time ago. Anyway, I hope something profitable comes of it! And I was glad to hear that your trip to Chicago was to be funded by working for your passage. But do your hosts really expect you to pay to meet them? I call that Scroogie.*

    Back to Babe. *I think it's your masterpiece. Where do you go from there? It was fascinating to see how the action fleshed out the script, and how the whole thing won such concentrated attention. There was a budding critic just behind us. As the curtain rose on Act II, he muttered, "We've had this bit before!" But he was immediately won over and decided he was not being short-changed…*

> *Love – Frank*

DW sent his draft of *Heidi* to FW for his comments.

15 May

Dear David,

...It's absolutely first-rate. I generally deplore any attempt to make a classic 'more relevant' or 'more accessible' to a present-day public by vandalising the original, whether Shakespeare, Dickens or the Book of Common Prayer. Nothing is gained by transferring Romeo and Juliet or Esther and Pip from their original place and time to the 20th century. Leonard Bernstein had the good sense to realise this when he invented West Side Story. *He did not play down Shakespeare; he simply pinched his plot and used as much as he wanted. ... And the authors of* Kiss Me Kate *did not play down either. They simply abridged Shakespeare's boisterous piece and set it in the framework of a touring company of players. This was neither vandalism nor condescension. ...They... created a new work of art.*

This, it seems to me, is what you have done with your 'treatment' of Heidi *for a feature film. You have kept the original story intact, and set it in an equally original frame...*

You have contrived to meet the challenge 'to combine the charms of the original with a modern style to involve a wider contemporary audience'. ...if this approach is necessary, then it could not have been done more deftly or more respectfully than you have done it...

...There is only one moment that I'm not quite happy about. It's at the bottom of page 9. 'Heidi becomes Hedda. Suddenly she hears a voice, "Hurry up, child! Will you stop dawdling?"'

The return of the Aunt to the Teacher is admirable. But what has happened to all the elaborate search for Hedda (pp 4 & 6)? It seems suddenly never to have taken place. I know I'm not very bright at keeping up with the techniques of modern film and TV

drama, and I may be missing a link or two, but I may share this
disability with quite a few others!...

> *Love to all as ever –*
> *Frank*

DW was by now in Chicago, where all seemed to be going well, according to the postcard sent from there.

18 May

> *This is a splendid place – & working with students at Northwestern*
> *University has been excellent – they jumped on my suddenlies &*
> *positive negative theories with relish, & want me to be a visiting*
> *Professor in the Theater faculty! The Chicago Children's Theater*
> *production of* The BFG *was pretty good (and well received),*
> *though the title role was played far too lightweight!...*

> *Love, David*

A return to the UK saw the end of the *Babe* tour, and a little more progress with the opera.

10 Jun

Dear Frank,

> *...Thank you for your nice comments about* Babe, the Sheep-
> Pig *in Oxford. Since then, the tour has finished, at Swansea.*
> *On the Thursday, I went up to see them all and we had a happy*
> *day. After the 11am performance, members of the company*
> *performed their tap-dancing routine, learnt over the many*
> *weeks of touring. This was followed by the company rock*
> *group! Kevin, our Company Manager, used to be a professional*
> *guitarist in a group called The Move, whose record Flowers in*

the Rain *was the first record ever played on Radio 1! Both these entertainments were excellent, followed by yours truly doing a bit of magic! … After the evening performance of* Babe, the Sheep-Pig, *we all went to a restaurant and celebrated until the early hours.*

Although the business has not been as good as we had hoped, the tour was certainly successful. They were, as you noted, a splendid and happy company.

The Forest Child. *Last week, I heard from Derek Clark, the composer, who has virtually finished, apparently. And it seems that the first performances will be very soon, although nobody has officially informed me! Derek seems very happy with it all, so let's hope it leads to further performances and publication…*

…No news about The Story of Heidi. *My treatment was received with kind words and prompt payment! Since then, not a dickey-bird! I suppose the Producer is trying to raise money…*

…The Chicago Children's Theatre production of The BFG *was not the greatest, but it was pretty good. They had missed out all the danger and darker side. It was like watching the play performed above sea level, with no investigation into the murky depths below! What was good was that I was able to tell the company what I felt, without disrespect or rudeness. They wanted me to be honest, and I was!*

I met a publisher, who has made an offer to publish an American edition of my Theatre for Children book, *which is excellent news…*

…While there, the Executive Director of the Dallas Children's Theater flew in to meet me. They are doing Babe, the Sheep-Pig *and* The BFG *in their next season. Hopefully, they will invite me to Dallas.*

…Barclays and the Arts Council decided not to support Whirligig Theatre for 1998/9, which meant that we had to abandon our proposed tour of The Owl and the Pussycat Went to See… *We are now planning to just do one week of performances*

at Birmingham Hippodrome of Dinosaurs and All That Rubbish, my adaptation of the Michael Foreman book which employs two professional actors and 150 children! We must be mad!…

…The week before, I will be making a speech at the National! This will be at the launch of Action for Children's Arts, a new organisation of which I find myself the Chair!

…Meanwhile, Methuen are going ahead with Collected Editions of my plays. The first two volumes will include plays mentioned as examples in the Faber book, which seems sensible.

…Weinbergers, the publishers, suddenly decided they wanted to re-launch Rock Nativity and offered to pay for the recording of a new 'demo'. It was decided to ask the National Youth Music Theatre, an excellent company, to provide the voices. Tony [Hatch] flew over from Spain and I joined him in Worthing, of all places, for the rehearsals. The NYMT had just performed a musical in Brighton, and simply stayed on over the bank holiday weekend to rehearse Rock Nativity. The following weekend, we were all in a studio in London. The result was very exciting and may well give the show a new lease of life. What was particularly reassuring for Tony and myself was the fact that all the participants hadn't been born when the show was written! Yet, they all seemed to enjoy it enormously and never gave the impression that they were working on a museum piece!…

Yours,
David

16 Jun

Dear David,

…The re-launch of Rock Nativity is splendid news. I always felt that it didn't meet with the success it deserved because it was overshadowed by Superstar and Godspell. Now perhaps it may come into its own, although the rivals are still around.

And the possibility of another adaptation of Roald Dahl! I don't know The Twits. *Not a very appealing title, but I'll look for it in the Winchester Children's Library – and also the* Spot *books.*

The Action for Children's Arts is surely a great idea. Who thought of it? The involvement of Trevor Nunn and the National should fly a flag for it and demonstrate that Children's Theatre should be taken seriously as an art in its own right and not merely a poor relation to be patronised...

Frank

22 Jun

Dear Frank,

...No news re: The Story of Heidi. *The producer is trying to raise the money. The next stage would be for me to write the screenplay, for which I would be well paid!...*

...Since writing to you, I am afraid that the Dinosaurs and All That Rubbish *project in Birmingham has collapsed. Our budgets showed we needed £60,000 to do it. Unfortunately, the theatre was only willing to pay £35,000! We managed to trim the budget rather ruthlessly and get it down to £45,000, but there was still a £10,000 shortfall. Unfortunately, in the time available before publicity announcements had to be made, it would have been impossible to raise the money and so the whole thing was called off. A shame.*

*...*The Twits *is one of Roald Dahl's shorter, less epic, books. It is really rather unpleasant! But children love it. The problem is, it has very little structure and needs shaping and re-thinking for the stage, in my opinion. So I will probably be thinking about that over the summer.*

Action for Children's Arts was initiated by two or three of us having a moan one day! It will be interesting to see whether the launch achieves any publicity at all.

All for now,
David

1998 The Forest Child –

Schools. Welsh National Opera Education Dept. – 1998
The Forest Child has been raised by the animals of the forest. She is captured by a hunter and taken back to 'civilisation' where she is treated badly, before being rescued by the hunter's son.

Summer 1998 saw the first performances of *The Forest Child* and a trip to Dallas for DW.

14 Oct

Dear Frank,

… Dallas was great fun. I was very well looked-after and the production of Babe, the Sheep-Pig *was really very faithful and enjoyable. It lacked the edge of my own production, but maybe this was just as well, because the audiences were very young.*

I went into four different schools doing my storytellings and talks, and everybody seemed very pleased, I am glad to say. I did virtually exactly the same as I do at home, and the reactions were exactly the same too! It is very reassuring that children don't seem to be very different from country to country.

The Dallas Children's Theater, short of money like all of us in this business(!), manages to produce 11 productions a year, which is pretty remarkable. They have a full company of actors, some of them semi-professional, and many of them teachers who also work on behalf of the Children's Theater Company in schools, doing special classes…

Yours,
David

Getting news from Texas led FW into one of his vivid reminiscences of travels in times past.

Dear David,

…The Southern Americans are so hospitable – almost overwhelmingly so. I gather you had no language difficulty in the Lone Star State. I once had a very brief stop-over in Houston and had great difficulty in requesting a dish of eggs and bacon because the waitress could not follow my all-British accent. I forget why the plane had to set me down there on my flight from New York to Bogota, but it was a pretty grotty plane. When we were over the jungle in Colombia, a fellow passenger whispered to me, "Don't look down now, but I think one of our engines has stopped!" It was no place, geographically speaking, for an emergency landing, being thick with trees and probably alive with creepy-crawlies and even wilder beasties. A nun who was beside us overheard his whispered warning and began energetically to ply her beads. They must have worked because the reluctant engine picked up and we completed our mission successfully after another rest in Panama. That was just after Peace broke out, in 1946, and 'planes needed frequent refuelling in those far-off days…

Love to you all as ever,
Frank

21 Oct

Dear Frank,

…First of all, I will bring you up to date on the Methuen Collected Editions.

I have now been appointed an Editor, who luckily is a fan as well!

The idea is that they will do two volumes to begin with, each one containing four plays. They want a balanced 'programme', bearing in mind that there are original plays, adaptations, pantomime substitutes and family musicals…

… Yes, the Dallas Experience was exhilarating indeed. It is very nice to be greeted as a prophet from another land!…

The production of Babe, the Sheep-Pig *itself was pretty good, as I may have said. They soft-pedalled some of the more potentially frightening moments, but they did certainly tell the story well and fluently. You mentioned accents. The amusing thing here was that they all tried to use English accents, with mixed results! The very first speech of the play is, if you remember, the TV Commentator who, in my production, uses a West Country Phil Drabble-type voice. The Dallas Commentator had a beautifully-studied, resonant BBC news announcer's voice!*

The flights there and back were very good, unlike your 1946 epic voyage! Indeed, coming back, I was rather surprised when, as I was boarding, I was asked to wait behind a moment. …I was to be upgraded to Business Class. I think Dallas Children's Theater had rung the airline saying that I was a very important person! I wasn't complaining…

…Going back to the play, the costumes and scenery were pretty good, though they obviously had spent much less money on them than we had. The play was only running for four or five weeks. But it was all quite presentable…

…I am enclosing the latest synopsis for the proposed tv animation version of The Selfish Giant. *…Now we have an animation producer (cartoon) who has managed to get some money from Granada to take the project a stage further. He has encouraged me to update everything, which is a little bit worrying, but I would be interested to see how you think the treatment reads.*

…Things are busy, as you can tell, although nothing much in the children's theatre line. We still await news as to whether we have the funding to revive The See-Saw Tree *next year…*

With love from us all,
David

FW was quick to respond to the suggestion of updating *The Selfish Giant*.

25 Oct

Dear David,

...I'm in favour of the updating. Oscar's original is altogether too twee. Your treatment is dramatic, exciting, suspensive and in every way more suitable for the present time. It should make admirable viewing. The only thing that worries me is whether, having modernised the setting and the children, the Giant and his garden should not have been updated too, perhaps into some plutocratic Property Developer, rather than retained as the traditional Giant of traditional fairy stories. Will he not strain credibility in his new setting? However, if the animators can bring it off, it may score by emphasising the contrast between past and present social conditions, and by suggesting that though the 20th century's 'Little horrors' have lost their innocence, they may still retain something of the blessing of imagination which William Blake regarded as the Holy Spirit (of Animation!) in humankind...

...I do hope you manage a revival of The See-Saw Tree. *It's more relevant than ever...*

Love to all,
Frank

9 Nov

Dear Frank,

...Thank you for your thoughts on The Selfish Giant. *It is interesting that you feel it might be an idea to change the traditional Giant into a more modern plutocrat. You may be right. But I still feel he has to be a physical misfit as well as an on-the-surface baddie. I think, too, that the producers feel that we have to fulfil the obligations of the title! Everything has gone*

quiet on The Selfish Giant – *all to do with contracts not yet signed. I have been very clear that I won't do any more work until contracts are agreed. Often in the past I have gone ahead with the writing, only to find that the whole thing has fallen by the wayside...*

...I have a meeting in Oxford in ten days' time ...at the Playhouse, where we hope to mount the première of Spot's Birthday Party *in the spring of 2000. I think I mentioned that I had the rights on the* Spot *books. Did I send you a copy of the first treatment I did? If not, I will. Eric Hill, the creator of* Spot, *has said OK, although he doesn't like one particular sequence, which I may have to change.*

... It looks as though I will now do an adaptation of The Twits *by Roald Dahl. This will be for the Belgrade, Coventry. They will do their own production. I will have no directing input. Scheduled to open next March. It is a strange book. Rather repulsive, really! But children love it. I have an idea whereby the whole thing will take place in a circus. When I finish the synopsis, I will send you a copy.*

I have now had the official invitation to go back to Chicago next year and work as a sort of Visiting Professor with a group of students for a concentrated week's course. This will be at Northwestern University. Then, the following week, I will address the Conference of the Association of American Theatre and Education (AATE). Hopefully, my Theatre for Children *book will be launched in America – officially – at the same time.*

So things are quite busy...

Yours,
David

DW then sent off the draft of *Spot* and was soon reading the usual detailed response.

26 Nov

Dear David,

*…*Spot's Birthday Party *is a great joy. And HURRAH for 'Book music and lyrics' by David Wood! Mary agrees with me that it is a marvellous treatment for that very young age group. We both think that the sequence Eric Hill dislikes is the introduction of the disco lighting. This seems too sophisticated for the kindergarten and reception-class age – not to mention the destruction to the theatre seating by the dancing on it. The little dears might easily end up wrecking the whole auditorium under that so-called 'psychedelic' influence…*

Love to you all as ever – Frank

DW's reply raised once more the topic of *Peter Pan*, always a fascination to both men.

1 Dec

Dear Frank,

Today, I'm sending you …an interesting article about Peter Pan *… by …Peter Hollindale. He spoke extremely well at the Conference I went to the other day, the one where they launched the Children's Laureate scheme. He was talking about Barrie and Dahl, making very interesting comparisons between the two, suggesting that much of the anti-adult feelings displayed in their books, as well as the subversivness, can be put down to their respective heights. Barrie, of course, was less than five feet tall, Dahl was approximately six foot seven. Both were teased about their height when they were small, and both had strong relationships with their mothers, strong yet troubled. Barrie, as you know, tried to 'become' his deceased elder brother, while Dahl was sent away to a tough British public school (from Norway). Interesting.*

I wrote to Peter Hollindale saying how much I had enjoyed his lecture. In the introductory notes to his session, I had seen that he had written quite a lot about Barrie and Peter Pan, *so decided to find out more. The result was the enclosed, which I enjoyed reading and hope you do.*

Going back to Spot's Birthday Party. *I am delighted you and Mary enjoyed it. I was worried that it was too entertainment-based rather than story-based, but I'm beginning to believe that, for this very young age group, it is inappropriate to try to spin out a story for a full 90 minutes. The problem is, of course, that the theatres where a show like this might visit insist on having an interval, because they don't want to lose ice-cream sales! So there have to be two acts, and each one really has to be at least half an hour long.*

The section which Eric Hill, the creator of Spot, *doesn't like is not the disco sequence, although I think you may have a point here; it is the* Cinderella *section. He feels that to superimpose other characters on to the* Spot *characters would be too confusing. I have to say I think he is wrong. The whole nature of play and dressing up to become somebody else is very natural, and I think children of 3 and 4 not only understand it but do it themselves. Furthermore, the story of* Cinderella *is the best-known story in the world. Every time I visit a school, even the youngest children know about the magic of the pumpkin turning into a carriage, the unpleasantness of the sisters, etc., etc. So I think I will probably fight them on this question. The show needs a change of gear in the second half, and it needs a bit of real storytelling.*

Yours,
David

Dear David,

...Peter Holindale first. I'm very glad you wrote to him and had such a response. I was much intrigued by his article and shall probably invest in the World's Classics editions for which he wrote introductions. I like his very well-balanced view of Barrie and he has prompted me to read again The Little White Bird *from which* Peter Pan in Kensington Gardens *was extrapolated. (Is that the word I want, and, if it is, have I spelt it right?) That episode provides six chapters which do not sit quite so easily into the preceding and following as they might, arousing a suspicion that they might have been written first and subsequently framed in the main plot. I must admit that the whimsy did strike me as a bit much on this re-reading, and the sentiment as cloying. And yet – how original and imaginative the whole thing is, how subtly witty and ironic! Those five Davies boys left Barrie with no illusions about childhood as the Preface to the published script of* Peter Pan *makes clear. I was specially interested to learn that this differs from the play as performed. And what a joy it is to read prose that has style!...*

... The Little White Bird *offers a number of clues to the genesis of later works, however, and it is fair enough to note them. The germ of* Mary Rose *is there, and of* Dear Brutus, *as well as of a lesser work,* A Kiss for Cinderella. *I remember Barrie's claiming somewhere that the period of gestation for* Mary Rose *was 25 years. She haunted him until he finally exorcised her at the end of the Great War. All sheer genius and utterly inexplicable.*

Now to Spot *and his* Birthday Party. *I did suspect that* Cinderella *might be what Eric Hill jibbed at. But I think you are quite right to fight for it. He is probably underestimating the capacity of the expected audience...*

Frank

1999

A new year began with the discussion of a new draft, for DW's adaptation of *The Twits*.

6 Jan

Dear Frank,

...First, Spot. *I think I might get away with the* Cinderella *section; at least the powers that be have now said they are willing to consider it within the whole piece when it is written!*

I can't remember whether I have sent you a synopsis of The Twits. *I certainly told you that the Belgrade, Coventry were interested in me adapting it. Well, the Dahl Estate, uncertain about the rather radical treatment I was suggesting, said I could go ahead with the adaptation, and that Coventry could go ahead with the production, but that they would reserve judgement until they saw it as to whether it could be released for future exploitation. Coventry then took me a bit by surprise by saying they wanted to go into rehearsal on March 1st! As a result, I hastened to my hotel room retreat outside Bexhill on December 28th and put my head down! The result is enclosed. I feel quite pleased with it and hope that everybody else does too. The actual story is, even for Dahl, really rather repulsive! But children love it, so I decided to go with the flow and not hold back on the yuck factor! See what you think!...*

Before Christmas, I went to Birmingham and, in two days, saw five shows! First was a rather good adaptation of Dahl's George's Marvellous Medicine *at the Old Rep. (the Barry Jackson one) – the producer of this wants to do* The Witches *next year, and take it on tour. I'm inclined to let him go ahead...*

Next day... I set off for a primary school outside the centre of the city, where my children's opera, The Forest Child, *was being performed. Welsh National Opera had brought along three professional singers and three musicians, who had worked with the children (every single one of them of Asian descent) and mounted the show for pupils and parents in the school hall. In many ways, it worked well, although I found to my amazement (and the Musical Director's frustration) that Asian children seem to have no idea whatsoever of rhythm or pitch, certainly western-style rhythm and pitch. They were absolutely delightful, apparently tried ever so hard to get things right, and had a ball, but, when it came to it, couldn't deliver! Nevertheless, the piece seemed to work all right, to my relief.*

Yours,
David

Dear David,

Huge thanks for The Twits. *I have enjoyed it enormously despite the 'yuck' element, which I'm sure will delight the children but perhaps disturb their parents. I say 'perhaps' because they will mostly be pretty young parents to whom the 'yuck' is less out of place than it must be to their parents. The dialogue, particularly in the first Mugwump scene, is outstandingly good. The only thing that troubles me is the dependence upon so much acrobatic skill and mechanical contrivance. How on earth do you hold a pyramid upside down long enough – and be upside down in the cage through pp39 and 40? And the glueing of the furniture in the caravan plus the revolve of the room? I can't quite visualise how the child-puppeteers will manipulate their birds on the branches of the tree and the caravan roof. I haven't seen Dahl's book, but I suppose your framing of the action in the circus ring setting is what the Dahl Estate calls 'radical treatment' and is unhappy about. Maybe their visualisation is limited (like mine) and they will be convinced of its justification when they see it actually working. It is all very exciting and the story has powerful momentum mounting with the more-than-usual audience participation. The narrator/musician is an admirable innovation. From the director's point of view, and the stage-manager's, it is probably your most demanding yet…*

…I should like to see what the N.T. has done with Peter Pan. *At least J.M.B. retains his footing in the credits…*

…It was good to hear that The Forest Child *has taken the floor effectively. I'm not surprised that Asian children should have a different conception of rhythm from Western when one thinks of some of the very odd noises that emerge from the East. What does surprise me is that the Chinese and Japanese so quickly master European music and make as good or better performers than those born to it…*

Frank

8 Feb

Dear Frank,

… I'm now looking through your enjoyable letter. Thank you for all the nice comments about The Twits. *I, like you, feel that I have asked actors to do the impossible, particularly in the acrobatic department. However, the director assures me that all this will be possible, or at least something approximating! She has found a couple of children to be the young monkeys – both of them are champion gymnasts! The revolving of the room is another matter – the designer seems to have some very clever idea, whereby things can be lifted and then slotted into a ceiling. I'll believe it when I see it! You make a very good point about the child-puppeteers manipulating their birds – how can they do it upside down?! The director pointed this out to me too! I think they are going to have some extra bird puppets made, which will be attached to the rods upside down. Nobody could say this play was boring!…*

...Interested to hear that you are continuing your way through the works of Barrie. I must admit I haven't read Sentimental Tommy, *although I really should. The other day, we went to see* Peter Pan *at the National. It was really rather disappointing, I felt. Wonderfully extravagant and beautifully staged, but I fancy the actors were not giving their all. And the auditorium was only about half full. Also, as I may have said before, Trevor Nunn has re-worked the play to include a character who, I suppose, is meant to be a sort of Barrie figure, wandering through reading out the stage directions! Sometimes, he adds a bit from the original novel version of the story. Why on earth this is felt necessary, I can't imagine. It keeps on holding up the action. And Michael Bryant, an actor I normally like very much, seemed to be bored rigid by the whole thing! Having said all that, the production is a darn sight better than a lot of the panto-style versions we are getting these days. In fact, we have just agreed that* Peter Pan *shall be the Christmas production at Wimbledon Theatre for 1999/2000. It will probably be ghastly, but will undoubtedly bring the punters in.*

Yours,
David

Once again, mention of *Peter Pan* led the conversation away from matters of the moment...

16 Feb

Dear David,

...I was very interested in your reaction to the National's Peter Pan, *though I can understand the temptation of trying to find a place in performance for those entertaining stage-directions – especially that sinister and revealing one at the end of Act V.*

Sc.1. After Sentimental Tommy *and* Tommy and Grizel, *I've been re-reading all the 'works' in chronological order. I suppose the necessity of providing these volumes led to the prolixity of those two novels. In the earlier books which were put together from the articles he contributed to such acclaim in the* St. James' Gazette, *the construction is altogether tighter – in* The Auld Licht Idylls *and* A Window in Thrums *especially – and* Margaret Ogilvy *is an unqualified masterpiece – though his family and neighbours in Kirriemuir were not very happy at being exhibited in public. One critic complained that he was portraying the little town and its inhabitants not as they were contemporarily but as they had been back in 1840. This was quite true. He based those pieces so much on the stories his mother told him of her childhood. But it is the subtle humour of the telling, the masterly style, that chiefly distinguishes them. And it was the drama, not the novel, that was his especial forte. There he was a master of construction, though his creation of character was never very deep although, I suppose, sufficient for his purpose of delighting and charming his audience. However, for all his phenomenal success, I think now that it is only in* Peter Pan *that he was 'not just for an age but for all time', as Ben Jonson recognised in Shakespeare. And Barrie falls below the highest – Shakespeare, Hardy, George Eliot – because like Dickens he fails to 'hold up the stars in their courses and make them give some account of things'. He shares with Dickens a miraculous skill in holding his reader with spell-binding language, but that cannot compensate for his failing the ultimate challenge of philosophy. The puritanical certainties of his mother and the Auld Licht were too deeply engrained. I'm reading Janet Dunbar's book –* J.M. Barrie…

Ever –
Frank

12 Mar

Am here [Coventry] for 16 hours for Twits *rehearsals! Going well, I think. Today, I go to Bristol to see a perf. of* The Forest Child...

David

20 Mar

...I'm delighted that you're being so fully employed! I do hope The Twits *goes to great acclaim, in Coventry, and it's very good to know that* The Forest Child *is being repeated...*

Love to you all –
Frank (& Mary)

1999 The Twits –

Belgrade Theatre, Coventry – 25th March 1999
Set in a circus where, bored with playing silly tricks on one another, Mr and Mrs Twit turn their attentions to capturing and training a family of monkeys for a circus act. The monkeys' cruel incarceration in a cage is avenged when the Birds trick the Twits into believing the world has turned upside down. The audience help in the trick by pretending to be upside down too (they put their shoes on their outstretched hands).

27 Mar

Frank – thanks for card and good wishes – Twits *opened very well!* G. Man *rehearsals in full flight (for Dubai) – and* Swallows and Amazons *radio adaptation written in between ... – sorry ...been up to our eyes, so no time yet for a full letter! Expect one soon, though!*

Love to you and Mary –
David

Three cheers for The Twits! *I'm delighted that all the little horrors of Coventry responded so well and hope that a tour may be forthcoming to take in* The Mayflower. *I do hope the* G. Man *doesn't take a drop too much in Dubai or land in the middle of a civil disturbance!*

The adaptation of Swallows and Amazons *for radio is very good news. We'll keep an ear open as well as an eye on* The Radio Times…

Love to all from self and Mary,
F.

After this flurry of postcard messages, there was finally time for a more detailed update in early April.

6 Apr

Dear Frank,

…I am in Dubai! Things have been very hectic for the last few weeks. Rehearsals for The Gingerbread Man *have gone very well, but have obviously been time-consuming. The cast are splendid. They have all done it before, and indeed this cast is exactly the same as the Birmingham cast from the year before last…*

… The Twits *is going really well in Coventry. I'm really delighted with the production, which is full of energy and understanding of how to do it. The director has been very faithful to my text, while exploiting all the physical possibilities, however demanding they might be! Inside the cage, five Muggle-Wumps do actually stand upside down for quite a long time! Kathi, the director, has found some excellent acrobatic children, as well as splendidly physical actors to play the main cast. The business is extremely good and, hopefully, the Dahl Estate folk will like it enough to allow a tour to happen before too long. I'm enclosing another review for your collection!…*

…The Forest Child was given another performance, this time in Croydon, the other day. Unfortunately, I couldn't go, because of Gingerbread *rehearsals. But Derek Clark, the composer, went and enjoyed it. He was seeing it for the very first time. Future productions are announced, including one in Southampton. Might you be interested to see it? I'm not sure quite when it is, but it will certainly be on a weekday at about 2.00 in the afternoon. It lasts about 40 minutes, no more! It will be in a school in Southampton…*

…I was asked a while ago to write a radio adaptation of Swallows and Amazons. *Two episodes, each of one hour's duration. Eventually, the commission was confirmed and I realised I had to deliver it in the middle of my Dubai excursion. This meant writing it at the beginning of March, to get it out of the way. So back I went to my little hotel room in Bexhill and, thank heavens, managed to get it done in four days. We have just sent it off, and hope to goodness they don't want any re-writes! You will remember I did the screenplay of* Swallows and Amazons *some 25 years ago. It is just as well I hoard everything. I had all my scripts and original notes, making life much easier. I have never written for radio before, so it was interesting closing my eyes and wondering if they would understand various scenes and expressions. Let's hope it works okay…*

…Also, Oxford Playhouse have finally confirmed that they want me to do a play about Spot, *the very popular little dog, whose adventures are in lots and lots of books for the pre-school audience. Of course, I sent you the synopsis of* Spot's Birthday Party, *so you know what I am talking about! Well, it seems it will go ahead in the spring of next year, so I will have to put pen to paper soon. They are also interested in me doing another production, this time for lots of children to take part in, alongside a couple of professional actors. This would be based on a lovely story called* The Lighthouse Keeper's Lunch, *something I found a couple of years ago. More of that anon…*

I have also secured the rights of Tom's Midnight Garden, *the classic children's book by Philippa Pearce. I think I told you I went to meet her in her home near Cambridge not so long ago. Anyway, it looks as though Unicorn Theatre would like to commission this, again for next year...*

...Then it won't be long before I go to Chicago to do my teaching stint at Northwestern University, followed by various sessions at the American Association of Theatre and Education. ...Not only that (!), we have just been invited to take The Gingerbread Man *to Troy, in the State of New York, for a week of performances at the beginning of November. Off we go again!...*

Yours,
David

11 Apr

Dear David,

...I'm delighted to know English is the prevailing language in Dubai. I meant to ask – did you have to take the set with you on the plane? It must be the most far-flung scenery in the business. I trust the G.B. will not encounter any language problem in the State of New York...

...I've just read in our local rag that Patricia Routledge is to tackle Lady Bracknell at Chichester this year. I do wish some powerful producer would grasp the opportunity of staging The Boy David *there with a male David. It would be splendid for the play to have a chance of speaking for itself without being submerged beneath too much cumbersome scenery and star performers competing with each other at the author's expense...*

...We shall look forward to Swallows and Amazons. *How wonderfully that survives – like* Earnest *– long after its world*

has vanished. And Pooh *is another. What about an 'Expotition' with Christopher Robin & Co?…*

And finally – Well done, The Twits!

Ever,
Frank

19 Apr

Dear Frank,

…Dubai proved an extraordinary experience. The temperature was 112 degrees most of the time! Thank heavens for air-conditioning, say I!…

750 seats in a raked auditorium, with a conference-style stage, which was fine for The Gingerbread Man, *but wouldn't be much use if you wanted to have things in the wings or flying pieces coming in and out. Access to the building was dreadful – no proper dock door, so a team of bearers were employed to carry the set from the container in the car park, through the front door, up a non-working escalator, across a landing to another non-working escalator, through the back door of the auditorium, down one of the aisles, and up onto the stage! We also managed to create a black box effect with some curtains we had been clever enough to take along just in case!*

Everybody worked very hard on the technical side, and in the end the shows looked very good indeed. The cast were brilliant. They are all past masters of their craft, and it was interesting that the show gained about 6 minutes simply from their extra clarity and measured delivery, to make quite sure that all the children understood. And they did understand, oh yes, they did!…

Yours,
David

In his next letter, FW returned to the topic of Barrie's plays.

25 Apr

...After Dickens, my next early discovery was Barrie. My mother, in a moment of frustration, with her limited domestic ambiente, carted me off one afternoon, by tram, to the Grand Theatre, Croydon, where a touring company – a No.1.Coy – was giving Quality Street. *She said afterwards, by way of excuse, that it was time I was introduced to Theatre...*

> *Love to you all at Wimbledon and elsewhere,*
> *Frank*

FW's questions about the language used in Dubai led to some further thoughts from DW about original productions of his plays.

30 Jun

Dear Frank,

...Dubai seems a long time ago. In retrospect, the experience was highly enjoyable. However, there is a slight reluctance on my part to enthuse wholeheartedly about the enterprise, because we are still waiting for most of the payment from the Dubai promoters! We are owed £7,000, most of which, of course, we have already paid out to the participants...

In your April letter, you talk of The Boy David. *I have it by my bedside and have in fact read and enjoyed quite a bit. But I have to admit I haven't finished it yet! The idea of it being played at Chichester is intriguing. The space could be ideal...*

In May, you wrote to thank me for the Methuen Collected Editions. My pleasure, as they say! Since then, I have seen them in several shops. Indeed, the National Theatre bookshop devoted a whole shelf to them for a few days!...

You ask in what language The Gingerbread Man *was played*

in Japan. In Japanese…

The translation of the plays into other languages is, of course, something that is virtually impossible to monitor. This is especially true, I believe, with my stuff, because I use a lot of nonsense expressions; also, the fantasy ideas in many of the plays must be totally foreign to the translator! The use of puns must be particularly difficult to maintain. The Plotters of Cabbage Patch Corner *is quite popular, for instance, in Germany. The Red Admiral character is, as you may remember, in the original, a butterfly who is also a retired naval officer! But the German translation doesn't yield the same double meaning. It doesn't seem to have affected the popularity of the play, I'm glad to say. The translator of* The Gingerbread Man *in Germany is, in fact, bi-lingual. She is English, married to a German, and has lived in Germany for many years. Her translation has helped* The Gingerbread Man *to become the most popular children's play in Germany over many years. But heaven knows what happens elsewhere! We have just sold the Greek rights of* The Selfish Shellfish *and the Danish rights of* Cinderella*! Who knows what they will be like?*

I think I told you I was adapting Swallows and Amazons *for Radio 4. The recording took place in early June. …I did attend one delightful morning when we recorded the character ADULT TITTY. …As a device, it seemed to work well. When they asked me who I wanted to play the part, I immediately suggested Jean Anderson, with whom I worked a couple of times and who, as a child, I really loved when she played Mother in* The Railway Children *on television. Luckily, Jean was available and did the job beautifully. She is now ninety-one years old!…*

…I have several new projects to think about. I have already mentioned Tom's Midnight Garden *for Unicorn and* Spot's Birthday Party *for Oxford Playhouse. (This is now confirmed for spring of next year!) I have also been asked to do a new play for the Crescent Theatre, Birmingham, an amateur company of*

some standing. They want me to do a play on a larger scale than I might normally be able to do for professionals. And I am also meant to be thinking about a one-man show for Anthony Pedley (who played the BFG) – this would be a show in which he plays Roald Dahl and would be the story of Dahl's life, as seen through his writings…

Love and best wishes,
David

8 Jul

Dear David,

…I'm glad you have The Boy David *at your bedside. Granville Barker's preface is masterly. The difficulty for producers is the series of 'visions' which constitute Act III. But as with all Barrie's plays, the final curtain is superb, I think.*

I'm looking forward – Mary too – to Swallows and Amazons *on Radio 4. And what a brilliant inspiration and what a stroke of luck to engage Jean Anderson! We've been her admirers ever since* Tenko, *that series about the women's prison camp in which Stephanie Cole also played so memorably…*

Love – Frank

6 Sep

Dear Frank,

… Am back from a few days trying to finish the Spot *first draft. I think I have done enough now – enough for all the powers that be, copyright holders, etc., to have a look…*

Love to both,
D

Postcards from travels kept the pair in touch over the summer, before one of DW's regular updates followed in September, preceded by an excited note that he had found an acting edition of *Peter Pan* in a second-hand bookshop in Hastings, leading to a similarly enthusiastic response from FW.

7 Sep

Dear David,

I say, I SAY! What a fascinating discovery! I remember Hastings used to be a favourite haunt of mine for second-hand bookshops, all situated on a single street in the old part of the town. Gradually, they succumbed to economic pressure and gave up, much to my disappointment.

It is surprising that French should have produced an 'Acting Edition', which as he admits is no such thing. That 'publisher's note' confirms my opinion that the first production failed because of what he calls its 'immensity'. Too much scenery, too many star actors, not enough reliance on the text…

[Mary] sends her love with mine to you all –
Frank

13 Sep

Dear Frank,

…this reply is somewhat overdue. Sorry about that.

…I have been struggling with Spot's Birthday Party. *I can't remember whether I ever sent you a synopsis of this one. I know I have talked about it. Hopefully, it will come together, but it hasn't been a very enjoyable process (mind you, it never really is!). The problem is that it is aimed at a very low age group – pre-school children. By using the birthday party as a structure, there is no need to have a complete, through storyline which, for*

this age, would be too taxing. But, as you know, I really like to have a good story, and Spot, *with its succession of party games and fun, has been tricky to accomplish without being very bland and boring! Another problem is that the characters of Spot (the puppy) and his friends are virtually non-existent in the original books. So there is very little to work on. Oh well, maybe it will all come out okay in the wash!*

...I met quite a lot of interesting people at the Conference. What I learnt above all was that children's theatre is regarded with academic seriousness by the American Universities. ...In the UK, of course, there is not one university that shows any interest whatsoever in theatre for children!

There is a downside, in my opinion. Most of the people who work in children's theatre in America seem to be academics rather than practising 'artistes'. Some of them are very talented, I'm sure, but have never had to work in the real world...

...Now we are preparing for The Gingerbread Man *in Troy, New York State.*

...This Friday, [we] are meeting the Dubai impresario, who is over here for a few days. He hasn't yet said whether he is bringing a nice cheque. I have a feeling he will be pleading poverty and asking us to accept only a proportion of what he owes. However, I think we have every right to refuse this, because the reason he is over is to discuss arrangements for the forthcoming visit to Dubai of the Regent's Park Company in Twelfth Night. *The man who runs Regent's Park has kindly said that they will not go unless our debt is honoured, and, indeed, the debt of Polka Theatre, who also went to Dubai and weren't fully paid. I will fill you in on the next instalment of the saga in my next letter...*

... Action for Children's Arts continues to do its bit, although until we have proper funding and an office and paid employees, it will be impossible to do as much as we would like.

However, we managed to have a meeting with various

departments of the Arts Council the other day, to try to push for more attention for children's arts. The meeting seemed to go well.

Yours,
David

15 Sep

Dear David,

…The review of Theatre for Children *makes very good reading. I hope it will do something to make up for the lack of promotion which should have accompanied your personal appearance in the U.S. Her 'minor quibble' is not really justified, though. That 'repetition of some ideas' keeps them in mind as the reader proceeds from one example to another. It's the very good reason which the preacher gave to the parishioner who complained of his saying the same thing every Sunday. "And what do I say every Sunday?" "Er – er – " said the parishioner. "Exactly," said the preacher, "that's why I say it!"…*

Frank

The pair met up for lunch at the end of the month, and a draft of *Spot* followed soon afterwards.

26 Sep

Dear Frank,

…I am sending you a copy of the first draft of Spot's Birthday Party, *even though I have been rather rude about it! See what you think. I have to keep telling myself that the audience is going to be aged 3 on average! Hopefully, it will work. I'm quite pleased with some of the songs…*

Yours,
David

1. DW and FW at FW's home in Winchester, 2001.

2. FW, 1996.

3. West Sussex County Council Youth Drama Summer School, Lodge Hill, 1960. FW front row centre, DW middle row, second from the right.

4. DW at Sussex Youth Theatre Summer School, Burwash Place, 1961.

5. FW, c1945.

6. FW (left) and Ralph Kerns on the porch, Tehran, 1945.

Frank Whitbourn – "dearly my delicate Ariel!"

James Porter – "bravely my spirit".

THE TEMPEST

by

William Shakespeare

The Persons in the Play:

CHORUS	Mehedi Forough
PROSPERO, the rightful Duke of Milan	Frank Whitbourn
MIRANDA, his daughter	Madge Monypenny
ARIEL, a spirit, servant to Prospero	Ralph Kerns
CALIBAN, monster, slave to Prospero	A.Z. Ghaffari
FERDINAND, son to the King of Naples	James Porter
GONZALO an honest counsellor	Albert Berseghian
ANTONIO, brother to Prospero and usurping Duke of Milan	Manuel Aratunian
ALONZO, King of Naples	Kenneth Le Page
TRINCULO, a clown	Adrian Grant
STEPHANO, a drunken butler	Jim Arigona
A BOATSWAIN	E. Manshai

Spirits called up by Prospero-
JUPITER	David Fox
CERES	Lucille Nicholson
REAPERS	Wilma Protiva Diana Grant Aida Akhoonzadeh Dorothy Leppman Irena Mikeladze

Miranda's love to dainty Ariel!

life is like a mirror,
If you smile,
Smiles come back to greet you
If you're frowning all the while,
Frowns for ever meet you

The Action of the Play takes place on a ship at sea and on an enchanted island.

The Play will be presented in two parts, with an interval of 15 minutes between them.

Aida

[Handwritten across top:] ...ve seen lots of sprites – but my goodness – what a "sprout" our ariel – Ceres Nickie

THE TEMPEST — by William Shakespeare

[Handwritten:] To Ralph the ariel of our & Shakespeare's dreams – Jupiter Fox

The Play directed by Frank Whitbourn and James Porter

[Handwritten left margin:] "You are such stuff as my dreams are made of ...." Phil. "Where the bee sucks – there such I – will haunt, Thanks – This one for ever, Doretta — To you Doretta Jefferson"

The Setting designed by W.W. Ramsay and built under the direction of J. K. Caton.

The costumes devised by Monica Le Page and W.W. Ramsay, and executed by Josephine.

The Music under the direction of David Hicks and Parviz Mahmud.

"Come Unto These Yellow Sands" and "Full Fathom Five" composed by David Hicks.

"Where the Bee Sucks" composed by Dr. Arne.

Flute Accompaniments played by Leppman.

[Handwritten right:] See you again in West Hampstead

The Dances arranged by Lucille Nicholson.

Lighting and Sound Effects by P.R. Glanville.

Spotlights kindly lent by the Management of the Tehran Theatre

Programme Cover designed by R. Hill

[Handwritten right margin:] Best wishes to you, from Roger Gill

Stage Manager	)		M. A. Issari
Assistant Stage Manager	) for the		George Barker
Wardrobe Mistress	) A.I.D.S.		Monica Le Page
General Business Manager	)		W. T. Messeter

[Handwritten:] Bonheur et joie de Hélène Rikakdré

The Producers wish to extend their sincere thanks to the Directors and Staffs of the Anglo-Persian Institutes at Tehran and Tajrish, and to many other friends of the A.I.D.S. for the whole-hearted co-operation which has made this production possible.

8. The Tempest, *FW as Prospero, Ralph Kerns as Ariel, Tehran 1945.*

9. *FW performing a speech from Marlowe's* Dr Faustus *in his recital, Tehran c1945.*

11.5.93

Dear Frank, You've no idea how
chuffed I was to receive your NODDY
reaction — it's not just that you flatter me
with your kind comment, it's so warming
to see how 'seriously' you have taken
the piece, & how well you have understood
my intentions. You always latch on to
the salient points like a homing pigeon!
I'm delighted you like it. Gillian Baverstock
(E.B's daughter) will see the script tomorrow,
I'm told. Fingers crossed she will feel
it works, is faithful, and echoes her mother's
belief that Noddy represents the young
fledgling child emerging into the 'real
world', where there are dangers and
folk cannot always be taken at face
value. I'm sure she was right to
include Noddy's tantrums — 'it's not fair!'
as well as his basic 'goodness'.
     I value your skittles thoughts —
you're quite right, they are a little cabaret
incursion, mainly devised to give work to the
ASMs and increase the 'citizenship' of
what is (for financial reasons) a rather

10. DW letter to FW, 1993.

14 Francis Gardens
Winchester Hants
SO23 7HD

3 Feb 2000

Dear David—

Hurrah for your splendid package! It dropped in with a most auspicious PLOP!

I've been wondering what you've been up to. Now I know. I haven't read Philippa Pearce's book. A good thing because, as you say, I'll be able to approach your Tom's Midnight Garden as a play in its own right. 'It's very different' you say. I can't wait. I'm just going out in my gardening gear to take advantage of a mild morning for some necessary tidying up after the frosts we've been having, then I'll get cracking.

We've managed to keep clear of the 'flu. Have you all? We hope so. It's a particularly vicious strain.

Lots of love to all the Wordes, from Mary too, and huginimus thanks!

Frank

12. The Gingerbread Man, *Old Vic, 1977. L to R – Salt (Tim Barker), Pepper (Vivienne Martin), The Gingerbread Man (Andrew Secombe), Herr Von Cuckoo (Ronnie Stevens).*

13. Meg and Mog Show, *Unicorn at the Arts Theatre, 1981. L to R - Mog (Vincent Osborne), Owl (Carrie Simcocks), Meg (Maureen Lipman), Zookeeper (Andrew Sargent), Stegosaurus (Ben Robertson, Pamela Power, Mary Roscoe).*

14. a. Abbacadabra, *1983. Publicity leaflet.*

b. Abbacadabra, *Lyric Hammersmith, 1983. Carabosse (Elaine Paige).*

15. a. The Old Man of Lochnagar, *1986. Publicity leaflet.*

b. The Old Man of Lochnagar, *His Majesty's Aberdeen, Sadler's Wells, Albery Theatre, 1986. L to R – Nagar Maid (Katrina Ramsay), Lagopus Scoticus (Percy Copley), The Old Man (Iain Lauchlan), Nagar Maid (Lucy Allen).*

16. Save the Human, *Arts Theatre Cambridge, Sadler's Wells, 1990. L to R - Chas Chimp (Adam Stafford), Norman (Neil Smye), Father Bear (David Bale), Norma (Mandy Lassalles), Becky Bear (Jenny Galloway), Mother Bear (David Burrows), Freda Ferret (Wenda Holland), Patch Badger (Robert McKewley).*

17. The BFG, *Wimbledon Theatre, Aldwych Theatre, 1991. L to R – The BFG (Anthony Pedley), Sophie (Fiona Grogan).*

18. The Witches, *Lyceum Sheffield, Duke of York's Theatre, 1992. The Grand High Witch (Dorothy Ann Gould).*

19. Noddy, *Wimbledon Theatre, Lyric Hammersmith, 1993. L to R – Big Ears (Eric Potts), Sally Skittle (Sara Jane Derrick), Noddy (Karen Briffett), Tessie Bear (Amanda Macdonald), Bumpy Dog (Michael Seraphim), Sam Skittle (Graham Breeze), Sly (Jonathan Bex), Mr Plod (Roger Bingham).*

20. Babe, the Sheep-Pig, *New Victoria Woking, 1997. Fly (Mary-Ann Coburn),
Babe (Karen Briffett), Farmer Hogget (Anthony Pedley), Sheep 1 (Emma Clayton).*

21. Theatre for Children – A Guide
to Writing, Adapting, Directing and
Acting, *1997. Book Cover.*

22. Tom's Midnight Garden, *Unicorn
at the Pleasance, 2000. Tom (Dale
Superville).*

23. Spot's Birthday Party, *Oxford Playhouse, Lyric Hammersmith, 2000. L to R –
Marco (Daniel Tomlinson), Spot (Dale Superville), Helen (Denise Kennedy), Sally
(Joanna Van Kampen), Sam (Alexander L'Estrange), Steve (Matthew Harvey),
Tom (Daniel Robinson).*

24. Clockwork, *Linbury Studio
Theatre at the Royal Opera House,
2004. Publicity leaflet.*

Note

In the foregoing lines may be detected echoes from the last 2,000 years, viz: The First Book of Kings, xviii 43–45, (with enigmatic variations), Ecclesiastes, i 2–3, The Canterbury Tales, ancient liturgy, and The Book of Common Prayer.

25. FW's 'Poem for the Millennium', one of his characteristic Christmas cards, 1999.

David, Jacqui and the Gub —
This is my Special Offer — Two for One — and I shall sleep With my way through the Millennium Midnight fireworks! Enjoy yourselves!

Every Good Wish
for
Christmas
and
The New Year
love
from
Frank and Mary.

1999
14 Francis Gardens Winchester.

A BIDDING PRAYER

The patient process of a myriad years
Marks time for an arbitary moment. Let
No man forget at the century's turning all
The tread of her pursuant shadows; all
The unstinted mourning and the tears; all
The uprooted, drifting, hungered, dying; all
The salient suppurating scars of her
Insatiable, unnecessary wars.

But then look Eastward. There, beyond
The challenging horizon of a dark,
Indifferent, tumultuous sea, behold a cloud
No larger than a Child's hand, affirming
An under-achieving Star! The sun also
Ariseth, quickening the march; and warning.

FW.

26. FW's bookplate.

FAMILIAS · FIRMAT · PIETAS

FRANK WHITBOURN

5 Oct

Dear David,

'SPOT ON!'

Huge thanks for your latest masterwork – it's nothing less – and has kept myself and Mary chuckling loud and long. The concept of the Birthday Party, providing sustainable stretches of concentration with masses of participation, establishes that it was the only way it could be done. The impression of inevitability is always one of the signs of artistic success, no matter what the medium. You have cunningly linked each step in the sequence with the next, for example, the squashing of the cake at the end of Musical Chairs naturally leading to the baking of the eventual cake. Nevertheless, without a sophisticated storyline, you have provided a scheme of continuity with the planting of the sunflower seeds, a recurring moment of expectation every time they are watered – when children plant seeds they always expect immediate results and are ever ready to dig them up to see if they are growing. In much the same way, after only the first five minutes of a car journey, they ask, "Are we there yet?" These moments also provide time for settling down after the excitement of each episode. And the play of Cinderella provides a notable climax before the beautiful, quieting scene of the sunflower coming into bloom. Quite truly magical – and true to life. "I can't go to sleep without my teddy" and the crafty "Can I have a drink of water?" – Anything to postpone Mother's final departure!

The choice of octosyllabics for Cinderella, instead of the usual 'iambic pentameters' for the couplets, is very cunning, too. They increase the pace and give emphasis to the rhymes, some of which are hilarious – 'sisters-resist us', 'here-idea', 'in for-in law'. I laughed and laughed!

How well do you suppose to-day's 3-5-year-olds will know the story? And how well will they know the traditional nursery rhymes? I take it you don't expect to use all those you have printed out – it's a pretty extensive anthology!

205

The lyrics are excellent. The frequent repetition of lines and phrases makes them easy to grasp and remember – you won't need 'song sheets', even if these were feasible for such a young audience. Incidentally, you are well on line with the latest governmental thinking on what every child should know from year to year. In 'Like a Statue', I found myself wondering whether line four of the verse, 'But when the whistle', should not perhaps include 'blows' from the next line, thus:

But when the whistle blows
You have to stop!

The suggestion of a free handout of cake, ice cream or lollies in the interval is a notable way of providing the ultimate in audience participation. It would take some organising, and if members of the cast undertake distribution they won't get much of a break after all the energy they have had to burn up on stage. They'll need to be an exceptionally talented lot with a special gift for improvisation to cope with the unexpected. The addition of Marco, the Rabbit, to the usual characters is very neat. His acting as MC with a command of sleight-of-hand helps to tie the sequences together, and he's an arresting character in his own right. I remember your being bothered that the Noddy character and more especially Rupert Bear were very bland, but Spot's chums have plenty of individuality – I particularly like the Crocodile's tears!

For the leaving handout at the end, Mary wonders whether a 'Spot' biscuit might be provided, like The Gingerbread Man, *if a biscuit manufacturer could be found to sponsor it. I suppose, though, any such manufacturer would need the guarantee of a long run to justify him in setting up the necessary 'jigs', or whatever machinery such businesses require, to turn out a special pattern. They would certainly make for ease of distribution, as would the option of ice lollies in the interval. There might be a lot of lolly-sticks to be cleared up afterwards but no matter. They might be one of the less harmful consequences of audience participation. Playing 'Statues' and 'Dancing in the Stalls' (that suggests a title for a play) may leave the auditorium requiring some renovation. Perhaps you should take out an insurance policy against this consequence. But I fear the premium would be high!*

I have always defined a work of art as the achievement of a deliberate aim in a creation which provides aesthetic pleasure, which is, in brief, a 'thing of beauty'. For me, Spot's Birthday Party *does just this.* My only regret is that, the literary and theatrical circumstances being as they are, it will not receive the recognition it deserves. Is there any other management to take it beyond the Oxford Playhouse and provide an extensive run? I hope Eric Hill approves it as much as I do.*

* But of course full realisation can only come in performance…

As ever –
Frank

12 Oct

Dear Frank,

…I can't tell you how much it means to have somebody like yourself read 'seriously' my plays. Your comments are so reassuring, because you are quite honestly the only person who notices things within the structure, or the way my mind has approached the piece. Because I tend to do the actual writing quite quickly, I think some people assume that the whole thing is thrown together without too much care. If only they knew!…

So far, there has been no reaction from Eric Hill or Penguin. The Oxford Playhouse have, somewhat non-committally, said they enjoyed reading it, but that is all. Fingers crossed we don't have all sorts of problems from the copyright holders.

…we have many hurdles to scale yet with Spot's Birthday Party. *We need to get the right cast together and hopefully prove that the show works in front of little punters of the year 2000!*

…The use of the Cinderella *story is, I suppose, debatable. But I really felt… We needed to get into the realm of theatre, using the imagination to tell the story, employing props we have already seen and pretending, as children always do, that they are something else. To do this needed a story which had as much familiarity as possible.* Cinderella *seemed the obvious one. I'm quite sure there will be a lot of tiny tots for whom the whole thing is a bit of a mystery, but hopefully by then they will have accepted the characters and the actors playing them, and will enjoy the continual movement and rhythm of the play within a play.*

The nursery rhymes will probably not be used at all. …The idea really was to show that I wanted there to be some form of activity before the show proper begins. …That is not the most pressing worry – if necessary, we don't bother to do anything, and just start the show with Sam and Sally entering and introducing themselves.

I think you might be right about the 'I blow the whistle' line in 'Like a Statue'. The reason that in the second verse I separated the word 'whistle' and the word 'blows' is that, in the first verse, the equivalent line is 'I blow the whistle' followed by the next line, 'And you all stand still'. In other words, in the second verse, the word 'But' is a stressed syllable, like the 'I' in the first verse. I think, following your comment, I should change them both, so that the first verse will read…

*I BLOW THE WHISTLE AND
YOU ALL STAND STILL!*

And the second verse would read…

*BUT WHEN THE WHISTLE BLOWS
YOU HAVE TO STOP!*

Thank you for that!

…I'm glad to say that Oxford Playhouse are intending to tour the production after it finishes its run in Oxford. They have also acquired worldwide rights, so that they might be able to secure a production in the United States, where Spot *is very popular and, indeed, in many other countries.* Spot *is translated into something like eighty different languages!*

…We start rehearsals for The Gingerbread Man *on Monday 18th October. Fingers crossed for the American Adventure!*

… Love and best wishes to you both, and once again, thank you so much for taking the trouble to read Spot's Birthday Party *with such care and attention to detail. It means an awful lot to me.*

David

17 Oct

Dear David,

…This is really just to say how pleased I am that my observations on Spot's Birthday Party *have proved useful. Yes, your revised version…*

> *I blow the whistle and*
> *You all stand still*

seems to hit the right note.

I think you're quite right when you say that if the little punters have accepted the reality of the characters from the books they will have no difficulty, with Cinderella, her Godmother, her Pumpkin and her Fairy Prince. It's the conviction carried by his characters that enables W.S. to get away with his (literally) far-fetched plots.

…I do hope the GB rehearsals will have got well underweigh by the time you receive this scrawl. America is Waiting!

Love –
Frank

The next correspondence covered the time when the US production of *The Gingerbread Man* was playing.

7 Nov

Dear David,

Many thanks for your card from Gingerbread Country. I calculate that you must, at this moment-as-ever-is, be preparing for the last performance of your visit. I do hope the whole experience has been worthwhile in every way and that you and the Company, though probably not the set, will be safely back in Wombledon this week…

Love –
Frank

24 Nov

Dear Frank,

…The Gingerbread Man got a wonderful reception, I'm glad to say. I'm enclosing a review. The New York State Theatre Institute treated us extremely well and very hospitably, and the audiences were excellent, particularly the schools' ones. We only changed one word in the play – 'sweet' to 'candy' and even the youngest seemed to have no problem whatsoever in understanding what was going on. In fact, the reaction was just as good if not better than over here!

Lots of people said we should be doing the play again in the United States, possibly touring. We have been talking to various people and maybe something will happen. I have to say that I thoroughly enjoyed being there and that the interest shown in the work from all sides was very refreshing and good for the self-esteem! The theatre was within a college, but run totally by professionals, all of whom were very competent and friendly. The whole visit was a total delight. We never overran on stage in the technical and dress rehearsal stage, nobody got in a state or threw a wobbly! All very civilised, with lots of receptions, parties, organised trips and a very comfortable hotel too. Our elderly company (four actors in their 50s or 60s, plus two striplings in their 30s and 40s) sailed through with flying colours. The energy level was huge and we had no problems with voices or strained muscles!...

...I've been back nearly a week, and everything seems extremely busy and back to normal. Meetings are going on about Spot's Birthday Party*. We have a designer and hopefully a choreographer. As I think I told you, I am working with totally new people, provided by the Oxford Playhouse, who want to develop their new children's wing. It will be strange not having the resident team, but maybe it will be invigorating and 'good' for me.*

The publishers have come back with some comments about the script. They want Spot to narrate the Cinderella *section, rather than play the Prince. They feel this puts him in a better light. They may be right. But I still think he should play the Prince, even if he narrates as well!*

Meanwhile, the producers are being 'hands-on' as well! They have come up with the idea that the Cinderella *sequence should be transferred to the end of Act 1, and all the business with the birthday cake to the end of Act 2. I will wait to see their proposals in detail, but I fancy they are wrong. The whole point about the* Cinderella *sequence is that we go into a different kind of fantasy. It wouldn't work as well to do that and then return to the original status quo for the second half... We will see!...*

... Jacqui and I have just been to Cardiff for a couple of days to see the opening of The Twits *there. It is the same production as in Coventry, re-mounted for a Christmas season in Cardiff. Very enjoyable.*

Meanwhile, Birmingham Stage Company are touring The Witches, *in a new production using my adaptation. I haven't heard reports of it yet, but I know the business is very good in Birmingham, where they play for about ten weeks over Christmas.*

Yours,
David

The discussion of children's theatre in the USA reminded FW of some of his theatrical experiences when working for the British Council in Iran, and the people he met there.

29 Nov

Dear David,

...I am surprised that Children's Theatre in the U.S.A. is even less well funded than ours. I suppose the Men with Money see no immediate return on investment and haven't the nous or the imagination to look ahead... They certainly take their 'community theatre' very seriously and aim at a very high standard. I have a chum in Carolina who is closely concerned with it. I came to know him when he was a G.I. in Teheran and I was working for the British Council there. He played Ariel to my Prospero in a lavish production of The Tempest *which I directed in a wonderful open-air setting in Shemran, the village in the foothills above Teheran where the wealthy have their villas to escape the summer heat – a sort of Simla. The Embassy had a summer residence there, providing a natural theatre banked with flowers and a guarantee of perfect weather. I also put on* A Midsummer Night's Dream *and a Persian-speaking officer (intelligence) from the Embassy produced Flecker's* Hassan *in a Persian translation – with real camels to take the Golden Road to Samarkand! ...Those were my Glory Days!...*

...Now – Spot. Who is the clot of a publisher that cannot appreciate that your script should not be tampered with? You must resist, tooth and nail. It's so absolutely right as it is, with the birthday party and the making of the cake providing the necessary climax to Act One. To bring Cinderella *forward would destroy the marvellous build-up for the end of Act Two and the whole play, so cunningly held in reserve to introduce a new and unexpected, spectacular element – a sort of equivalent of the Grand Transformation Scene and Walk Down which climaxed the traditional pantomime. I agree – they may have a point that*

Spot should narrate the Cinderella *section, but I don't see how that puts him in 'a better light' than his appearing as the Prince.*

I'm delighted The Twits *are enjoying a Christmas Season in Cardiff and* The Witches *in Birmingham. Does 'a new production' mean new sets and machinery as well as stage direction?...*

Ever –
Frank

6 Dec

Dear Frank,

...Various meetings have now taken place about Spot's Birthday Party. *The publishers had a few comments, some of them rather strange! In the 'Welcome to My Party' song, they didn't want the characters to actually sing words which implied they were a monkey, a crocodile or a hippo. Apparently, Eric Hill feels that they are really children, not animals at all! This is totally illogical, but I have adapted the words hopefully to satisfy them...*

Although I did at first resist the idea of swapping round the Cinderella *sequence with the 'baking a cake' sequence, I was willing to give it a try. My producers felt that it was better to have all the cake business in the second half, leading up to the celebratory 'Happy Birthday' at the end of the show, rather than just before the interval. I could see the logic in this, although I was worried that the* Cinderella *sequence really needed to be at the end, because we were going up a gear in terms of fantasy and theatricality.*

Anyway, I have written a second draft, in the knowledge that we can always go back to the original if we feel it is better (and my first instincts often are correct, says he modestly!).

I would be very grateful if you could have a read of it and let me know what you think. I actually think it works okay, but would very much welcome your opinion...

Love and best wishes,
David

8 Dec

Dear David,

Many thanks for your offering of the new draft of Spot's Birthday Party *for my delectation. It landed on the front door-mat this morning...*

I find this Eric Hill's wanting to change the words of the Welcome song quite pointless. Surely the children accept Spot and his friends as animals, not children like themselves, don't they? That's the whole point of anthropomorphic animals. They are compatible with humans but are nevertheless animals, and that's what makes them special. However, if he wants the change, I don't think it matters, the children will still re-act in their own way, and you've effected it very neatly just as you have spliced the re-location of the Birthday Cake and Cinderella.*

I can see the logic of this. The making and cutting – and eating – of the cake may be the climax of the party, but it's not the end of it. And the blowing out of the candles and consequent black-out might make some of the audience feel that the entertainment was over, so that voices might be heard asking, "Do we have to go home now?" However, the coming-on of the house lights and the offer of cake or ice-cream as well as the exodus to the loos should settle that.*

But the introduction of Cinderella *at this point brings an entirely different element into play, and reverting in Act II to the sort of fun and games which preceded it, will be in danger of seeming anti-climatic. It's the icing on the cake, which should be kept to the last. It does occur to me nevertheless that the deftness of the parody of traditional pantomime couplets is something that may appeal to parents rather than their children, so some of its speciality may be discounted. But your instinct is right. It is best where it is, though I think the piece will work despite the switch, if less effectively. I suppose only an actual performance will demonstrate this, and that'll be rather late in the day! You're right to 'give it a try' even if you have to avoid saying "I told you so!"*

It seems to me better for Spot not to be a narrator as well as the Prince. The children might find this duality confusing. Marco as MC of the whole party is surely the most suitable to be the link man.

I don't think you should need to go back to the drawing-board again. Either way, it will be very effective, I'm sure. My only anxiety is for the theatre upholstery with all those infant feet beating time on it! Does the Oxford Playhouse have the sort of seats that tip-up when you're not expecting them to do so?…

Love to you all –
Frank

The year ended with DW considering how to revise *Spot's Birthday Party* alongside working on his adaptation of *Tom's Midnight Garden*, based in his usual writing retreat.

30 Dec

Dear Frank,

Do hope you & Mary had a good Xmas – thanks for your splendid poems – and your last letter, to which I will respond properly soon – Meanwhile, I'm in my attic hotel room in Bexhill trying to adapt Tom's Midnight Garden *by Philippa Pearce – it's a real challenge! Xmas was fine – both my mother & John (he is increasingly frail) came – HAPPY MILLENNIUM!!*

Love to both,
David x

2000

The first letter from DW for the new century included a draft of *Tom's Midnight Garden.*

31 Jan

Dear Frank,

...Here, at last, is the first draft of the latest opus!

I don't know whether you have ever read Philippa Pearce's book, which, written in the '50s, is now considered a classic of its kind.

If you haven't read the book, that might be rather good, because you could be totally objective about the play!

It is very different from most of my other plays, and hopefully offers lots of theatrical opportunities!...

David

3 Feb

Dear David,

Hurrah for your splendid package! It dropped in with a most auspicious PLOP!

I've been wondering what you've been up to. Now I know. I haven't read Philippa Pearce's book. A good thing because, as you say, I'll be able to approach your Tom's Midnight Garden *as a play in its own right. "It's very different," you say. I can't wait. I'm just going out in my gardening gear to take advantage of a mild morning for some necessary tidying-up after the frosts we've been having, then I'll get cracking...*

Lots of love to all the Woodies, from Mary too and hugissimus thanks!

Frank

Within a few days, the script had been read and FW sent his detailed responses.

7 Feb

Dear David,

I don't know Philippa Pearce's book (published by O.U.P., I notice, that's a hallmark of quality), so I have necessarily approached Tom's Midnight Garden *as an original play in its own right.*

I find it spell-binding. Clearly, it aims at an audience older than those for whom most of your past work has been designed. Are they Tom's contemporaries? He seems very mature for his age, Peter too, but the letters are a very successful way of maintaining the narrative, and the degree of literacy Tom displays is acceptable under the terms of poetic licence. Both characters are convincingly established and my belief is that if characters in a play or novel are convincing then any activity in which they take part will be credible too.

As you say, the fluency of the narrative is essential and therefore you are quite right to offer no act divisions, or any interval* because any such interruption could break the spell which is cast from the very first moment of Mrs Bartholomew's entry down the stairs to wind the clock, the symbol of Time, and the chorus of off-stage voices. Absolutely gripping. I find myself wondering whether it might be best for these to be recorded by other actors than those in the play, but perhaps they should be represented as presences surviving in the house. In your introduction, you ask, 'Is it a ghost story? Is it exploring the supernatural? Is it about the power of the human spirit? Does it suggest that an old house can retain memories of the past? Is it about time? Is it about freedom?' And you rightly answer, 'It is about all these things. And what makes it a classic is that it is also believable'. It creates in the words of Coleridge (I think) 'a willing suspension of disbelief '.

*The older spectators shouldn't need 'to be excused', should they?

So I am a little troubled by the suggestion of the introduction of puppets for the geese and other animals. Could not these be boldly imagined? If the actors see them, the spectators will see them also...

All this supports your belief in the necessity of simplicity in the setting. The introduction of revolves or wagons would be shattering. As I was reading, I found myself visualising a setting with a central Victorian staircase leading to the 'first floor back' on an upper level, with Tom's bedroom central too, so that it might dominate the action along with the clock, fitted with bed, cupboard and 'practical' door for him to prop open with his slipper. And I suppose a table for the breakfast scene on the same level, like the bedroom, a permanent part of the 'minimalist' set.

Then I began to picture a front door in a wall to my right (stage left) through which Uncle Alan would bring Tom to stay, affording a glimpse of the street beyond, extending perhaps behind a gauze wall. Though so much is established by verbal description, I felt that a limited visuality would not come amiss.

On the other side was the door to the garden. Now, in such a Victorian house, this would have been a 'garden door' from a lobby where those going to the garden would change into outdoor shoes or put on galoshes. Victorian houses did not provide direct access from living-rooms to the garden, though Georgian houses allowed a way out through tall sash windows for persons prepared to stoop a little. The 1850s house, just demolished, across the way from us, had a very prominent door leading to the garden and the park. So I visualised just such a door, a 'practical door' for Tom's way into the garden. And it seemed to me if this ponderous and prominent means of ingress and egress were set in a wall of gauze similar to that on stage left (my right), the sudden misty lighting-up of a view of the garden might provoke the sort of gasp of surprise achieved by the sudden appearance of *the magic wood at the end of the first act of Barrie's* Dear Brutus. *…This would allow Tom, having stepped out through the door, to make his way back for extended action in the central stage area, round the lower end of the gauze flats. The action in the garden is going to require as much space as possible, and Abel and his greenhouse – to be imagined and mimed – will have to be there also, will they not? Likewise, the cathedral tower.*

…The garden door, perhaps draped or colour-glazed, as it probably would have been, might well be added to establish the Victorian scene. And perhaps a telephone table by the front door would clarify the presence of the 20th century on that half of the stage.

But I have rambled on enough and detained you too long with my impertinent comments and fancies. I may get hold of the book, or I may not. It might disappoint me after experiencing such a spell-binding text as you have presented me with…

Frank

Crossing with this letter in the post was an update from DW on other projects that were in progress.

8 Feb

Dear Frank,

…Before Christmas, you wrote beguilingly about your productions of Shakespeare in Teheran. What extraordinary days they must have been! I wish I could have seen your Prospero!…

…After Christmas, you kindly responded to the second draft of Spot's Birthday Party. *I have begun to get used to the changes – it looks as though the second draft will prevail! I still, like you, feel that the* Cinderella *sequence should be where it was originally, but everyone else seems to be happier with the change, so, at least for the time being, I will succumb. We are*

now having auditions and casting. We have seen some quite interesting people who, hopefully, will accept the offer to come aboard! Rehearsals start on March 13th, which is really rather close. We found a young designer, who has come up with an interesting set. I have a new Director of Movement (the phrase he insists on using!): who has worked a lot at the National and the Royal Opera House... My new Musical Supervisor is not totally new – he started his career with Whirligig back in 1980.

... A few days after New Year, Jacqui and I went to see Maureen Lipman in Peggy for You. *You may have read about this tribute by Alan Plater to the legendary Peggy Ramsay, who was my agent for many years. ... I always remember her phoning me having read my adaptation of* The Old Man of Lochnagar. *She said she thought the first half was better than the second half, but that probably didn't matter. Then she said she thought we might have a problem with the lavatory! She thought the Palace might object. When I pointed out that it was in Prince Charles' book, she said breezily, "Oh, that's all right then! Bye!"...*

Yours,
David

DW also told the woeful tale of a less-than-impressive (though financially successful) pantomime version of *Peter Pan* at Wimbledon Theatre, and this met with an exasperated response from FW in his next letter.

13 Feb 2000
(I like doing all these noughts but
I'm never quite sure when to stop)

Dear David,

Oh, I say, what a lovely long letter!...

...I'm sorry that the commissioners of Spot's Birthday Party *are blind to the advantage of reserving* Cinderella *for the climax. It'll be interesting to see how the second version works out in practice in its effect upon the audiences. And it'll be even more interesting to see how your new Oxford team graduate...*

...I'm delighted that Wimbledon Theatre finds itself in the black, but I do wish people, even with the best of intentions, wouldn't try to improve on Barrie. I should like to start a Society for the Protection of Persecuted Playwrights. I wonder whether Peggy Ramsay would have approved the idea. Probably not...

Love to you all from both of us,
Frank

DW's next letter was in response to FW's critique of the draft of *Tom's Midnight Garden*.

16 Feb

Dear Frank,

...I'm rather pleased that you didn't know the book. That means you didn't fill in any gaps simply because you knew the original! Am very pleased you found it readable.

Yes, I think this is for 10-year-olds upwards, including adults.

In fact, there is an interval. But I decided to offer scene divisions rather than act divisions to keep the flow. The interval comes at a good moment in the story, when Tom is terrified he can't actually get back to the present.

I think you are absolutely right about puppets. I think we should imagine them.

Thank you for imagining the set in such detail. Your description is very much as I imagined it, except that you have suggested that the bedroom be on the top level in a central area. This is much better than my original thinking that it would be on one side. It is so integral to the story, that it should definitely be as visible to everybody as possible.

I'm afraid I won't be directing the first production – Tony Graham, who commissioned it for Unicorn Theatre, has already reserved that right! But he seems clever and sensitive and hopefully will do it well. One thing he feels strongly is that there should be a very haunting musical content, underscoring in particular. He is beginning to feel that the voices of the house should be almost sung. He seems to be talking cello and flute at the moment, which could be rather nice!

The day after your lovely response arrived, I had a phone call from Philippa Pearce, who was, I'm relieved to say, very pleased with the script. She has found a dozen or so small things to discuss, however. The main one is quite interesting. She pointed out that Tom cannot catch the apple in the scene where he helps Hatty by making one of the cousins look silly in the Hatty-in-the-middle game. This was a scene I invented. She is absolutely right. Nowhere else in the book or the play can Tom actually touch or pick up objects. Having said that, quite honestly, I don't think it matters whether he can or can't, certainly not in the play. But I think I had better find an alternative for her!

One lovely thing she said was that she wished she had started the book in the way I have the play! I think she means that I start the story later than she does, which makes it more immediate, and doesn't make us wait as long to get to the exciting part when he goes into the garden. Philippa has quite a long preamble in which we see Tom at home with his mother and brother, having to get ready to leave. There is then the drive to the aunt and uncle's house/flat, seeing Ely Cathedral on the way. She liked the way I had telescoped all that information into about four lines! She also liked the ending very much, which is slightly different from hers. It is always a good sign when the original writer enjoys certain things being different, as long as they are in the spirit of the original.

...As you read this, I should be in Bexhill yet again, trying to cobble together yet another play, this time a thirty-minute musical piece for two professional actors and sixty children! It's for the Oxford Playhouse again, based on a nice children's book called The Lighthouse Keeper's Lunch, *by Ronda and David Armitage.*

All for now, love to you both, thanks again.

Yours,
David

Within a week, a draft of *The Lighthouse Keeper's Lunch* was on its way to FW, and he was as prompt as ever in his reply.

24 Feb

Dear David,

Well! WELL!! Oh MY!!! Bexhill-on-Sea-and-Solitary certainly came up with the goods! The whole thing is a wonderful idea – 'concept' if you favour the 'in' word. Where, When and How did it originate? From the Oxford Playhouse? I hope it won't be just a 'one-off' there, but will be taken up by other local theatres, Nuffield, Salisbury, for instance, which made a valuable point of educational work with local schools. The whole undertaking should be tremendous fun if local school managements and staffs are not too chary of time, too obsessed with the 'national curriculum', that tiresome straitjacket, to take advantage of this imaginative tonic.

I'm especially pleased that you've undertaken the music yourself. The 'cumulative' song, if that's the right word for such memorabilia as 'The House that Jack Built' and 'I have a Song to Sing-O', makes a rousing finale. When do you expect it to take the stage at Oxford?...

Love to all as ever – and from Mary,
Frank

Dear Frank,

...Glad you approve of The Lighthouse Keeper's Lunch. *I think it will be fun. Whether or not Samuel French will take it up, I just don't know. It is so clearly something that schools or youth groups could do...*

We will be doing five performances at the Oxford Playhouse, opening June 26th. Each group of children will come in for the day, culminating with a performance round about 4.00pm. Different children every day!...

Yours,
David

Attention then moved to preparations for the launch of *Spot's Birthday Party* in Oxford.

14 Mar

Dear Frank,

...Am enclosing a Spot *leaflet, plus a tour schedule, just in case it is going to be possible for you to see it. Rehearsals begin on Monday 13th. We had a nice day on Wednesday, when the entire company came to Oxford for lunch, measuring for costumes, publicity photos and a read-through. They seem a delightful lot.*

Business for the Spot *tour is apparently coming along extremely well, which is encouraging...*

Yours,
David

Dear David,

…The prospect of Spot's Birthday Party *actually reaching the stage of being staged is most exciting – especially the tour. I had hoped that Pat might be able to take us to Oxford but she is already over-committed for that week and so we are aiming at Poole, which is probably easier to reach and to park at…*

Frank

2000 Spot's Birthday Party –

Oxford Playhouse – 6th April 2000

From Eric Hill's popular stories, using a simple plot where the audience are treated like guests at the party.

25 Apr

Dear Frank,

…You will be pleased to know that [Spot's Birthday Party] opened very successfully after a really enjoyable rehearsal period. The company worked hard and well, and everybody on the technical side took the whole thing very seriously, so that, by the time we got to the theatre, everything was ready and we never got behind schedule. There has been one Oxford Mail *review, which was very good, and which I will forward to you as soon as I receive copies. The business has been excellent too. And, indeed, we are told that the advance bookings throughout the tour are excellent.*

Working with my new team of people, most of them suggested by Oxford, has been very productive. It was strange at first, but everybody worked really well and listened carefully to what I wanted to achieve, and there were no arguments or differences of opinion to cloud the atmosphere.

I hope very much that you, Mary and Pat will enjoy the production in Poole. Sadly, I won't be able to join you as I will be rehearsing The Lighthouse Keeper's Lunch, *back in Oxford.*

Last Monday, I spent the day with Peter Pontzen, getting the music done for The Lighthouse Keeper's Lunch. *As usual, I had written out my top lines in a somewhat amateurish fashion, and Peter does the arrangements for the tunes. Having done this for thirty-odd years, he is very quick at hearing what I can hear going on underneath the main tune. This speeds up the whole process! I'm really quite pleased with the songs I have written for this one, and hope that the children will enjoy singing them. As I may have told you, the forty-minute musical is written for two professional actors plus sixty children. We are doing it with five schools, each of whom provides sixty children for one performance. So we do five performances with five different sets of children. I have cast The Lighthouse Keeper and his wife. They are both performers I have known for some time and seen before quite often, but I have never actually worked with either of them before. Am looking forward to it. The performances in Oxford are each weekday from June 26th. I think 2.30pm will be the time of performance…*

Love and best wishes,
David

FW's reply included a flurry of reminiscences that showed once again his connection with theatrical notables of the past.

4 May

Dear David,

It was a great joy to receive your latest yesterday. Huge thanks for it and the truly magnificent programme for Spot's Birthday Party. *Your essay (it has to be accorded that dignity) was Alpha+,* and Eric Hill's account of the conception and development of Spot was fascinating. Talk about acorns growing into mighty oaks … Here's hoping The Lighthouse Keeper's Lunch will take off as happily. …I look forward to hearing how the Lunch works out in practice. I'm delighted that you've done the lyrics and music. N. Coward, that not inconsiderable music maker, employed a qualified musician to flesh out his numbers, so Peter Pontzen provides a well-recognized co-adjucentory. And Irving Berlin, I believe, couldn't read a note of music…

…the Young Vic …leads me to the Old Vic and my friendship with Harcourt Williams and his wife, Jean Sterling Mackinlay. This came about because their son, John Sterling, was my colleague as i/c Music at Clayesmore School in Dorset – my first teaching job. Jeannie's mother was Antoinette Sterling, a famous Victorian contralto who was asked by Sullivan to launch The Lost Chord. She turned the offer down, saying, "I canna sing that! 'Tis all on one note!" Indeed it was – and is – but had she taken up the offer, it would have brought her a rare heap 'o' siller' in royalties, and she lived to regret her rejection of it.

John invited me to stay at his parents' cottage at Ebony, near Tenterden in Kent – and Ellen Terry's home at Smallhythe. I became a close friend of them both. After an initial nationwide success in a play called Sunday, which did not lead to the offers she had hoped for, despite the admiration of G.B.S, she set out on a career as a 'diseuse' singing and acting folk songs in a most enchanting manner. There is a picture of her by – oh dear, Memory is letting me down, Hugh Somebody, I think, in three of her most successful songs, The Piper o' Dundee, Is My Team Ploughing (Houseman) and another which escapes me, a triptych now – or it was once – in the National Portrait Gallery.

She and Billee (as H.W. was known to his friends) were close friends of Ellen Terry, whom they always referred to as 'Gandy'. A long time after their wedding, ET drove over from

Smallhythe with a beautiful round oak table as a wedding present, explaining that she'd not made them an adequate offering on the wedding day itself. I remember riotous evenings during my many subsequent visits to Ebony playing Scrabble (then known as 'Kan You Go') by lamplight. There were no 'mod cons' then, though these were installed after the War. Water was pumped up from a well under the kitchen sink. On one of my visits during a terrible drought, this was in danger of running dry until suddenly the 'heavens opened' in the middle of the night and we all rose in our night-attire to gather up as much of the mercy as we could in whatever vessels we could lay hands on. When it was all over and we sank exhausted round Gandy's table, Jeannie exclaimed triumphantly, "Oh! But wasn't it exciting!"

Her recitals took her all over the country. A regular 'date' was at Warwick Castle where she became a great friend of the then Countess of Warwick. At Christmas time, she and Billee presented a series of Children's Matinees at the Rudolf Steiner Hall in Baker Street where I served as ASM and played small parts.

You – and your work – would have had a lot in common with Jean, and Billee, who complemented her songs by telling stories in front of the curtain. These were his own versions of Andersen and Grimm which he eventually published as Tales from Ebony. *He battled hard with the LCC to adopt a more light-hearted attitude to sending parties of schoolchildren to plays other than those pedantically prescribed for examinations, texts of which were sent out to the schools for study. He suggested, "How about sending them to see a play they have not studied, about which they know nothing?" "Oh, wouldn't that be rather a joyride?" was the reply. He also resisted Miss Baylis's custom of sending understudies on for the principal parts in the matinees for children, arguing that children must be given the best.*

I went to stay at Ebony shortly after I came home from Iran in 1946 and my visit co-incided with the first post-war revival of *the celebration of Ellen Terry's birthday in the Barn Theatre which Edith Craig (Gordon's sister) had established at Smallhythe. On this occasion, there was a reading of* Macbeth *by John Gielgud, Casson, Sybil Thorndike and Harcourt Williams. It provided the most thrilling presentation of the 'Scottish play' that I have ever attended. Macbeth and Lady M were taken by Gielgud and Sybil. Casson and Billee filled in all the rest. It was spell-binding. All the glitterati of the Stage were there but I was happy enough in the company of Jeannie, Sybil and John Gielgud. I met both of the latter subsequently, Sybil most memorably when she was playing in* Yes, My Darling Daughter *at Wimbledon, as I think I related when I spoke to the Friends there. "That's all very well if you're a genius," she said, "but for people like you and me, my dear ...!"*[*]

Billee had acted with Irving, but more often in Frank Benson's Touring Company. He described how Benson, who was reputed to be keener on cricket than drama, would dash into the theatre about twenty minutes before curtain-up, breathless from watching or playing his favourite game, cry, "What's it tonight, then? Lear? Right – give me my wig and beard. Tell them to ring up. Where's my crown?" just in time to stride on stage as Kent and Gloucester concluded their opening dialogue, with, "Attend the lords of France and Burgundy, Gloucester."...

Ever – Frank

FW saw *Spot's Birthday Party* when the tour reached Poole.

27 May

Dear David,

Oh, we did enjoy it! We loved every minute and the cast were quite enchanting. I can't imagine how they can exude such warmth and exuberant energy, making immediate rapport with

---

[*] *She also wrote me a testimonial for a job I was after.*

the audience. We have to thank you not only for the play but for splendid seats to watch and hear it from. I reckon the theatre – which seemed to be larger than I remembered it from our visit to Save The Human – was about three-quarters full. One or two of Spot's fans were very young, probably under-age – but they obviously all knew the books and needed no inducement to join in from the start.

It was fascinating to see how you had developed the whole from that first draft. I do think you should always direct your masterpieces yourself because I'm sure no one else could realise their potential so completely. I didn't quarrel with Cinderella's transfer to the first half because it worked quite well there, even though the splendid pantomime couplets were rather lost – but then of course only adults in the audience could really appreciate them – and the brilliant visual finale of the outburst of sun-flowers was quite stunning.

I'm inclined to think that the cleverest element in the whole piece was the introduction of those sun-flower seeds under cover of the birthday parcels. The successive waterings and inspections provided a continuity of suspense and expectation, a definite storyline in what would otherwise have been simply a series of episodes, exciting though each was in itself. Musical Chairs was sheer joy and Hide-and-Seek in the dark provided a notable contrast. There was a piece in The Times yesterday saying that schools should be banned from indulging in such games as Musical Chairs because they encouraged children to be aggressive. The Times pointed out that competition is essential for a child's development and the aggressive instinct is a necessary one. How dotty can educationists get? Where should we all be if we weren't prepared to stick up for ourselves in a hostile environment?

…What a splendid Christmas show for the younger children Spot's Birthday Party would make. Is there any chance of such a development? … I haven't enjoyed myself so much in a theatre *for ages. Thank you again – and here's wishing a similar success for* The Lighthouse Keeper's Lunch…

More thanks and love to you all –
Frank

12 Jun

Dear Frank,

…Talking of Tom's Midnight Garden, *I had a lovely day with Philippa Pearce, the author, last week. We went through the first draft and she suggested a few changes and ideas, none of them too big or structural. She is a delight. Just 80 years old (a mere chicken!) and full of enthusiasm. She lives yards away from the house which inspired the book, the house in which she lived for more than twenty years as a child…*

Thank you for expanding on your friendship with Harcourt Williams. What a fascinating group of people, including Ellen Terry, no less. Which makes me think of John Gielgud, without whom the world is a dimmer place… Sybil Thorndike too! Did I ever tell you that when I was at Oxford she came, with Lewis Casson, to the New Theatre in a play, the title of which has completely disappeared from my memory. Having met her a couple of times when I was an extra in The Workhouse Donkey *[at CFT] (she and Casson were, of course, in the second year of* Uncle Vanya*), I felt bold enough to invite her to lunch with the OUDS Committee. She was, I think, well into her 80s, yet wrote back saying sorry, she was unable to come to lunch, because she and Lewis were booked up for lunch every day of the week. However, would I like to pop in for a cup of tea at the Randolph on Friday afternoon? I did, of course, and I wish to heaven I could remember the conversation. I do remember her shouting at Casson quite a bit – he was pretty deaf and didn't join in the conversation much!*

So delighted you enjoyed Spot's Birthday Party. *I must say it is doing well. Richmond was a splendid week, with vast hordes of little children pouring through the doors. The decision has now been taken that the production will return to Oxford after its stint at Hammersmith. And I think they will try to organise another tour later this year or early next year.*

Which brings me to another bit of good news. The Belgrade, Coventry, have won a grant to tour The Twits *next year. Apparently, a very good tour has been lined up, including a Christmas season. I'm pleased about this, because, as you know, I didn't direct the production, yet thought it was extremely good. The tour will allow it to be seen more widely…*

Yours,
David

                                                          26 Jun

Dear Frank,

It's the morning of the first perf. of Lighthouse. *Fingers crossed we are ready. The children arrive at 9.00 and we go up at 2.30. My pro. actors have been wonderful in the schools…*

D

2000 The Lighthouse Keeper's Lunch –
                          Oxford Playhouse – 26ᵗʰ June 2000
Each day, seagulls steal Mr Grinling's lunch as it is being pullied across the sea by Mrs Grinling from her cottage to the lighthouse. Mrs Grinling comes up with a plan to foil the seagulls.

28 Jun

Dear David,

…I'm delighted that Spot's Birthday Party *is doing so well and is to return to Oxford from Hammersmith. And a tour for* The Twits*! That's splendid. It would have been a wicked waste if it had merely begun and ended in Coventry.*

Ever,
Frank

5 Jul

Dear Frank,

The Lighthouse Keeper's Lunch *was, I'm delighted and relieved to say, a great success. Very hard work in the sense that there was very little time, and children seemed to need to go to the loo more often than adults… But the whole experience proved very rewarding and worthwhile…*

All the schools had a great time, I think. Considering that the two classes from each school had not been chosen because of any interest or experience in drama, the results were tremendous. And the Playhouse team really pulled out the stops. We had a beautifully built and lit set, and the whole production really looked very professional. My team – Assistant Director, the Choreographer, Musical Director, a Designer and a Stage Manager entered into the spirit of things with great skill and commitment. And the two actors playing Mr and Mrs Grinling were, as I knew they would be, wonderful, both in schools and on the stage. They are both very experienced at working for and with children. They have both worked a lot at Polka. In fact, Richard Tate, who is about 60 now, played Cuckoo in the Nuffield, Southampton production of The Gingerbread Man *twenty years ago! I'm enclosing an article about the project and also the* Oxford Mail *review. All in all, it was a very invigorating spell which I thoroughly enjoyed, although it was very intensive and exhausting!…*

> Yours,
> *David*

25 Jul

Dear Frank,

…Talking of Lighthouse, *there are no plans to produce it again, although the Oxford Playhouse have kept the set just in case. Such a project is, of course, non-cost-effective. It cannot be done without sponsorship or subsidy. Most of the seats in the theatre were given away to the school that took part, and all the other seats were sold for only £2 each. And employing the team for a number of weeks, going into schools etc. cost money. But it is just the sort of work that theatres should be doing, in my belief…*

…On to your second letter. The possibility of adapting Harry Potter *has already arisen in a way. A producer rang me asking if I would be interested. In fact, he used to run Unicorn years ago, but now runs an independent company. I said I might be interested, but not hugely… He told me that the agents relayed to him information that Ms. Rowling has said she is not against the idea of a play, but would want it to be an original plot, rather than an adaptation of one of the existing books. I rather respect her for that. I have read one of the books, but wasn't really overwhelmed. They do seem to have a huge appeal, though. What is surprising is that they are so traditional in many ways – the boarding school setting, the idea of an academy for wizards (very like the Jill Murphy* Worst Witch *series), all very much in the line of* Billy Bunter *in some ways! I don't know. I suppose somebody will do it one day, but whether it will be me, who knows?!…*

> Yours,
> *David*

10 Aug

Dear David,

…I'm not surprised that French should hesitate about Spot's Birthday Party *because excellent though it is – and in spite of Vivien Goodwin's enjoyment of it – they must feel that the age of the audience it is designed for must necessarily limit the frequency of production. The problem with* The Lighthouse Keeper's Lunch *is not quite the same. The limitation must be posed less by the age of the audience than the difficulty of finding schools with the time, energy and resources to tackle it, no matter how much they might like to do so…*

> *Love to you all as ever –*
> *Frank*

4 Sep

Dear Frank,

…Samuel French have now decided to publish and take the amateur rights of Spot's Birthday Party, *I'm glad to say. No news yet on* The Lighthouse Keeper's Lunch, *mainly because nobody from French's was able to see it, and we have been waiting for the video to arrive, so that they can take a look at that. We are also talking to Scholastic, who publish the children's book upon which my musical was based. They may be interested in doing some sort of educational package, which might inspire schools to put on the play. This would really be the ideal situation. I don't think there are going to be many professional or even amateur companies who will want to do it, other than youth theatres (or younger) and schools.*

Rehearsals started last week for Tom's Midnight Garden. *Fingers crossed. Quite frankly, I think some of the casting is rather odd, but I will give them the benefit of the doubt! I like the*

Director and have decided to trust him! There is rather a clever musician working on it who will provide some atmospheric incidental music. I'm enclosing a leaflet giving times of the public performances, plus a photocopy of the times of the schools' performances. Just wondering if there might be a way of getting you (and Mary if she would like to come) along to see it. If there is a particular date that might be possible, then we could try and sort out the transport. Maybe I could come and pick you up and take you back!...

...Spot's Birthday Party went very well at the Lyric, Hammersmith, I'm glad to say. The weather was very hot, but business was brisk and the reaction excellent. Edward Snape, a young Producer who has always shown interest in children's work, came to see it with his young daughter, who, at the age of three, apparently turned to him in the interval and said, "I think we had better transfer this one, Daddy!" As a result, there are now plans to bring the show into the West End for Christmas 2001. It will be what I call a West End sandwich – a tour throughout the autumn and another tour in the spring with the West End season nicely in the middle. Fingers crossed all that will happen. The same Producer is involved with The Twits tour, which, as I think you know, the Belgrade, Coventry are arranging. It looks like a very good and long tour to major theatres. No date list yet, though.

Not only that, Unicorn have told me that they wish to tour Tom's Midnight Garden *in spring of next year. They have applied for Arts Council money to do this. One of the theatres they will visit will be Poole! If we hear positive things soon, perhaps we should postpone your visit until then.*

It is ironic that Coventry managed to get money from the Arts Council for The Twits, *Oxford managed to get money from them for* Spot's Birthday Party *and now, hopefully, they will cough up for Unicorn and* Tom's Midnight Garden. *It is ironic because, as you know, Whirligig found it impossible to get anything out of them if my name was attached to it! It was as though they felt I had had my day, or was too much of a one-man band. Fate decreed that I started working for other companies and it seems to have paid off. While in Cornwall, which proved very pleasant, even if the weather was a little mixed, I managed to finish* The Witches: Plays for Children *for Puffin. I'm enclosing a copy of the manuscript for your perusal, if you feel up to it! It is, of course, based on my full-length adaptation, but aimed at schools and youth groups who might want to just perform a short play rather than a full-length one. I did a similar volume of* BFG *plays a few years ago…*

All for now. Love and best wishes to you and Mary. Hope to see you soon,

David

13 Sep

Dear David,

…I'm delighted that French are undertaking Spot's Birthday Party. *I can foresee amateur groups, like ours here, having great fun with that, specially as a Christmas show. I can understand hesitancy over* The Lighthouse Keeper and his Lunch *because that would be very much an in-school production – lots of fun with teachers undertaking the two adult roles, but would they have the time, harassed as they are by the demands of the bureaucratic National Curriculum? I loved the story of the three-year-old at Hammersmith by the way. An impresario and an entrepreneur in the making. It's splendid to think of* Spot *gracing the West End in a sandwich, and* The Twits *on an extended tour.*

We are very eager to see Tom's Midnight Garden, *and your offer of carrying us to and from the theatre in Islington is more than generous. And if no tour materialises – it is easy for us to get across to Poole, as we did for* Spot…

237

And so to The Witches: Plays for Children. *These are excellent – I particularly love the dialogue between Boy and Bruno – but I am a little puzzled by the logistics of presentation. No piece is really complete enough in itself to be performed separately.* Real Witches *and* The Tree House Witch *might be done in the classroom by children familiar with the book, as most of them would probably be, but the following ones call for the space of an Assembly Hall which would mean offering them to a larger audience. And each ends with a note of expectation. The audience will feel cheated if the expectation is not satisfied. They are a series which needs to be on offer on a single occasion, not served up over an extended period as it might be on TV.*

And there is also the problem of expense. One or two wigs might be available from parents who followed the fashion of a few years ago of covering their natural hair with a wig, but would be unlikely to have bald pates on offer. And in the central scenes of The Grand High Witch, The Witches' Annual Meeting *and* The Boy Mouse Defeats the Witches, *a considerable number of wigs would need to be hired, as well as smoke machines and special furniture such as the trolley for the tureen, and the cheese. An art or craft department at school might once have furnished these, but are they now within the limitations of the national curriculum amid the pressures of league tables and Ofsted inspections? Oh, thank Goodness I'm not teaching anymore! If I were, I should want to do the lot of these delightful extracts in one Gorgeous Go with parents being charged for the privilege of watching their offspring perform to cover expenses – including French's fee and your slice of it!...*

Love to you all as ever – from Mary too, of course,
Frank

28 Sep

Dear Frank,

...No further news about the Tom's Midnight Garden *tour. The play opens on Saturday September 30th. I am hoping to go on October 5th (the first date available!). Also, Jacqui and I will be going on Saturday October 14th, which is the day when Philippa Pearce herself is coming. If you and Mary wanted to come then, we could I'm sure pick you up at Waterloo. The performance starts at 2.30 pm. But don't worry if it sounds too complicated a day.*

I have been to a couple of rehearsals, and saw a run-through last Thursday. It seems to be working well. The cast are good, I think, and care very much about the story and telling it faithfully. The surprise casting was that of Tom himself. The director has cast Dale Superville, last seen playing Spot! He actually plays the part very well, in spite of the fact that he is thirty years old! And the fact that he is a black actor doesn't really seem to jar at all. The ensemble feel of the production means that hopefully the audience will take it in their stride...

All good wishes,
David

2000 Tom's Midnight Garden –

Pleasance Theatre, London – 30th September 2000
Tom travels from the present to the past and meets Hatty, a ten-year-old girl. Over a short period of time, although Tom remains the same age, Hatty grows into a young woman.

4 Oct

Dear David,

...I'm delighted that Puffin are taking up The Witches: Plays for Children. *Yes, I think teachers – if they have any time – will*

enjoy making use of them in class without aiming to stage them fully. And of course the children will be familiar with the story and the characters. Your editor at Puffin must be rather genteel to object to the vulgarity of the Jenkinses. Surely that's the whole point of them?

It would be lovely to join you and Jacqui for Tom's Midnight Garden *on 14 Oct. But having chewed the proposal over, Mary and I think it would be rather more than we could cope with, so we're keeping our fingers crossed for the tour and a stop-over at Poole…*

Well! Yes! I do call that casting of Dale Superville as Tom surprising. But I can see no objection to his being played by a black actor. I think that using such a one for Romeo is stretching political correctness beyond reasonable bounds, though for Othello, of course, an advantage. I hadn't realised his colour as Spot – one didn't see a lot of him under his mask.

Frank

9 Oct

Dear Frank,

…I quite understand that it would be a little too much for you and Mary to come to Tom's Midnight Garden. *I'm actually rather relieved that you have come to this decision, because when I visited the theatre for the first time the other day, I found that not only was it up a rather long flight of outside steps, it required even more mountaineering skills when you got inside the building. The theatre is a converted warehouse, and you enter from the top of the auditorium. So once you have got up there, you have to come down the steps to your seat, assuming you are not sitting in the very back row!*

The production opened a week or so ago, and I managed to see two performances on Thursday. I'm really very pleased with it. There are a few quibbles, but I think the director has been very clever. The set is even more minimalist than the one you suggested, but actually seems to work well. All the mimed activities and props and furniture seem to be quite understandable to the audience. And the audiences I joined on Thursday were all inexperienced theatregoers aged about nine or ten, from wildly different cultural backgrounds from the world described in the book and play! But the magic seemed to hold them most of the time. There was a slight problem in that Mrs. Bartholomew is played by a 77-year-old actress, who, quite frankly, hasn't got the vocal strength any more to reach the back row – to reach the front row, if I'm honest! She also plays Aunt Grace who, I suppose, should really be in her 40s. The director has admitted that he just wasn't thinking very straight when he did his casting. He almost forgot that Mrs. B also played Aunt G! The young actor playing Tom (who played Spot, you remember) has pulled it off really very well. He is immensely likeable and very energetic, and the audience really respond to him. It made me realise how important it is to have an experienced actor playing the part, rather than an eight-year-old boy. The latter would be fine on television or on film, but would not be able to 'carry' the play in the theatre. I'm still hoping there will be a tour and that you will be able to see it.

…The last week, it has been back to reality and I must now think about doing a synopsis for James and the Giant Peach, which is the next Dahl to go into production for Christmas 2001. Actually, I may have to start on another one before that, because I have just been asked to do yet another Dahl, Fantastic Mr Fox, for the Belgrade, Coventry for spring 2001. Discussions are taking place about this…

David

14 Oct

Dear David,

…I trust the proofs of The Twits *did not require much correcting. I remember that S. French edited my stage directions with his insertions of UL, DR, etc., but I was too happy to cash his cheques to bother. I am more ready to take issue with Jeremy Kingston for describing Barrie's stage directions as 'soppy'. They are generally so illuminating and amusing that one wishes an audience might have the benefit of them – I believe there has been a production of* Peter Pan *which attempted this. That little piece at the end of Act V is quite terrifying. It shows that Barrie had no illusions about children – the Davies boys left him none…*

…It's great that you've been asked to do more work for Dahl. I won't detain you any longer except to say thank you again for a wonderful letter.

Love – in which Mary joins me – to you all,
F

The discussion of Barrie's *Peter Pan* was followed by a visit by DW to a production of another of his plays, *Dear Brutus.*

25 Oct

Dear Frank,

I sat in the auditorium of Nottingham Playhouse on Saturday night wishing so much that you could have been beside me to witness what I truly think is a wonderful production of Dear Brutus*… A full house was, I think, amazed at how funny it was, how powerful it was, and how moving it was. As far as I could see, Jeremy Sams had not tinkered too much with the text (which I had re-read before seeing the production), and the whole cast performed it without any trace of tongue-in-cheek.*

242

It worked a treat. The moment when Dearth realises he has not got a daughter after all was heartstopping – you could have heard a pin drop... And, as you probably read, they added a chilling moment at the end when Margaret tries to get in the French window, making everybody think of Peter Pan. *I must say this worked extremely well, particularly as the girl playing Margaret had been so good in the second act. ... Something that was demonstrated beautifully was the sheer theatricality of Barrie, and I think it is this aspect which surprised many of the younger members of the audience, who had gone along expecting something rather whimsical and fey. They came out shattered! One girl in her twenties, who works in the marketing department somewhere, couldn't get over how tingly the whole thing had been. I suppose it is the extraordinary blend of the day-to-day – 'ordinary' people in a room – with the supernatural, the 'what if' motif and the fact that (rather like in* Tom's Midnight Garden) *there is never a feeling that you are watching fantasy. Both realities are as haunting and as frightening as each other...*

...Now to some of the points raised in your letter. First of all, Tom's Midnight Garden. *On the very day you were writing your epistle, Saturday 14th, Jacqui, Katherine and I set off to see the show, which was also attended by Philippa Pearce, her daughter and her agent. My agent also came, plus several other celebrity types, especially invited because Philippa was going. They had laid on a special tea for everybody and were treating it as a sort of gala performance. Imagine the anguish and embarrassment when it was discovered that the lighting board had completely gone down. Not a flicker, not a single beam of light was forthcoming, except for a couple of working lights on stage and the house lights in the auditorium. In such boringly untheatrical mode we had to witness the performance. As you can imagine, lighting plays a significant part in the production, so it really was frustrating. Having said that, the actors really came up trumps and proved how strong the story*

is (which delighted Philippa!) and, though I say it myself, that the adaptation was enough to keep the attention of everybody above the age of seven or so. People were most complimentary, I must say, and Philippa was really excited. She has agreed to come and see the production again next week, when hopefully the gremlins will stay away!...

> *Yours as ever,*
> *D.*

28 Oct

Dear David,

...oh, what a shame that the lighting apparatus should fail on such an occasion at The Pleasance. (I forebear from jests about the unpleasantness!) The single consolation must be that though the audience of celebrities – including your agent and the authoress – could not appreciate the skill of the production, they must surely have been able to realise the excellence of the text. I wonder how many of them were already acquainted with the book?...

...How I wish I could have been with you at the Nottingham Playhouse... Your graphic account of Dear Brutus *was most exciting. Perhaps with the present interest of young folk in fantasy, Barrie may – tactfully updated – enjoy a come-back. ...I'm not so sure about the reappearance of Margaret at the window at the end. Very effective, no doubt. But it seems to continue the dream world of the second act beyond its proper limits...*

> *Love – Frank*

Attention then moved to the next proposed Dahl adaptation, *Fantastic Mr Fox*.

9 Nov

Am back in Bexhill trying to knock out a quick synopsis for an adaptation of DAHL'S Fantastic Mr Fox, *suddenly requested by Belgrade, Coventry, for production in APRIL! WHY CAN'T I EVER SAY NO??!!! Do hope you and Mary are well – love to both – I'll reply to your last letter next week!*

Best, David x

14 Nov

Delighted to hear that you've booked in to Bexhill for another Dahl effort! That'll be another piece to look forward to or (if you insist) to which to look forward…

Keep on Dahling! Love to all,
F.

15 Nov

Dear Frank,

…I'm delighted to say that on November 4th, Philippa Pearce saw Tom's Midnight Garden *complete with all its excellent lighting, and once again expressed her delight at the production. Plans for the tour apparently proceed apace. No concrete list as yet, but am hoping very much that Poole will retain its week on the schedule. These things do change around alarmingly. …I'm enclosing the current list for the tour of* The Twits *next year… Anyway, have a look and see if anywhere looks possible! I'd love you to see that one. Talking of which (again!), I spent three days in Coventry attending rehearsals of* The Twits. *It will be opening early in December at the University of Warwick Arts Centre. The cast seemed very talented. Mrs. Twit is doing it for the third time! And for this production she is being joined by her real-life husband as Mr. Twit. Rather a nice story for the newspapers.*

...I enjoyed your comments about Dear Brutus. *You are probably right about the reappearance of Margaret at the window at the end. However, I must say it was quite cleverly done. Everybody else left the room, the lighting changed, so that you felt you were back in the dream world, and then Margaret appeared. She was not, of course, observed by anybody in the play, only by us, the audience. I think it unlikely that Barrie would have wanted this, but I must say it worked theatrically and was really rather moving, as I'm sure you can imagine.*

...While [at the Belgrade, Coventry], I had a meeting with the two people in charge, who persuaded me (oh, why can't I say no!) to interrupt everything and do a quick adaptation of Dahl's Fantastic Mr Fox *for production at the Belgrade in April of next year. I think something must have fallen through, giving an empty slot to be filled. I, of course, said I would have a go, so last week spent three days in my usual hotel room in Bexhill trying to knock out a synopsis. I managed to get something done, which hopefully will work. If it all goes ahead, I have to try to write it before Christmas!*

This still leaves James and the Giant Peach, *and I have promised to deliver a synopsis of that by December. Heigh ho!...*

Yours, as ever,
David

By this time, the relationship between the two men was of such mutual trust that FW felt able to share his misgivings about *Fantastic Mr Fox* and the proposed adaptation.

20 Nov

Dear David,

...Now I come to Fantastic Mr Fox – *not one of Dahl's more successful pieces, I think, because of the somewhat doubtful ethic*

noticed by Badger – and Badger is more sympatico, I feel, than Mr Fox as a hero! It strikes me that the logistics of the production are pretty formidable – the children and youths will need a lot of patience on somebody's part, and the two doubles may not be very easy. The setting seems more elaborate than usual, too. I cannot quite visualise how the 'huge wooden table' will work. If it is to be raked and revolved – as I think it must be – will not the rake be very steep if one end of the table is to be at normal table height – 27"– 29" I believe – and the other, the upper end, to be high enough to allow for the fox's den underneath? It will need to have head-room of at least 5 feet, surely? 5'3'. Then how will the animals be able to sit round it? Will they be on sloping benches? Will it not be very cumbersome? It will need to afford a generous area for the action taking place on it.

It's clear that overground and underground must be simultaneously visible – as they have to be for Act IV of Peter Pan where the problem is solved horizontally, with a two-tier setting – devised long before Alan Ayckbourn had the idea of presenting several rooms at once, with interaction between them. There could still be communication between the two levels by trap doors, and the foxes could dig, dig, dig sideways.

Maybe I'm unnecessarily bothered and the whole thing is less complicated – and costly – than it looks on paper. I suspect the three farmers will probably steal the show! They're so beastly but endearing, though the very young fox who is left behind will have everybody rooting for him! I'm reminded of a 2½-year-old fairy I had in an open-air production of A Midsummer Night's Dream in Teheran who failed to 'skip hence' on cue and had to be fetched by an older fairy before the play could proceed. It was a huge success! But the infant never managed to repeat it in subsequent performances...

...I look forward to James and the Giant Peach. Heigh-ho, as you say! Don't take time off to answer this scrawl, but I thought I ought to let you have my misgivings about Mr Fox, *though they're probably merely my inadequate imagination and visualisation of the 'staging' in the synopsis.*

Ever –
Frank

Dear Frank,

This is a very short letter which will hopefully arrive before Christmas, but, with the post in the state it is in, I'm not sure!
Please find a copy of the new book... Also the first draft of Fantastic Mr Fox *for your perusal.*
I am aware of the fact that I haven't answered your last letter yet, but that will have to wait until the New Year!
Thinking of you and Mary.
Love and best wishes from all of us.

Yours,
David

29 Dec
Dear David,

Huge thanks for your letter and the draft of Fantastic Mr Fox. *I've enjoyed it very much, though I still can't visualise how the animals are to sit round the table! But I'm sure you'll make it work. The dialogue and the building of concerted speech is splendid and the 'curtains' for both parts (especially the couplet for Act I) very neat. On page 7, I was suddenly pulled up by Bean's "My dear Boggis–". This didn't seem in character. On the whole, I suspect the nasty farmers will upstage the animals! The morality of the plot seems to me questionable but that's Dahl's responsibility, not yours! It makes a very exciting narrative anyway with bags of 'suddenlies' and suspense.*
The schedule for Tom's Midnight Garden *was welcome too,*

with confirmation of the date for Poole. ...it's an easy run with easy parking...

> *Love to you all as ever –*
> *Frank*

31 Dec

Dear Frank,

...Thanks for your Fantastic Mr Fox *kind words – I agree "My dear Boggis" is odd – it is Dahl's line, in fact... maybe it is meant to be delivered with sarcasm! As to the animals sitting round the table, I'm waiting to see what the designer has come up with!! Maybe they'll end up sitting on the stage around the outside of the acting area...*

> *Love,*
> *Dx*

2001

The early months of 2001 saw further developments on current projects, as well as ongoing tours of earlier shows.

23 Jan

Dear Frank,

...I have no news on Fantastic Mr Fox. *People are strange! I delivered the script on December 21st. It is now January 16th and I have heard not one word from anybody at the Belgrade, Coventry. I have just decided to contact them, although I really feel I shouldn't! I think it is so rude, apart from anything else. What does it mean? Do they hate the script? Do they love it?*

Are they working away getting ready for a production? But not to acknowledge its arrival or its reception amongst the people meant to be putting it on, it seems extraordinary to me…

…As I dictate this, I am getting ready to go to Oxford for a few hours. I have been asked to see a production of Arabian Nights *at the Old Fire Station. I also have a meeting at the Playhouse about the forthcoming* Spot's Birthday Party *tour.*

Yours,
David

29 Jan

Dear David,

Another splendid news-crammed packet from you, for which many thanks. Fascinating stuff!

…The review of The Twits *is splendid. I hope the tour of* Spot's Birthday Party *is now well on the way…*

Love to you all,
Frank

15 Feb

Dear Frank,

…Coventry are happy with Fantastic Mr Fox. *After waiting five weeks before hearing from them, it turned out that the Producer lady had thought she had sent me a fax. She obviously hadn't, and admits now that she didn't, but at the time, 'it was in her head' …Rehearsals start on March 5th. Meanwhile,* The Twits *is in rehearsal again and opens at the large Milton Keynes Theatre next week with a huge advance at the Box Office, I'm glad to say. In fact, business everywhere seems to be very brisk.* Tom's Midnight Garden *starts rehearsing next month too!* Spot's Birthday Party *is now scheduled to start rehearsal on September 3rd, for an autumn tour, plus a West End season. Fingers crossed.*

...Early in March, I am setting off to my little room in the hotel at Bexhill to try to conquer James and the Giant Peach, *which I have recklessly promised by Easter to both Cardiff and Birmingham, whose productions will be this coming Christmas. I haven't quite got the synopsis right yet, and I must do that before I actually go to the hotel; otherwise, valuable time gets wasted!*

...The other day, I went to the Royal Court, not to see a play, but to witness the presentation of the first Children's Award for writing plays for children, organised and sponsored by the Arts Council, believe it or not. A very welcome move in the right direction, although the only people present to witness the presentation of the prize to the esteemed Mike Kenny were children's theatre practitioners! No press or practitioners from the mainstream theatre. This has led me to write a letter to the Arts Council suggesting they try to incorporate it within the Olivier Awards to give it a bit more profile and status. But it is a step in the right direction...

Yours,
David

23 Feb

Dear Frank and Mary,

Forgive me for being lazy and not writing an individual letter to everybody – thank you so much for remembering my birthday – much appreciated!

...Now it's back to business as usual – I have Fantastic Mr Fox *going into rehearsal soon;* The Twits *is on tour;* Tom's Midnight Garden *will be on tour from March (in New York in October). There is another play to write before Easter, plus schools to visit (storytellings), meetings to attend, etc., etc. – and all in all, things go well!*

Love,
David

25 Feb

Dear David,

…Anyway, I shall be looking forward to James and the Giant Peach. *Why do theatre managements always approach things in such a rush? Don't they ever take a long-term view and work out what their requirements will be? But, at least, serving Cardiff and Birmingham simultaneously should save time and labour. Two visits to Bexhill for the price of one, as it were!*

…I think your idea, submitted to the Arts Council, that Children's Awards should be incorporated with the Olivier is excellent. Do you know any influential friends of that body who might undertake to back it? It really would be a giant step in the right direction…

Love to you all as ever,
Frank

19 Mar

Dear Frank,

*…*Fantastic Mr Fox *is into its third week of rehearsal in Coventry. I went to the read-through, which revealed a very talented cast. I didn't stay to meet the forty or more local community cast. I'm hoping to see a run-through at the end of this week.*

The week before last, I was in Bexhill – hopefully, you got a postcard – and managed to finish the first draft of James And The Giant Peach. *This project rather crept up on me, in as much as I only did a very, very brief synopsis, which didn't even warrant sending to you for comment, it was so bald and basic! However, the two producers in Birmingham and Cardiff were happy, and suddenly the deadline – Easter – approached and I felt I had to get a move on! …Hopefully, we will be on target and deliver it before Easter. You will of course be sent a copy for perusal.*

Tom's Midnight Garden is also in rehearsal. I haven't had time to visit them yet! Hopefully, I will see a run-through during the week. They open at the Cochrane next week. The tour is booking well, apparently. And the tour of The Twits is doing wonderful business, I'm delighted to say…

Yours,
David

26 Mar

Dear David,

…I'm delighted that The Twits is doing so well. I can't be sure whether or not I'll manage to get to Tom's Midnight Garden at Poole Arts Centre, there are so many 'variables' as I believe they are called, but I'm keeping my fingers crossed – they're getting a bit stuck crosswise these days.

Domestic duties call me. The nice young Cleaning Lady is de-frosting the Freezer and I must go and assist. She's just announced it's ready to receive its contents which have been under wraps and 'cool bags' in the 'snug'. I just hope nothing will have 'gone orf!'…

Love – love – love,
Frank

The draft of *James and the Giant Peach* was sent to FW at the end of March and his response was soon on its way.

2 Apr

Dear David,

I've hugely enjoyed James and the Giant Peach. The characterisation is marvellous and the dialogue outstanding.

I especially enjoyed the Queen Mary scene, though I doubt whether children will really appreciate the parody of seamanship! Earthworm is quite adorable.

It will make great demands on the designer and stage management and the doubling will need to be very nifty, but the idea of beginning in New York and introducing the insects as performers of the play within the play is brilliant, besides giving a very satisfactory sense of form to the whole. It must be the most difficult of all the jobs you've done for Dahl.

I've only one small suggestion to offer. On my first reading, my dimming wits were confused by the shift of the action from Central Park to U.K. On p.6, James could say either

"I lived happily with my father and mother in England..."

or

"We had a beautiful house by the sea in England..."

'England' being the last word in either case to emphasize the change of location.

When the peach stone house becomes the aunts' cottage, I take it that the façade will be differentiated in some way, perhaps with roses round the door or some such Anglicanism!

I notice that many of the stage directions offer 'suggestions' which are optional rather than authoritative, thereby leaving much to the director's ingenuity. I think that's very useful and it will make comparison between the two productions even more interesting.

I'm in favour of the verses being sung, provided none of the words get lost. I have always thought that the reputation of the D'Oyly Carte Co for clarity of diction depended not just on their skilled enunciation but the care with which Gilbert provided words that could be clearly enunciated – the selection of vowels and consonants – and Sullivan's rarely providing more than two notes to any one syllable except when he was deliberately parodying grand opera. Both librettist and composer ensured their works should be heard. In Grand Opera generally it doesn't matter what language is used – the words are never distinguishable in any known lingo and the whole piece might just as well be bellowed forth on 'ah'! B. Britten does better than most but even in Peter Grimes, *surtitles are not to be sneezed at.*

Congratulations on the Peach. *It will tax the ingenuity of directors and casts but you have marvellously transferred it from the printed page to the stage…*

Love –
Frank

2001 Fantastic Mr Fox –

Belgrade Theatre, Coventry – 3rd April 2001

The farmers try to get rid of the fox, who regularly steals food from their farms, only to be outwitted by Fantastic Mr Fox at every turn.

4 Apr

Dear Frank,

Many thanks indeed for your lovely response to James and the Giant Peach. *I'm glad you liked it.*

Thank you, too, for your excellent suggestion about reminding the audience that James starts off in England. A very good point indeed.

The Birmingham producers have responded positively to the script. I haven't heard yet from Cardiff! Yes, the set will require ingenuity. But I think it is all possible.

More possible than the set I described for Fantastic Mr Fox. *You pointed this out very astutely! You couldn't understand how a false stage could be created to look like a table, without having a very unrealistic rake! Having just returned from the first night of the production in Coventry, I can tell you that you were spot on!*

The designer, in the end, came up with a revolving structure, which allowed us to see underground and above ground at the same time, as well as providing a network of tunnels for the foxes. It all works reasonably well, and the toppling of the tree at the end of Act 1 is very effective.

The whole stage is covered with peat! So real earth appears to be dug at regular intervals, and the whole thing has a very rural and earthy feel, beautifully complemented by the music, by John Kirkpatrick, who is a noted folk musician. He plays the squeezebox in various outfits like the Albion Band, as well as performing solo. He has come up with some lovely folky music, which works a treat.

The opening performance was not straightforward, although the audience will not have noticed anything untoward. But when I arrived, the day before, for a dress rehearsal, I was told that this would be impossible, because the technical, which had been going on for five days, still wasn't finished. This was partly because a lighting designer had to be got rid of, having wasted so much time creating lighting states that didn't work… Apparently, the poor man had had a bereavement recently, but was protesting that it wasn't affecting his work! Alas, in the end, he was despatched and another one brought in, but for the whole company, including the many children taking part, the whole experience was like wading through treacle…

Not only that, the day after I arrived, which was the day of the actual opening, the Stage Manager 'on the book', arguably the most important person in the building at this stage of a production, having to call out all the lighting, flying and sound cues, didn't turn up for work! It turned out that her husband had tried to commit suicide and she didn't dare leave the house. Much more drama off the stage than on it!

It ended up with the director calling the show, something I admired tremendously – I don't think I could do it – and the curtain going up three-quarters of an hour late. But everybody seemed to enjoy it very much and I think, once things settle down, it will be good.

Going back to James, *I think I agree about the rhymes/ songs. If the songs can be accompanied simply, possibly by the Grasshopper, then we will hopefully be able to hear the words. Whether or not I will write the tunes, I don't know. Probably I should, to give some sort of consistency...*

...I was sitting in the theatre in Coventry last night, trying not to worry (!), when I suddenly realised that also opening the same evening was Tom's Midnight Garden *in Brighton and* The Twits *in Wolverhampton! What a triple! Hope they all do well this week.*

Love and best wishes, as ever,
David

7 Apr

Dear Frank,

Here's a nice review! – the production is selling out, I'm glad to say, as is The Twits *and* Tom's Midnight Garden*! A happy treble –*

Would you like me to take you to T.M.G. in Poole on either April 26th or 27th – 10.30 perf? We would leave at, say, 8.30 AM! I would collect you...

Best,
David

9 Apr

Dear David,

...The reply to that is OH YES! What a lark!! And either date will do, with the 27th preferred. I'm sometimes a bit shattered on Thursdays after my shopping expedition on Wednesday with Sheila. I'll be ready and waiting by 8.30 am!

What a splendid review of Fantastic Mr Fox, *especially after that traumatic first performance. And the* Guardian *notice of* TMG *is very satisfactory and useful, though I do think DW should have been named therein. I do hope you'll undertake the setting of the songs for* James. *A simple violin accompaniment by Grasshopper would be fine. What a delightful character he is!*

...Congrats again on the Triple Crown of FMF, TMG, *and* TT!

Love to all,
Frank

Family issues then intervened, including the death of DW's stepfather and ongoing hospital treatment for Mary, FW's sister. DW also returned to the USA to see a production of *The BFG* at Dallas Children's Theater.

3 Jul

Dear Frank,

Several weeks have passed since I last wrote to you. I'm hoping that things at your end are improving and that Mary is progressing...

...Meanwhile, workwise, I am casting The BFG *for its Christmas season and long tour and also* The Gingerbread Man *for its 25th anniversary season in Maidenhead. We have found quite a few good people, but need a few more! There are more auditions this week.*

Last week, I went to Dallas for three days to see the Dallas Children's Theater production of The BFG. *I had a very enjoyable time. I like the people there, and they work very hard and enthusiastically. As usual, the production was rather short on Dahl's darker imaginative touches. The giants lumbered on rather like refugees from* The Muppets, *or even a Disney roadshow! There was little sense of threat, which, to my mind, lessens the theatricality and excitement. However, the audiences responded very well and it had a very good review in the Dallas newspaper...*

…Have been asked by Unicorn to adapt a splendid book called Coram Boy, *by Jamila Gavin. I think you would enjoy the book, which, although written as a children's novel, is really rather adult in content. I'm still not sure whether I want to do it, but will take it to Cornwall and read it a few times more.*

The Twits *comes to the end of its tour in a couple of weeks' time. It has been very successful, I'm glad to say. Very large houses and very good reviews. I saw the production again at Richmond Theatre the other day. I feel it has broadened somewhat, as often happens on a long tour. It is rather remorseless now and lacks any of the subtlety it once had! But the bare bones are still very much in place and the audience responded well…*

With love,
David

Another US visit for DW followed in August, when he was in San Diego.

28 Aug

Dear David,

Huge thanks for The Witches *plays. Puffin has presented them very attractively and I'm sure young Dahlites will be eager to do them. The only one with real difficulty may be the* Annual Meeting *because of the wigs required coming expensive. I notice in the list 'Other books by Roald Dahl' opposite the title page, under 'Plays',* Fantastic Mr Fox *(adapted by Sally Reid) and* James and the Giant Peach *(adapted by Richard George). Who are these interlopers? And how come?…*

Love to you all (from Mary too) –
Frank

Dear Frank,

…Glad you approved of The Witches: Plays for Children *– already a professional company in Northampton is using it as a schools' touring production for 5 actors – (quite how they will distribute the roles, I don't know!)…*

…The Richard George and Sally Reid Dahl adaptations you saw listed were written some years ago – for children to perform – …Dahl himself sanctioned them and they sell quite well – I'm hoping that my James, *and* F. Mr Fox *will both grab some of the market from them!…*

> *Love and best wishes to both,*
> *David*

Discussions of children's theatre took a back seat for a while when FW reported, not totally enthusiastically, on the restoration and reopening of the Theatre Royal, Winchester, before a letter from DW reported on his San Diego experience.

11 Sep

Dear Frank,

…Our American trip now seems long ago! It was most enjoyable, though not the most relaxing holiday! We were on the move quite a lot. First of all, we went to San Diego for a children's theatre conference. The city is delightful. Nice temperature most of the time, on the sea, a wonderful public-funded park, interesting buildings and things to do, including the famous zoo, which we visited briefly and admired hugely. The conference itself was very enjoyable, and we managed to meet up with a lot of old friends, some from Chicago, some from Dallas and some from New York. Most of them are in the academic world, teaching students to

write, act and direct for children. One or two run their own theatres. As I may have said before, the interesting difference between the UK and the US is that children's theatre is taken seriously over there by the academics. Over here, it is totally ignored by that sector. So most of the people who do children's theatre in America either do it within a University setting or learn about it there, and then do it professionally. There are a certain number of key University professors that I am now cultivating, in the hope that my plays will appear on more and more booklists over the next few years!

My acting/directing workshop was attended by about 80 people, quite a few more than were expected. People had to rush around grabbing chairs from other rooms in order to accommodate everybody. This was gratifying, as you can imagine. And the twenty copies of my Theatre for Children *book, sent over from Chicago by the publisher, sold out within minutes of the end of the workshop! We were relieved by this, because we had visions of having to carry them all home in our luggage! Sadly, Samuel French Inc., the American arm of the company, did absolutely nothing to help publicise my work during the Conference. My numerous messages to the Los Angeles office and the New York office went unheeded. Luckily, the London office came to my rescue and sent over a whole lot of playscripts for me to give away, and made me a couple of nice display boards to take over. I am discussing with the Samuel French people over here how we can get more positive action from their American counterparts…*

…Back home, things have returned to normal. We are still casting The BFG *and* The Gingerbread Man. *The process seems to be taking forever. Several people have been offered parts and then turned them down, which is very frustrating! Fingers crossed we are just about there…*

Yours,
David

In his next letter, FW mentioned a local open-air production, leading him to remember a very different setting for alfresco theatre.

16 Sep

Dear David,

...Mottisfont, an ancient abbey now celebrated for its rose garden and Rex Whistler's tromp d'oeil decorations of one of its salons. It's near Romsey and is used by a Southampton group of amateurs to present open-air productions which generally require the spectators to up their rugs and cushions during the action which shifts from one front of the building to another. When they put on A Man for All Seasons *they cunningly made use of the River Test, which flows serenely through the grounds, for the King's arrival to see Thomas More in Chelsea. The chancy weather of course is always a problem because if it rains the spectators – and actors – have to scarper. The actors can retreat into the house, but the audience can only retreat to their motors in the car park about a quarter of a mile away. I've always felt that open-air productions are too risky in this country. In Iran* I put on* The Tempest *and* A Midsummer Night's Dream *in a superb setting and knew that the weather would co-operate. We also did Flecker's* Hassan *translated into Persian with real camels en route to Samarkand! But I invited local talent to direct that one!...*

* then called Persia.

...Which reminds me. Were Mr Burton's [Lance Burton, Magician] – oh no! I'm thinking of the Siegfried and Roy Show [in Las Vegas] – white tigers roaming the stage, real tigers, like my British Council camels, or were they an illusion? I should have mentioned the acting space for those open-air productions was designed as a tennis court, rather wider than any at Wimbledon,

and our stage was a broad bank, smothered in flowers, at one end of it, about five feet high. The width created a sort of wide-screen effect which could present problems. As part of a gesture of Anglo-Russian solidarity, I staged there a scene from Hamlet *and a scene from* The Seagull *– in English, of course. The audience, a very cultured lot, were expected to follow the action without translation, having all been properly schooled. The occasion was graced by Chekov's widow, Olga Knipper, once a famous Russian actress. She marched to centre stage after the plays and held forth in Russian, equally of course, and of course there was no simultaneous or any other translation, so nobody understood a word. Having done, she rolled up her script and marched off stage right, hotly pursued from stage left by the British Council Representative with a vast goodwill bouquet. It was like that famous scene in* Uncle Vanya *and evoked lively applause. I think he caught up with her in the shrubbery which provided wing space – and had sheltered the camels for* Hassan. *Oh, I did have a lovely war!...*

*...Have I ever told you that one of my first pupils became the father of Antony Worrall Thompson, the TV cook?*** *His parents ran the Watford Rep, but he took to the stage as Michael Ingham and appeared with the likes of Edith Evans and Donald Wolfit, but ended as an Equity representative in Wales. He died several years ago. Another was Michael Balfour, who made a splendid Sir Toby Belch at Clayesmore, became a successful character actor in early TV, toured for years as the chimney sweep in Dorothy Sayers'* Busman's Honeymoon, *haunted by Sayers throughout the tour, and sadly took to the bottle, whether to escape D.L.S. or not I never knew. And then there was Stephen Joseph, whose mother was Hermione Gingold. He was responsible for my first publication (I got 8 guineas for it) by Samuel French. It was called* Ask a Policeman *and I wrote it for his puppet theatre. In*

** *Not that I had anything to do with this!*

the course of a Geography lesson*** he put up his hand and asked, "Please, sir, will you write me a play for my theatre?" I said, "Yes, of course. Just keep on drawing a few more maps and I'll see what I can do." And did...

So, with love to you and all yours, in which Mary joins me, ever yours,

Frank

2 Oct

Dear Frank,

...Meanwhile, it is back to reality and preparations for The BFG and The Gingerbread Man.

Much enjoyed reading about your productions in Persia. Lovely to have real camels, even if you didn't direct the play! What a shame that part of the world now seems so remote, almost alien. I suppose it was good to see that they were joining in this so-called coalition, but in the minds of many there will still be suspicion, albeit less than with Iraq...

...Yes, the white tigers of Siegfried and Roy were the real thing, and are apparently the only ones left in the world, thanks to the breeding programme undertaken by the two magicians. There are none left in the wild, it seems. I must dig out an article about them for you!

I loved your story about Chekov's widow holding forth in unintelligible Russian! Talking of Chekov, the Uncle Vanya, starring Tom Courtenay, at the Royal Exchange, Manchester, has had some wonderful reviews. I wonder if they will transfer it.

Much enjoyed your stories about Stephen Joseph. As you know, he influenced hugely the young Alan Ayckbourn, who has named his theatre in Scarborough after him, and who insisted on it being a theatre in the round, partly as a tribute to Stephen Joseph, but

---

*** My method was applicable to any subject whether I was qualified for it or not.

also because he loves the freedom it gives him. Presumably, it also means that they spend less on scenery for the productions!…

Yours,
David

Dear David,

Oh, HURRAH! Tom's Midnight Garden *arrived this a.m. to put a little cheer into a very dismal morning. Huge thanks for it…*

I hope preparations for The G.B. *and* B.F.G. *are going well and that casting problems have been overcome…*

Mary says send… her love. Here 'tis! With mine,
Frank

Dear Frank,

…Jacqui and I are, if all goes according to plan, off to New York on Saturday the 20th. It is not the ideal time to go…

However, the company will be out there, already performing Tom's Midnight Garden, *and I feel we must show solidarity. I also have a storytelling to do at the University, plus several meetings.*

We now have a full cast and crew for The Gingerbread Man *and* The BFG. *Rehearsals for the latter start on November 19th and for the former on November 5th. The overlapping weeks will be the test!…*

Love and best wishes,
David

After a successful US visit, despite it coinciding with the dreadful events of 9/11 – the attack on the World Trade Centre – it was back to overseeing ongoing productions.

12 Nov

Dear Frank,

I'm dictating this the day before rehearsals commence for The BFG. *The next six or seven weeks will be fairly intensive! In week 3 of* The BFG *rehearsals, we begin rehearsing* The Gingerbread Man. *The technical week for* The BFG *overlaps with week 2 of* The Gingerbread Man! *At least I have the support of Sheila and Adam, my Choreographer and Associate Director, both of whom have worked on both shows before. Indeed, Adam has been in both as an actor, and has directed* The BFG *once. And I think we have a very good company of actors for both shows.*

Last Thursday, I did the Magic and Music Show *(twice!) at the Norden Farm Centre for the Arts, Maidenhead, the theatre where we are taking* The Gingerbread Man. *It really is a delightful venue, newly opened, following lottery funding. A kindly farmer, whose family had owned a farm on the outskirts of Maidenhead for a century or so, offered the council the farm upon his demise, as long as they dedicated it to local community use. They had the vision to turn it into an arts centre. The new theatre, built next door to the original Georgian farmhouse (now used as offices) is small, but beautifully designed, in my opinion. Modern, yes, but friendly and technically very advanced. I enjoyed my two performances, and am looking forward to seeing* The Gingerbread Man *there.*

…We had splendid weather in New York. It was really warm the whole time. No rain. Rather like the last few days in Wimbledon, and hopefully Winchester!…

Now to our New York trip! Jacqui and I were somewhat

daunted by the idea of going, following the horrors of September 11th. Our main concern, I think, was that something might happen here, and that we would find ourselves the wrong side of the Atlantic. Anyway, all went extremely well. We almost felt guilty how much we enjoyed our week in the Big Apple! Tom's Midnight Garden *had been very well received upon its opening the week before, and business was very good, even though a few schools were cancelling. This was mainly due to the fact that they were over the other side of the bridges leading to Manhattan Island, and parents quite reasonably didn't want their children to be stuck the wrong side, should the bridges be attacked. But the public performances in the early evening all did extremely well, I'm glad to say. We had a nice review in the* New York Times, *which I will send you. And there were a few other good reviews, too...*

We took the cruise round the bottom of Manhattan Island, from where one could see smoke rising from Ground Zero, plus the cranes and arclights. This was a sobering experience, although we found it quite extraordinary that more damage hadn't been caused by the collapse of the Twin Towers. If they had fallen sideways, they would have knocked over several adjacent buildings. All these are still there, and, to be honest, from the water, one can hardly see the gap...

We visited Professor Lowell Swortzell and his wife, Nancy. I had been wanting to get to know this man for many years. He is a world authority on children's theatre, and has written a biography of Aurand Harris, who is sometimes compared with me – he is, or was, the major American children's playwright. Twenty-five years ago, we were interviewed, in the back of a taxi in Piccadilly Circus, for some extraordinary reason, for the Radio 4 programme Kaleidoscope. *He was older than me, but we got on immediately, both of us thinking in much the same way about the importance of children's theatre. Lowell Swortzell managed to evade me for several years, before I*

*was introduced to him in London, funnily enough, earlier
this year. Then we met again in San Diego at the Conference
I attended. He lives in New York and works at the University.
Jacqui and I had a lovely lunch and afternoon with him and
his wife. Various coincidences emerged. One, which was quite
extraordinary, was that the pair of them stayed in our house
in Wimbledon thirty or so years ago, when they were asked
to dog sit by a friend of the then owners, William Mann
(Music Critic of* The Times*) and his wife. They remembered
the house well, and the garden! What are the chances of that
happening?!…*

> *Love and best wishes,*
> *David*

DW's report of his visit to New York reminded FW of his much earlier
stay there.

16 Nov

Dear David,

*…Your letter delighted both self and Mary and we were
especially glad that your trip to New York (why is it called The
Big Apple?) was so enjoyable despite the recent disaster. I'm
sure your activities were a morale booster. Thrilling to have*
Tom's Midnight Garden *staged on Broadway and evidently
being well received. Some years ago, I seem to remember, there
were all sorts of difficulties involved with Brits appearing
in the US. I take it these no longer obtain. What size of
playhouse is the New Victory Theater? I remember The Radio
City Music Hall and those energetic Rockettes. The ones you
saw must be the grandchildren, or even great-grandchildren
of my lot!*

*I also took in the Met, for the ballet (can't remember what
it was) and a John Van Druten play in which the most exciting*

moment was at the breaking of half-a-dozen eggs on stage to make an omelette!! Having just arrived from UK (it was late in 1946) where rationing was still the norm, I could only just prevent myself from shouting out "You can't do that!" and creating a riot or a shower of shushing! I hope you'll get that invitation to teach a course at the University there in 2003, which will be upon us before we can say 'Jack Robinson'. (Mem: who was J. Robinson? And why should we say him?)

Were there any difficulties in flight, or at the airports? It was certainly a memorable time to go. I can appreciate the concern people feel about the bombing, but at whatever cost. These determined terrorists must be stopped. I have long suspected that bombing may be an over-rated military exercise. I was an airman at Southend in 1940 and the airfield – a Fighter station – was attacked with tremendous sound and fury but the place wasn't put out of action at all. I was part of a team manning an anti-aircraft gun which wouldn't work, because it had come from Sweden minus a vital part. So we just ducked for cover!…

Ever – Frank

2001 James and the Giant Peach –
Sherman Theatre, Cardiff, 16th November 2001
Old Rep, Birmingham – 21st November 2001

James narrates his own story, helped by his insect friends. It begins in New York, where James and his friends now live. They explain how they came to be living in Central Park in a giant peach stone, having escaped from the horrible Aunt Spiker and Aunt Sponge.

11 Dec

Dear Frank,

… At last, both The BFG *and* The Gingerbread Man *are up and running and I have a day off! Both shows have gone well, I'm glad to say. However, we did have problems with* The BFG, *because of a lack of readiness of some of the important props. I won't go into too many details, but the gist of it is that our producers employed a production management company, who quoted a price for how much it would cost to stage the production. Our producers accepted this quote and secured all the investment for the production. The production management company then turned round and said that the budget was higher than they had first said. Our producers, unable to return to the investors and change the agreed deal, told the production management company that they must bring the show in for the originally agreed amount. This meant that every maker and provider was squeezed, in order to save money. They changed the set builders. Other makers were told to refurbish old props rather than make new ones, etc., etc. What a recipe for disaster. And, of course, many people suffered the consequences of things not being right or not even being there! However, we got the show on, and it has been very well received. Unfortunately, the repercussions will echo for a long time, because, as the tour progresses through 2002, all sorts of problems will emerge with the set and the props! But at least the show has been well received and the cast are very good.*

The Gingerbread Man *has gone relatively smoothly so far. A splendid cast, performing very well in this brand-new theatre in Maidenhead…*

…On Thursday I return to Warwick Arts Centre to look at The BFG, *and on Friday I go to Birmingham to see, for the first time,* James and the Giant Peach, *which is breaking all box office records. What is slightly worrying is that they seem to have*

abandoned the concept of James and the Insects *telling the story. I am off to investigate!*

Love and best wishes,
David

Dear David,

...I'm delighted BFG *and* GB *are well and truly launched. Maidenhead seems an unlikely place for a new theatre, but no doubt deserves it, and I hope the merry maidenheaders support it. I'm concerned about the liberties taken with* James and the Giant Peach. *How dare any director presume to gild the lily!...*

Love to you all and a Very Happy Christmas from self and Mary,
Frank

20 Dec

Dear David,

This is a Post-Scriptum Supplementary to my scrabbled note of the other day...

In that haste, I didn't manage to tell you how particularly impressed I was by the BFG *programme. They have always been ingenious but I thought this one was specially well laid out – the particulars of the production which probably don't mean much to the children – centre for mums and dads. Who originated this layout, transforming a programme into a magazine? Is it done by the same team for whichever company is launching the production? Presumably, the Road Dahl Foundation collects a royalty as a spin-off.*

I found the Norden Farm Centre programme interesting too, not only for its references to the Young Master, but because it offers the sort of thing we may expect at the Theatre Royal...

Clearly, the reviewer of James and the Giant Peach *was not an absolute Dahl fan – vide penultimate paragraph – but this made his tribute to the play and its performers all the more telling.*

...Love and thanks as ever, F

2002

The new year began with some difficult situations to resolve, as DW reported.

9 Jan

Dear Frank,

...Thank you for enjoying the programme for The BFG. *What happens nowadays is that there are specialist firms creating programmes, taking all the work away from the Producers! They even do the research and invent the games! They have resident designers, who make the whole thing look co-ordinated. They organise distribution too. ...Children don't particularly like programmes anyway, as you said. Far better to give them something they can enjoy, linked to the production, or make it fairly simple!*

...The day after Boxing Day, I found myself back in a rehearsal room. One of my BFG cast had decided to be boring and difficult and resign from the production. The problem started when he questioned the fact that no retainer was being paid to the company for the weeks in between the resident season at Coventry and the beginning of the tour. Everybody is on two separate contracts, which is perfectly normal. Everybody had embarked upon the

enterprise with full knowledge that there would be three weeks without payment in the middle. Yet he really got his knickers in a twist about it and decided to leave. The repercussions, of course, are huge. Everybody has had to drop everything and start again, in order to find and rehearse a new actor in. Next week (the week in which the New Year falls), I have to return to Coventry for four days and get the new boy in, so that he has at least had a chance to do a couple of performances before the tour. To further complicate things, the ASM/understudy decided to leave too. He was mortally offended that he was not offered promotion following the resignation of the other actor. There was nothing in his contract to even hint at possible promotion, and there is no way he could have taken over from this particular actor, being at least four or five inches shorter. Not only that, the actor leaving also understudies the title role and there is no way that the ASM in question could do that! But he was mortally offended and decided to quit. We still have, as I dictate this, no replacement, but I suppose we will find somebody in the end!

There have been some moments of high drama on The Gingerbread Man, too. The female understudy found herself playing the role of Salt on a Thursday and the role of Pepper only two days later! Both actors professed to have lost their voices, though this was a huge exaggeration. It really annoys me how some of the younger actors these days take performances off, as though it were their right. In my day (!!), we had no understudies and you had to be literally unable to move before you could be 'off'!

Anyway, both shows have been very well received, so I suppose I shouldn't complain.

I managed to do a quick whistle-stop tour to see several productions, including both James and the Giant Peach versions, which are as unalike as chalk and cheese! The Cardiff one is done as a sophisticated rock musical for nine-year-olds, the Birmingham one is more traditional and, frankly, less interesting, *though better for touring, in my estimation. I have sent several pages of notes to the Birmingham producer and director, in the hope that they will improve the show a little before it goes on the road.*

I also saw a lovely production of The Owl and the Pussycat Went to See…, *performed by the students of the Bristol Old Vic Theatre School. It really was very exciting seeing the audience responding in exactly the same way as they did over thirty years ago! It makes me feel as though I want to revive the play again myself!*

But not yet! I'm really feeling a little frayed around the edges with all this extra-curricular activity on The BFG. *Hopefully, I can take a few days off soon…*

Love and best wishes, as ever,
David

11 Feb

Dear Frank,

*…*The BFG *[tour] opened successfully. There were a couple of good reviews, which I enclose.*

While I think of it, I must tell you that we are crossing fingers for another tour of Spot's Birthday Party *this year. If all goes according to plan, the production will come to the Theatre Royal, Winchester for the week beginning July 29th! Fingers crossed.*

Last Saturday, I did a workshop for thirty amateur actor/ directors working in the Oxfordshire area. It all seemed to go well. People joined in and became giants from The BFG, *creatures from* The See-Saw Tree *and characters from* The Gingerbread Man! *They also bought quite a few of my books, which was kind of them!*

Tomorrow, I go to Bristol Old Vic Theatre School to give my annual mock auditions to the final-year students. I always enjoy this…

… James And The Giant Peach continues to break records in Birmingham, even though, as you gathered from my comments last time, it really isn't the greatest production. Such a shame, because it is the one that will be touring for two years! I have given them a great list of notes, but whether or not they will use them, I don't know. The Cardiff production was much more exciting, although I do feel it was a bit avant-garde to tour!

…Things seem to have settled down on The BFG tour. Hopefully, there will not be so many company meetings in future. One of the actors who has left proved to be very militant, questioning every clause in the contract when he could, and demanding things on behalf of people who didn't want things demanded! One of the technical touring crew, a female sound operator, has to assert herself all the time, it seems. She too seems to look for trouble. Occasionally, at company meetings, she has been known to say, "We are now one minute into overtime"! But even she seems to have mellowed since the Coventry season. I do hope so. You are right when you say that Tony Pedley is one of the old brigade! He has become the Equity deputy now, and is trying to make sure everything runs smoothly.

Yours,
David

13 Jan

Dear David,

Oh, I say! I say! What a splendid packet! Huge thanks for it. You must be absolutely whacked after so much to-ing and fro-ing. It's wonderful to see so much Wood that one can barely count the trees…

...And I don't think the review [by Charles Vance] of the published text of Tom's Midnight Garden *is over the top! 'Genius' is an abused word, but here I think it is entirely appropriate. 'Genius' is applicable to thinkers and artists who instinctively grasp possibilities and ways and means to achieve them which have not hitherto been realised. Which is what you've done...*

Love to you all –
Frank

14 Feb

Dear David,

...Three Cheers for The BFG *and those excellent reviews. I do hope the* James *company has taken notice of your notes. It's exasperating to feel that the play's full potential isn't being realised even if it's going well...*

Frank

1 Mar

Dear Frank,
...we are opening the tour [of Spot's Birthday Party] *at the Hexagon, Reading. This is one of those multi-purpose auditoria, built in the '70s, which do not have the full theatre facilities necessary to mount shows properly (in my opinion!). Whirligig took* The Plotters of Cabbage Patch Corner *there for Christmas 1979. It was the first-ever Christmas production in the theatre, and was reasonably successful, but we found it very difficult to fit the production onto the stage. Size was not a problem, rather the strange positions of lighting bars, and the inability to fly scenery. Anyway, I'm sure it will be fine in the end!*
...The BFG *Company has, touch wood, fingers crossed, don't make a sound, settled down somewhat over the past few weeks. I saw them at the Churchill, Bromley last week and they*

all seemed quite happy. The business was excellent, echoing the previous week at Sadler's Wells, when it was impossible to buy a ticket for any of the three Saturday performances!

This week, they are in Stoke. I will leave them to it up there! Next week, they come back down south to Richmond, where I will see them on the Friday, and also conduct an understudy rehearsal. The following week, they are at the Theatre Royal, Brighton. I will combine a visit with a Whirligig meeting – John Gould and our Administrator, Barry Sheppard, both live in Brighton now...

Yours,
David

10 Feb

Dear Frank,

... Since I last wrote, we have been casting Spot. We are having to find a completely new cast. The day before auditions, I went to see a Showcase by students at the Guildford School of Acting – the musical theatre course final-year students. Two of them struck me as being eminently employable. One was a short, bouncy boy! The other was an even shorter, bouncier girl! Within half an hour of their Showcase finishing, they had been invited to audition the following day, and by the following day had been booked to play Spot and Helen (the Hippo!). Very nice when that happens. They were so excited and had an infectious lack of cynicism! Casting continues this week.

...Meanwhile, there seems to be competition as to which of my two shows should go into the West End at Christmas! I should be so lucky! The BFG, on tour, as you know, is an obvious candidate. But the Belgrade, Coventry, who put on The Twits a couple of years ago, want to revive it. Technically, they have the right to do it, according to their contract, but I'm not quite sure whether the theatre owner/production company they want to work with is as keen as they say they are! I'm leaving it to the agents. But both parties keep ringing me up and asking my opinion! I'm feeling quite wanted! Why not put both on, I hear you cry?! Well, I don't really think there is room for two Dahls in the West End at the same time, even at Christmas.

...a very good children's theatre company in Seattle (the second best in the United States, apparently) expressed an interest in doing The BFG, but wanted to get rid of the birthday party framing device. I have managed to do this. I'm not sure that it will be as easy to mount as they think, but in order to get the production on, I decided (and the Dahls agreed) to give it a go. I'm sending you the revised script, just in case you have time to look through it.

While in Cornwall, we went to see James and the Giant Peach, which happened to be in Truro that week. I must say I am disappointed with the production. Maybe I have said that already! But it seems to be getting very good reviews and the audiences seem to like it more than I do! So I will shut up and happily receive the royalty cheque!

Last Friday, I went to Woking to see The BFG and to give notes. The backstage saga continues! Another two people have left – the sound operator and the technical assistant stage manager. I won't go into details, but we are better off without them! Their successors are doing extremely well. That means that since the first day of rehearsal, we have lost five people! Jacqui thinks that this will be the first tour in the history of the British Theatre to return to base with a totally different company from the one that set forth! Happily, the show seems to be in good shape and the business is still very good...

...Back to your letter. Yes, Philip Pullman has done the cause of children's books a great service. I think you would enjoy his trilogy. Clockwork, the book I may well adapt, is great fun and rather clever. It also has the virtue of being quite a short book! Very tightly written. As far as the libretto is concerned, I'm not quite sure how it will work yet. The composer has decided he wants to work from my synopsis. Fingers crossed.

I will send you a copy of the treatment soon. The first draft has already been discussed by all parties, including Philip Pullman, and there are a couple of changes to be made. I will send you the second draft!…

All good wishes,
David

The second draft followed later that month, with the usual rapid reply in response.

18 Apr

Dear David,

…Your 'structure' effectively tells the story. The telescoping of material, which in the original is a 'flashback' …successfully amalgamates the two story-tellers, Fritz and P. Pullman himself.

Looking first at 'Setting' and thence to the third paragraph of Act 1 synopsis, my eye was caught by 'Snow falls as Ringelmann and Karl, his apprentice, enter… They go to the inn …'

This implies that the exterior of the inn is visible. But surely we don't want to be aware of Kalmenius until the door is opened to reveal him to such staggering effect. Then under the 'Cast-proposed doubling'– I was glad to see that his only double was as a Clock Figure in Act 2. I think it very desirable that he shouldn't have to appear as any other body. And I should like the same to be arranged for Karl, so that nothing obscures the Kalmenius – Karl axis of the action – which seems to me the main-spring of the plot. The other, almost parallel, seems to me to be Gretl – Florian, but if she just plays Florian in the acting-out of Fritz's story, that seems fair enough.

I'm a little puzzled by the term 'Ensemble', the actors in which 'where necessary may take on other supporting roles'. Are these additional to the cast of eight listed above? Or do these people… sing the choruses as well as the solos?

Having the company in the inn act out the story as Fritz tells it is a useful device for providing some action …However, I should like to know why Fritz encourages his listeners to be actors. Is he hoping that they will help him to reach the conclusion which he has not prepared? Will they be like figures in a silent movie, leaving the words to Fritz to supply, as it were, the sub-titles? And is this acting-out justification for the pub people to act out in Act 2 what happened before the crisis described by Fritz at the beginning of his story in Act 1? And can we be sure that this time the acting is 'for real'? Perhaps they will no longer be silent.

That action is not going to be easy to represent as it 'brings Fritz' story to the point at which he originally started'.

The return of the action to the inn is less complicated, but the 'nightmarish sequence' of Gretl's climb 'inside and up the tower' will need some very artful stage-managing, but I'm sure you'll achieve that!

Which brings me to the Clock. To have that dominating the action with its remorseless 'tick tock' is superb. Time 'is of the essence' as PGW might say. To accommodate the life-size figures moving relentlessly in and out, it will need to be very large and very solid.

…I do hope the Man Who Puts the Words to Music will ensure that they can be put across intelligibly. …The arias should be eerie and scary but memorably hummable to command close attention just as Fritz's story had begun to grab the public at the inn. Gretl will, I imagine, be soprano, the Landlady/Princess (a bossy type) contralto. Might Prince Florian be a boy soprano?

I'm afraid none of these Incubations will be found very helpful. I look forward to the next stage of development. Huge thanks again. I must follow up Philip Pullman in that Trilogy just completed.

Love – as ever to all –
Frank

10 May

Dear Frank,

…The saga of The BFG *continues …in Wycombe, just over three weeks ago, they were having an understudy rehearsal. The new BFG understudy, who took over after Christmas, was inside the big giant puppet, when it started to topple over, due possibly to his over-enthusiasm. Various folk dashed in to catch it, pushed it back upright, but over compensated, so it crashed down in the other direction. The young man was in hospital for three days, had concussion, double vision and did something to a tendon in his knee. He is out of the show for at least a month. Meanwhile, the Deputy Stage Manager was whisked off to casualty as well, having suffered grazing and a bump on the head. And two others were very slightly injured. That evening, the Company Manager went 'on the book', the ASM/understudy took over the roles of the BFG understudy, and the other stage management shared out his duties between them. Within a few days, I had found yet another person to join the Company. This one had auditioned for me for* Spot *the week before! He arrived in Southampton on the Tuesday, was off the book by Thursday, and rehearsing with my Associate Director on the Friday! He is only there to understudy the one role, but apparently has made himself useful in other directions too, which is good to hear. On Thursday, I fly to Edinburgh to spend a couple of days with them, and we hope to have a complete understudy run-through, even though the main understudy won't be there! Dear oh dear!*

Glad you liked the new BFG *script. Linda Hartzell in Seattle felt that the birthday party framing device was too much of a cliché these days. Apparently, most American children's plays have this storytelling method. "Let's do the show right here!" At first, I pointed out to her that the framing device was the only thing that made the adaptation possible, in my view. But she persuaded me to have another look, and indeed I suddenly realised that it was possible, and that we could change the scale in both Acts by changing the scene as the characters look through windows! I think it's quite neat. Having said that, I think there will be problems in rehearsal, particularly when they are trying to make each location look 'real' rather than an adaptation of the bedroom. Anyway, that is their problem!...*

...Now to the big thank-you – for your splendid comments on Clockwork. *You are right when you say that we don't want to be aware of Kalmenius until the door opens. The idea would be that we would see the others outside the inn, then enter it, and the set would change to the interior only. If this proves impracticable, they will simply enter the inn from outside.*

The term 'ensemble' refers to the entire acting Company. All eight of them! They all have to double and treble like mad, except, obviously, for the times when it would be inappropriate, such as the ones you mention – Kalmenius will be a Clock Figure, completely disguised, but nothing else.

You ask, most perceptively, why Fritz encourages his listeners to be actors. Excellent point. My original idea was that he suggests the others take part to make the story more enjoyable. I had intended that they would indeed be able to speak in character, but would always be prompted by Fritz, who would take us from scene to scene in his narration. I suppose I envisage their acting to be somewhat stylised, almost melodramatic in this Act, whereas in Act 2, it will be more 'real'.

There is another possibility, and that is that somehow, through lighting, or even through costume, the storytelling in the first Act would be in 'black and white', whereas in the second Act it would be 'in colour'.

But the points you make are very pertinent and will be discussed with my director and composer next time we meet.

Yes, the clock will have to be quite something! On at least three levels, I fancy.

The way the writing is to proceed is that the composer

will now set out a suggested list of songs, choruses, arias, etc., following my treatment. He will even say 'four rhyming lines, here'. I have no idea whether this system will work, but we will give it a go! I think there may well be some spoken word as well as sung words. Not sure, though.

I so agree with you that the sung words must be audible and intelligible. The story is very important. Clarity will be extremely important. It may be that the word 'opera' is a little deceptive, I don't know. I would certainly like the music to be accessible, rather than alienating. The composer did the music for Tom's Midnight Garden, *which I enjoyed a lot. However, he does have classical leanings. I hope he doesn't lean too far towards the modern, atonal style. I don't think he will.*

Philip Pullman has responded positively to the treatment. I will try to remember to send you his reactions.

I may not have told you about a plan which has been in development for some time… the Ambassador Theatre Group, which owns many of the major touring theatres, as well as about ten West End theatres, have asked me to work with them for at least three years, directing one of my plays or adaptations each year for touring and West End presentation. They want to guarantee quality of product by producing their own productions to tour into their own theatres! They have seen the success of The Twits *and* The BFG *in their theatres over the last two years, and have now made this offer to keep me within their operation. One condition is that I deliver them two Dahl productions, in 2004 and 2005. This is not too much of a problem. I would try to revive* The Witches *and also mount a new production of* Fantastic Mr Fox, *which has so far only been seen in Coventry. In 2006, I would be allowed to do something else, as long as it was commercial enough (in other words, as long as the title was a strong one) to play 7pm performances as well as the daytime schools performances.*

The great thing about the Ambassador Theatre Group (ATG) is that all their bigwigs are passionate about theatre and not simply commercial animals. Many of them I know quite well. ...I am now in the process of telling all my colleagues, people who work for me on the Whirligig productions and others, exactly what is going on, in the hope that they don't think I am totally abandoning ship! Hopefully, this will be a new vessel on which several of us can sail.

Take care, lots of love,
David

19 May

Dear David,

...I'm glad you found my comments on Clockwork *treatment useful. I thought Philip Pullman's observations very interesting, especially his idea of using the Clock itself as narrator. But I'm sure your Fritz is better than a Talking Clock. The Clock should be indifferent to all that passes. I hope the Composer won't ask you to supply Words to ready-made tunes. Some spoken dialogue should be acceptable. Mozart made use of it...*

My niece Pat has recently become a Pullman fan and has lent me the first two books of his trilogy, His Dark Materials. *I can't tackle them just yet, because I'm involved with re-reading* The Lord of the Rings. *I had forgotten how terribly exciting it is. I have to put it down every so often because I just can't bear the suspense!*

The approach of The Ambassador Theatre Group sounds a wonderful proposition, and should further the noble cause of Children's Theatre. When they ask you to deliver two Dahl productions in 2004 and 2005, will already produced works be acceptable? Fantastic Mr Fox *has indeed enjoyed very limited exposure, but what of* The Witches? *No doubt you'll come up with something new. More Pullman perhaps, or Dick King-Smith? I presume you won't be exclusively committed to ATG...*

Frank

17 Jun

Dear Frank,

…The production of The Owl and the Pussycat Went To See… *at the Swan, Worcester – back where it all began 34 years ago! – was adequate but not much more than that, I'm afraid! The designs were good – borrowed from the Bristol Old Vic Theatre School production last year. Some of the performances were not bad, but some were pretty pathetic! Don't say I said so! They were all pleased that Jacqui and I had made the effort to see the show, and, as usual with any amateur dramatics, they were all incredibly enthusiastic and thrilled to be doing it. So, really, that makes it all worthwhile. I have always believed that most amateur theatre is, rightly, for the participants rather than the audience! It is a rare blessing when you get a combination of the two. Some school, university and other amateur productions I have seen have been a true joy. But most, if I'm honest, have not!*

I'm dictating this on the Sunday before we get-in Spot's Birthday Party *to the Hexagon, Reading. We open on Thursday. Rehearsals have been a real pleasure, with a talented young cast, for many of whom it is a first professional job. There have been various injuries to delay proceedings, but everything seems to have come together at the right time, with the final three run-throughs being very encouraging indeed. I hope very much you enjoy it!…*

Best wishes,
David

4 Jul

Dear Frank,

…It has been hectic here over the last couple of weeks. Once I had got Spot *on in Reading, it was necessary to go back to* The

BFG, *where yet another cast member had changed! This one was directed into the production by Adam, my No.2, but I haven't actually seen him working. I'm glad to say he is doing an excellent job. The tour continues for another few weeks. It has been the most eventful tour I have ever been involved with! Having said that, the reaction has been excellent, we have, touch wood, never missed a performance, and all the participants emerge with credit.*

Then I was back to Spot, *in Birmingham on the first leg of the tour. A few teething problems, but nothing much to worry about…*

Since then, I have spoken at a Conference on Creativity in Education, a rather high-powered event…

Anyway, there I was, sitting on a panel alongside Jude Kelly, the very public image-conscious director of the West Yorkshire Playhouse, and a lot of very distinguished educationalists, who spoke with very long words a sort of jargon I couldn't get my head round at all – I just told the Conference about the teacher at the infant school who told me that "There isn't time for fun anymore." I tried to suggest that the value of creativity and the arts could not be evaluated in a series of boxes which you tick or otherwise, but could be measured in the reaction of the participants… Joy, it seemed to me, was a perfectly acceptable indication of success. But I don't think that went down too well!

Love and best wishes to you and Mary, from all of us,
David

Spot's Birthday Party played at Winchester in August and FW was in the audience with young relatives.

Dear David,

…The Company Manager was charming and picked me out with no difficulty at all, me being quite the most antiquated object

among the crowds crushing into the Theatre Royal yesterday for the 2.30 performance. Not only was she charming, she was quite the most attractive young woman I've encountered for ages! We met again in the interval for a further chat. I suppose she will take up with another company when Spot *finishes?*

The House was full and I gather business has been good all the week – not only for Spot *but for the TR in general. As I looked over the audience, I reckoned that most of the parents – all young, of course – were not likely to be usual patrons of the theatre, so this has been a satisfactory promotion of play-going in general. And maybe many of them will take advantage during the overlong summer 'hols' to find profitable occupation for even these very young children in the various workshops on offer from the educational wing of the theatre.*

The whole thing went with a resounding bang and the young cast was absolutely first rate, displaying unflagging energy which fairly took my breath away. And the gasp of amazement at your final coup de théâtre was wonderful. How clever you were to think up those seeds as a continuing line of development in an otherwise plotless piece, with no conflicting baddies either. I think my favourite episode is the Cinderella *sequence. The monkey and the crocodile were especially good as the ugly sisters.*

Olivia, two and a half, was absolutely spellbound throughout and only recovered enough to join in the action towards the end. Victoria, three plus, responded straightaway with voice and gesture. Olivia and Victoria – who is bilingual – were meeting for the first time and it was fascinating to watch their cautious approach to each other. By the end of the afternoon, when we had returned to 14 FG for tea, they were bosom pals...

Huge thanks again, and love to all as ever,
Frank

6 Aug

Dear Frank,

...Delighted to hear that your Saturday party was a success and that Spot's Birthday Party *played its part! I haven't seen the production for a few weeks, so I was particularly glad to hear that the energy level was high. Also, I'm very pleased that Gilda welcomed you so warmly. She and I first worked together nearly twenty years ago, when she was a young ASM on* Meg and Mog Show *at Unicorn (the Arts). She toured for many years 'on the book' for Whirligig. Now she is Company Manager! She celebrated her fortieth birthday a few days before you met her!*

So pleased that the business was good at the Theatre Royal. It has not been quite as good elsewhere. Very glad that the sunflower sequence worked well! I love it when you hear genuine gasps from children. I like it best when the children try to wake Spot to let him know the flowers have grown. Sometimes it happens, sometimes it doesn't!...

Best wishes,
David

7 Jul

Dear David,

...I fully endorse your views on Creativity in Education. The obsession of Govt. with tests and tables is utterly useless. Teachers are left with no time to teach and the continual tests are a complete waste of time besides stifling creative enterprise. Your experience of teachers regarding your visits as a waste of time reminds me of an encounter which Harcourt Williams had with the LCC when he was directing at the Old Vic. He suggested that, instead of being limited to the texts of plays prescribed for dreary grammatical study for examinations, the children should be brought to performances

of plays they hadn't been forced to work on in such an off-putting way and have the chance to experience them for what they were directly in performance without off-putting previous study. "Oh, wouldn't that be rather a joyride?" was the reply!!!!

I believe that children should be taken to straightforward productions with only the briefest of instructions in the theatre, and allowed to receive the full effect of performance, letting the poetry do its work without any irritable reaching for meaning. Good actors can make that immediately accessible in a way that simply gazing at the printed page cannot. When Edith Evans as Rosalind exclaimed, "So this is the forest of Arden!", you knew immediately what she thought about it...

> *Love to you all – and Mother!*
> *Frank*

21 Aug

Dear Frank,

*...*Spot *continues its tour with reasonable audiences. We are in Oxford this week, and I will be spending a couple of days there. The following week, we have our four showcase performances at the Peacock Theatre in London. Then the tour closes with six performances at the Swan Theatre, Wycombe.*

Am now waiting to hear whether any cast members of The BFG *have decided not to join us at Christmas, in which case we have to search for new ones! Fingers crossed most of them will be pleased to return.*

I should have been working on Clockwork *for the last few weeks, but have somehow managed to avoid it! I really must try to do something soon. The composer is waiting!....*

You may remember that a year or two ago I went up to Nottingham, where the Playhouse were presenting Dear Brutus. *It was a splendid production and really proved that the play had not dated nearly as much as many people might have thought. The interesting news is that the same company are to revive* Mary Rose, *in October. I will make every effort to go!...*

A few days have elapsed since I dictated the above! I went to Oxford to see the Spot *company – it involved rehearsing in Spot's understudy, who is doing a couple of performances while the real incumbent is off rehearsing another show! All went well.*

...I have now heard, to my relief, that the entire cast, bar one, of The BFG *is returning for Christmas. That will save us a lot of bother, I must say.*

All good wishes, as ever, from us all.

Yours,
David

Dear David,

...I shall hope you can get to Mary Rose *in Nottingham and look forward to your report on it. It's such a perfect play. And with the present revival of interest in fantasy, maybe it will be very acceptable. I do think Chichester should have a bash at* The Boy David *with a real boy in it – how about your Tom? – and imaginative treatment of the tricky vision, instead of wasting time and money on mucking about with W. Shakespeare...*

Love to Jacqui and the girls as well as your 'goodself',
Frank

10 Sep

Dear Frank,

*...*Clockwork *is well behind schedule. I was meant to deliver the first draft of the first act by the end of August! I haven't written*

a word yet! Yes, I have thought about it a lot, but am finding it very difficult to discover the right tone. Being an opera, I don't have to make things rhyme, but as I have mainly written lyrics in the past, I keep getting tempted away from language which simply yet strongly tells the tale, towards the odd clever display of assonance or alliteration, and then decide it all looks too tricksy! Maybe something will click into shape soon…

*…*Spot's Birthday Party *ended up happily with four successful performances at the Peacock Theatre (formerly The Royalty) in London, and half a week at the Swan Theatre, Wycombe. I think the cast were quite sad to finish! They had all given considerable energy and enthusiasm to the project, for which I was very grateful.*

Later this week, I have to audition a new cast member for The BFG, *for the West End. Luckily, only one person is leaving. This means that we will have one week's rehearsal only, from November 4th, and open on November 13th for eight weeks at the Playhouse…*

…Last week, Anthony Pedley, of BFG fame… came to Belvedere Drive for three days to work on his solo Roald Dahl show. I may have mentioned this before. We had the idea over a year ago, and the Dahl family have given him permission to go ahead. We hope to open in Cardiff next year. The idea is that Pedley will 'be' Dahl, though won't try to impersonate him. The first half, which is quite dark, focuses on his early life, and also some of the adult writing. The second half is in a storytelling vein, more light-hearted, and concentrating on the children's books. The idea is that the second half will be totally self-contained, and will be able to be performed on its own for children in theatres, art centres, schools, libraries or festivals. …I have been helping him structure it, and will direct it for him.

I have been asked to write the book of a musical based on L P Hartley's The Go-Between. *I love the book, and I was very taken with the film version, scripted by Harold Pinter. But the songs for this proposed stage version are not really to my liking, and I think I am going to have to turn it down. For me, the story works because it is seen through the eyes of Leo, the child. The composer/lyricist of the musical (another book writer has already had a go at it apparently) seems more interested in the adult characters and what is going on inside their heads. This seems to me to be totally irrelevant. Maybe something in my reaction points to why I write for children!…*

…I must take a deep breath and try to get a bit of Clockwork *done.*

> *…Yours, as ever,*
> *David*

16 Sep

Dear David,

…Anthony Pedley's one-man show is a delightful idea. I do hope it really gets going – like Gielgud's Seven Ages of Man *recital which he was always able to turn on when other opportunities were slack. He might find our TR a possible venue, too. Why not?…*

> *Ever,*
> *Frank*

The first draft of *Clockwork* Act 1 was sent to FW at the end of October, quickly followed by an ever more detailed response.

6 Nov

Dear David,

Huge thanks for the draft of Act One of Clockwork. *It's a notable feather in your cap to have executed a tricky commission so effectively. Here are my reactions for what they may be worth…*

...I take it the 'songs' will be 'through composed' in the manner established by B. Britten in Peter Grimes. *This is much more dramatic than the old format of a series of stanzas designed to show off a singer's talent at the cost of holding up the action. You've stuck very faithfully to the original text. I think perhaps you might usefully have extended it in one or two places, which I'll indicate in a moment.*

The opening is splendid. The figures, I imagine, will be life-size, being flesh and blood. This means that Sir Ironsoul must be life-sized too, not the tiny, tinny figure referred to in the text. This should provide no problem so long as Karl is no weakling but a well set-up lad.

The opening provides the only ensemble passage, so your suggestion that the company in the tavern should provide a quartet on p.7, comparing the construction of a story to the construction of a clock hinted at on p.18 of the text, is a chance for another variation among the solo passages. I wonder whether the exchange between Fritz and Karl on your p.8 might not be made a duet? This would add significance to Karl's confession of his failure. It might include some enlargement of Karl's lines on Pullman's p.18. And then perhaps on your p.9 you might feature Fritz's confession that he doesn't know how to finish his story (a problem often confronting Sir Walter Scott) as an attempt to comfort Karl. In the original, this is merely an authorial intervention, but it would be useful if the audience in the theatre could be given the same insight as the readers of the printed page.

For the same reason, I would welcome an enlargement of the Burgomaster's 'Ah, yes!' (your p.5) by the inclusion of more of his speech on Pullman's p.13. I think it would be useful to emphasise and clarify the importance of an apprentice's obligation to produce an example of his mastery of his craft at the conclusion of his indentures. Today's audiences may not be familiar with the concept of apprenticeship as part of the tradition stressed by the Burgomaster. The reader has time to linger and grasp the significance of this, the spectator has not, he has to keep up with the ongoing action.

    I notice that you have used rhyme throughout but somewhat inconsistently. The unexpected introduction of rhyme in a generally prose – or unrhymed – passage, was a very effective Shakespearean device to highlight a particular point. You take advantage of this on your p.11:

First it would help if when I start
You all assist by taking part,
a novel idea, not in Pullman, that needs emphasis and explanation.
There is another instance on your p.19:
You came here
To peer
At me,
where it is especially effective in a spoken sequence.
But my ear is a little worried by two moments of inexact rhyme.
One is on your p.6, the Landlady's
He makes you hear the spooky wind
Whistling through the pines
And feel the ghostly fingers
Creeping up your spine.
The inexact rhyme 'offends the ear'. It could be remedied thus:
He makes us feel the spooky wind
Whistling through the pines
And feel the ghostly fingers
Creeping up our spines.

Again on p.4 your
Come, let's celebrate
The White House Tavern waits
might become
Come, let's celebrate
The White House Taverners wait

I fear the foregoing – if you can decipher it – is somewhat impertinent. It's the merest nit-picking. Your script admirably executes the composer's commission. However, the nits, if picked, might establish the adaptation as a drama in its own right without dependence on song setting, a true melodrama, its action simply supported by appropriate incidental music, so I hope you will accept all these suggestions, finding them, like the Police in The Pirates of Penzance:

> *Still it's evident*
> *These intentions are well meant...*

...I'm looking forward to Clockwork *Act II...*

Frank

7 Nov

Dear Frank,

I have started rehearsals for The BFG, *which opens at the lovely Playhouse Theatre, on the Embankment, on November 13th. I hadn't realised how delightful the interior of the theatre is. Last time I worked there, it was run by the BBC as a recording studio! I think they must have covered over much of the auditorium, for acoustic reasons. But it really is lovely. It seems, and you may well remember this, Gladys Cooper ran a company here many years ago. It is a lovely size, about 750 seats, and the set just fits. At least I hope it does. Everyone assures me it does!...*

...The Seattle production of The BFG *was very enjoyable. The framing device removal worked well, but only 80% of the time! The problem really was in the design. It was minimalist, to put it mildly. But there were some very nice wooden backcloths, of Buckingham Palace and houses with little windows in. It seems a bit odd to say wooden backcloths, I realise, but they were, in effect, sliding wooden curtains. A bit cumbersome, but*

quite effective. Particularly when there was light shining through the windows from behind.

The giants were done as puppet heads on the end of extended upwards arms. The actors' heads came through to the side of the enormous heads, and a false arm helped create the illusion that they were really tall. It sort of worked, but the effect was diluted when the giants opened their mouths! They were really rather pathetic and weedy, in my view! And when they ate all the children, which, when using the birthday party framing device, is easy, because there are lots of dolls and soft toys lying around the set, they resorted to miming picking up children and eating them, which was really rather unsatisfactory.

The little girl playing Sophie was very good.

Unfortunately, the actor playing the BFG was rather lightweight – a tenor when you really need a baritone or bass! But he was endearing, and I think the audiences liked him. Indeed, they liked the whole show. It has been extended twice, and now runs until mid- or late January…

All good wishes, as ever,
David

18 Nov

Dear Frank,

The BFG *opened safely and well on Wednesday, 13th November. The rehearsal week had been a joy, with a lovely atmosphere – something that had been lacking, sadly, in the original rehearsal period. Certain changes of personnel made this possible, I fancy. One or two of my original choices had proved to be rather negative and ultimately destructive. They are all happy bunnies now, I'm glad to report! And the Playhouse is quite delightful. The show fits beautifully, even though it is a little tight backstage. The technical rehearsals were hampered somewhat by the Lighting Designer being uncharacteristically slow and indecisive.*

She had done such a good job the first time, and had designed the lighting for Tom's Midnight Garden so well, that I couldn't understand why she had become rather difficult and volatile. It turned out that the poor girl had had a miscarriage only three days earlier, but didn't want to let us all down. Unfortunately, she didn't tell us until she had made us all rather prickly, thanks to her strange behaviour! She managed to finish lighting before the dress rehearsal, but then disappeared to see a doctor and hasn't been seen since. Luckily, her assistant knew the show well, and has ensured that it all looks okay.

The opening performances have gone well. The phones are ringing merrily, apparently. Fingers crossed for a successful season...

...To answer your Seattle questions – first of all, the whole cast spoke with English accents! This was admirable, except that nobody had told them about regional accents. This meant that the BFG had a delightful received pronunciation, rather than the country accent we give him over here! The Heads of the Army and Airforce were rather fun, straight out of a stiff upper lip movie!

Thank you for your Clockwork comments, all of which are extremely useful. Nothing is happening on Clockwork until December 19th, when the director and I go to meet the composer. Until then, I am not doing any more work on it or suggesting any changes. Let's just see what he comes up with!

You are quite right about the annoyingly imperfect rhymes. I will definitely change them.

It was an interesting experience. I felt quite free, in a way. But there were times when I knew I definitely wanted to use rhyme to increase the pace of the storytelling.

On the other hand, when I was doing a bit of 'blank verse', for want of a better phrase, I often found that words seemed to be rhyming themselves, and that it was worth using that to glue the sentences together. Sometimes, one of these 'nearly' rhymes *would come along, and I would think, "Well, really this isn't a rhyming section in the traditional sense, so a 'nearly' rhyme will be okay." In retrospect, I know this was wrong, and I know that if I don't change those rhymes I will forever look at them regretfully!...*

...Well, I must prepare for the week ahead. I have my first meeting with all the people at the Ambassador Theatre Group, with whom I might be working for three years, doing one play a year on tour and in the West End. Am also doing various radio interviews for The BFG*... On Friday, I go to Cardiff to see their production of* Babe, the Sheep-Pig. *Next week, various bits and pieces, including a visit to Leicester to see their production of* The Witches.*

...Then, on Monday, December 2nd, I set off once again for Bexhill and three days of work on the synopsis of Coram Boy. *Have I ever sent you a copy of this splendid novel, which Unicorn want me to adapt for the opening of their new theatre in 2004?...*

Yours,
David

26 Nov

Dear David,
...I take it the audience for the morning performances of BFG *are school groups, this being term time. Does this mean that the schools are able to undertake trips away from the classroom again and never mind the curriculum and those stupid league tables!*

I'm glad your agent is pleased with the first draft of Clockwork. *Yes, rhymes do have a way of turning up when you're not particularly wanting them. I've done some of my minor efforts with rhymes occurring casually throughout, not just at the end of lines. This can be quite pleasing and does help to bind ideas together. I think it might work quite well for musical setting...*

…Now, what is Coram Boy? *And was your 3-day purdah at Bexhill properly productive? How splendid to provide a work to open the new theatre. But I hope we shall all be whistling the airs from* Clockwork *before then…*

Love to all –
Frank

3 Dec

Dear Frank,

…Tomorrow, I go off to my attic in Bexhill to try to hack out a synopsis of Coram Boy. *I am sending you a copy of the book, which I hope you will enjoy. I think it is quite an achievement. The book won the children's Whitbread Award last year…*

The BFG *continues happily at the Playhouse. Schools business is not that good, and the fire fighters' strike hasn't helped, because some local authorities are telling schools not to take children on trips whenever the firemen are out… But the public seem to be coming in good numbers and the phone is busy. There have been quite a few reviews, copies of which I will be sending you…*

…Last week, I saw a production of The Witches *at the Haymarket, Leicester. It was pretty good really, though certain things annoyed me! I will send you a copy of the report I sent to the Dahl Estate. Don't bother to plough through it if it gets too pedantic!*

The week before, I saw a splendid Babe, the Sheep-Pig *in Cardiff. Most of the actors were actor-musicians, and they played all their own accompaniments. It was really very inventive and worked extremely well. As Ma the old ewe lay dying at the end of Act 1, the piano-accordion she had played throughout the Act echoed her wheezy expiry with brilliant appropriateness. And at one point a farmer stood leaning on what might have been his crook, but turned out to be his trombone! It all sounds rather gimmicky, but in fact it was beautifully worked out and, apart from the fact that the music was, for me, too loud, the whole thing worked beautifully.*

On December 20th, I go up to Manchester to see Tom's Midnight Garden...

...In the meantime, reports are coming in of a well-received production of Tom's Midnight Garden *at the Manchester Library Theatre.*

All for now, D

16 Dec

Dear David,

...Now I must give you a HUGE thank-you for Coram Boy. *It's TREMENDOUS! The most absorbing book I have read for ages! The pace is terrific, the writing so vivid and the character drawing so convincing that it has gripped me even more than* Lord of the Rings...

I'm very glad that your sojourn in Bexhill has enabled you to thrash out a synopsis for your dramatization, but HOW? I can visualize it as a film, but as a stage play? It is so intricately plotted. The first part consists of two stories – Meshak's and Alexander's – linked by Melissa. They are parallel stories. I'm put in mind of Elizabethan drama as a possible model for treatment, particularly Much Ado, *where our William adapts his usual formula of plot and subplot to run two equal plots, neither subordinate to the other. And the second part of the book, eight years after the first, suggests the structure of* The Winter's Tale. *And of course the seriousness of the theme and the action is for a considerably older audience than your plays hitherto. Can a dramatisation encompass the flexibility of action and structure of the novel? It was not too difficult for the author to fuse all the elements in her narrative, but in a stage action, how will you manage? It must present your toughest challenge to date and I'm dying to see how you have coped with it – as I'm sure you will have done! What a superb book it is! And what a wonderful picture of the reality of 18th-century England…*

Love to you all – and (of course) A Happy New Year!
Frank

These questions were answered when FW read the first draft synopsis, sent to him on 19th December.

23 Dec

Dear David,

Hugissimmus thanks for yours of the 19th (and the super Christmas card) and the schema for Coram Boy…

Now, Coram Boy. *Well, I really think you've cracked the problem by giving the vast, complicated tale a sort of cinematic treatment, contriving a fluid sequence of 'scenes' linked by narration. I assume that as narrators, Thomas and Meshak will maintain their characters as they are in the events they relate. I think it is important that Otis, Alex, Thomas, Meshak are not required to double. And I should prefer Isobel and Melissa to be similarly restricted, except perhaps as well-disguised ladies at Gaddarn's party.*

The concept of setting the whole in the Coram chapel is splendid and so is the use of Messiah throughout. Besides the choruses and solo numbers, there is plenty of purely orchestral music to draw on, though adaptations of some of the famous arias might be useful because they would be more immediately recognised. It should be made clear at the start, I think, that the audience is attending the acting-out of a story – the actors being seen as actors acting (as in the Elizabethan theatre), not as real persons on the modern stage. Their changing of bits of costume, handling of props, etc., will then be quite acceptable.

Now let me follow systematically your sheet of
Queries/Thoughts for Discussion

1. *Yes – if any actors can also play a musical instrument, this could be very useful.*
2. *Toby must surely be the only black actor, to emphasize his significance in the 18th century. It would, however, be nice (not quite the word!) to glimpse some black slaves at the dockside, but they would have to be restricted to that single appearance – boring for them and much too costly!*
3. *Mrs Lynch. It would be satisfying to resolve her story. I was puzzled by her appearance at the pub, and so soon afterwards at Ashbrook as housekeeper. Ashbrook is apparently some distance from Gloucester. How could she commute? It seems that the author has slipped up here.*
4. *The audience may recognise Gaddarn as Otis without in any way jeopardising the failure of other characters to spot him. Alex does, for a moment, think that he has seen him, or someone like him, somewhere before. The Shakespearean convention of non-recognition of one disguised character by another (Bassanio & Portia, for instance) is still workable even today, though perhaps the disguise is more sophisticated.*
5. *If Meshak/Mish recognises Otis, I don't think it matters. He is so much concerned about Aaron, his 'angel', and simpleton that he is can accept anything.*
6. *No, not strange at all. Thomas would certainly claw back Aaron as an ex-Coramite for the sake of his exceptional voice.*
7. *Yes. This is a problem! Could Alex do a falsetto like Hilda Bracket of the famous duo Hinge & Bracket?*
8. *This information would probably be best conveyed by Milcote or Lynch, who have had dealings with him.*
9. *I'm sure the little sister 'never would be missed'!*

P.S. And might not Mother Catbrain get the chop along with Dr Burney and Timothy Parfitt? Her prophecy gives Aaron some encouragement when he begins to recognise Alex as possibly his father, but with so many characters (all vividly depicted in the book), is this really necessary? Her elimination would reduce the doubling, and the less of that, the better…

Love as ever,
Frank

P.S. I'm looking forward to the first draft of the working script!

2003

The year began with a lull in letters caused by both participants dealing with illnesses and family difficulties. Meanwhile, DW began work on a new *Winnie the Pooh* project for Disney, a large arena show.

3 Mar

Dear Frank,

…I am enclosing a copy of the treatment for you to peruse. It is written, as I think I explained, for arena presentation, which means that it is in fairly huge and sometimes horrendous 'spaces', rather than theatres. But they erect a proper stage, and spend a lot of money on the costumes, the lighting, etc., making the main challenge to maintain the interest and the involvement of the very young audience to which it is aimed. Very often, these shows are glorified variety shows, with a lot of jolly singing and dancing, but little to grab the imagination or demonstrate the excitement of 'theatre'. The new Executive in the department, based in Los Angeles, is a theatre person, and she is determined to improve the quality of this kind of show. This, it seems, is why she asked me

to become involved. And, as you said in your letter, if someone is going to do it, it might not be a bad idea for me to have a crack at it.

Disney are notoriously mean in the financial dealings! It took ages to come up with a contract which seemed fair. Even now, if it all happens, it will not be a very lucrative job, but hopefully it might lead to other areas of discussion. We will see.

The first reaction to the treatment has been positive – from the lady herself. But now, of course, it has to go to a whole array of superiors, all of whom will feel compelled to thrown in their two pennyworths and suggest amendments and improvements! It will be interesting to see how frustrating the whole operation may become!

Meanwhile, there are developments on other fronts. Very soon, there will be a week of workshops with a team of opera singers, exploring Clockwork. The composer, it seems, likes my libretto. So far, no alterations have been asked for. I will attend some of the workshops, just to see what happens. Hopefully, I will then get the go-ahead to write the second half!

There is a meeting soon about Coram Boy, following my treatment. I think I will be asked to start work on the first draft soon, although I don't think production is anticipated until 2005! This is when they now hope the new Unicorn Theatre building on the South Bank will open – and Coram Boy is supposed to be the first production!

Meanwhile, going back to Clockwork, it seems that it is now fairly certain that the opening performances will take place in the Linbury Studio, which is the delightful smaller auditorium attached to the revamped Royal Opera House. So that could be nice!...

...I decided to offer some workshops based on Lady Lollipop, using the Lincolnshire children as guinea pigs (yet another pig reference!). The idea was snapped up by the teacher, so I was lumbered! I'm actually quite looking forward to it, and will report back in due course. Meanwhile, Walker Books, who publish Lady Lollipop, have agreed to publish a play version *later in the year. So that's something else I've got to settle down to write eventually…*

Yours,
David

9 Mar

Dear David,

…I was a little perplexed by the word 'arena' because to me that suggests the sort of vast space occupied by the Edinburgh Tattoo or the Royal Tournament at Earl's Court. The Disney concept with a 'proper stage' on which you can hang your gauze promises to be much more satisfactory. And the scene shifting by Rabbits' Friends and Relations is a splendid wheeze. The kids will enjoy that and it will allow them to recover from the rather long stretch of concentration required by the successive episodes. The use of Mother and Father as narrators is another brilliant idea. Between them, they will provide the forward narrative movement to a satisfactory conclusion with Christopher Robin preparing for school. The whole will gain immensely if it is not just a succession of independent stories. What age do the Disneys actually aim at with their 'very young'? There will certainly be plenty of action and participation. How much dialogue, I wonder? It strikes me that it would all fit very well into Chichester!

…I'm delighted to hear that matters are moving with Clockwork *and* Coram Boy, *though I'm sorry to hear that production of the latter is not expected before 2005!…*

Love as ever –
Frank

26 Mar

Dear Frank,

…The third draft of the Pooh *treatment winged its way over the Atlantic yesterday. Hopefully, this will be the last one! One of the problems of modern communication is that a whole script can be e-mailed to America by pressing a button… it arrives only seconds later. This means that they get to read it quicker, and react quicker, which means that the poor writer doesn't have a little period of calm before getting down to work again! In the good old days (!), a script had to go by post, which gave you a few days' grace!*

Anyway, since you read it, the nice framing device of the mother and father has gone – they felt it was too gentle! And, in fairness, there have been one or two improvements in the fluency of the show, particularly the second act.

As you imagined, the show is intended for large spaces. … Disney reckon it will play to audiences of no less than 3,000, and possibly a couple of thousand more! Much of the soundtrack has to be on tape, which frankly I dread. There is no easy way to allow for audience reaction, let alone participation. However, my Disney contact was very keen to do something 'with integrity', and kindly thought of me… we will see!

I suppose the audience will be similar to the family mix that attended Spot's Birthday Party. *The difference will be that the majority of them will not be the normal theatre-going public, which means that, apart from the occasional pantomime, they will all be first-timers. I must look upon this as a positive benefit! Having said that, for a three-year-old to experience live theatre for the first time from the back of a huge arena/auditorium is hardly likely to inspire them with a lifelong love of the drama!*

The show would be too big for Chichester! But you are absolutely right – it could be done at Chichester in a smaller production, and be rather delightful. Heigh ho!…

...Last week, there was a series of workshops on Clockwork. *These involved the director and composer, plus a repetiteur, plus seven real-life opera singers, working on the first twenty minutes of the opera. I popped in and out, and found it interesting, although I wish it could be a bit more tuneful! It's all a bit modern classical, somewhat atonal, and hardly what one might dare call catchy! Having said that, some of the dramatic moments worked well, and Tony Graham, who also directed* Tom's Midnight Garden, *is an experienced and sensitive director. ...The opera will be accompanied, I am told, by eight musicians from the London Symphonia (or do they spell it Sinfonia?). I must say I find it all a bit strange. On the first day, we had to go round introducing ourselves. I couldn't bring myself to say that I was the writer of the libretto, which sounded extremely pretentious! So I just said that I had done the words...*

As I dictate this, I am preparing for a Coram Boy *meeting tomorrow. I think it is the meeting when they will give me the go-ahead to start work. Quite when I will start this work, who knows? I still have Act 2 of* Clockwork *to prepare, and I'm quite sure that the Disney folk will be hounding me too! Never mind. Take a deep breath and keep in control!*

...The other day, an independent television producer rang up and asked if I was the person who had adapted Swallows and Amazons *for film some thirty years ago! I replied I was. Whereupon he asked if I had any other Ransome scripts tucked away. Lurking in a couple of box files, I found a six-part serialisation of* Pigeon Post, *which I honesty cannot remember writing! Also, there was a full-length movie version of* Great Northern?, *which I DO remember writing, but which never got off the ground.*

The producer, David Cobham, has now read them, likes them, and is approaching ITV with a view to producing them as 90-minute Sunday teatime events. Extraordinary! But I suppose the scripts, like the books, have not dated. Fingers crossed! As long as they don't want huge rewrites!

You may remember I told you that Anthony Pedley, the actor who played the BFG, was preparing a one-man show in which he would play Roald Dahl. He wanted me to write it, but I felt it wasn't my cup of tea, but I agreed to direct it. Also, to advise him… Unfortunately, the first draft of the script was not favourably received by the Dahls, but he has now revised the idea and truncated the script to become a 45-minute piece to be played in schools. The only requirements are a table and a chair, and it can be performed in a classroom or in the school hall…

Yours,
David

30 Mar

Dear David,

…I'm sorry Mother and Father have gone from Pooh. *Too gentle? Whatever do they want? Sex and violence in Ashdown Forest in lieu of pooh-sticks? I can appreciate that with expected audiences of 3,000, effects must necessarily be pretty broad. This scale makes me wonder whether* Pooh *is a proper choice for such a vast arena, but I suppose the movie version (which I've never seen) must be on a similar scale, except that the images can be in close-up and, however magnified, may still be contained and offer a sense of intimacy. If the audience – age-wise – is similar to that for* Spot, *will they have made contact with Pooh already? I would have thought that A.A. Milne was writing for an older readership than Eric Hill, whose stories are chiefly pictorial. But as you so wisely observe, 'We shall see'…*

…I'm glad that Tony Graham, who directed Tom's Midnight Garden, *is in charge of* Clockwork, *but the music does seem to be somewhat of the Kellogg kind – that's to say, of the 'snap, crackle, pop' type, which leaves one waiting for a tune to emerge. The producers certainly seem to be confident of it with such a tour lined up so far ahead. I like your modest admission of 'doing the words'.*

308

I do hope that the Coram Boy *meeting will have given you the go-ahead. Will you be going into purdah in Bexhill for all this?…*

Love to you all –
Frank

26 Apr

Dear Frank,

…Well – I'm not in New York!! – the Disney powers that be were unable to all assemble at the same time in the same place, so the meeting has been delayed – one of the problems seems to be that the producing company of the arena show will NOT be Disney. Disney will license the show to A.N. OTHER company, but 'retain control' – my presence at the meeting is, it seems, to enthuse A.N. OTHER to spend enough cash to do justice to the 'CONCEPT' – So – am waiting for more possible dates. The good thing is that the Disney folk now love what I have done so we are batting on the same wicket – I will send you a copy of the third treatment!…

…You enquire about my Bexhill hotel – I found it, like an oasis, some six or seven years ago, when I needed to write Babe, the Sheep-Pig *– my usual place in Hastings was full (I hadn't realised it was Easter weekend!!) – and I drove along the front of both Hastings and Eastbourne in search of a suitable spot – I need to overlook the sea!!*

Anyway, suddenly, outside Bexhill, when I had almost given up and was seriously thinking of heading home, along came the Cooden Beach Hotel – the receptionist showed me Room 208, an attic room overlooking the sea, and the rest is history!!! The staff know I write up there, but they don't know WHAT I write! Am booked in again next month – to start on Coram Boy!…

Lots of love,
David

30 Apr

Dear David,

...I was surprised to find that I didn't mind the elimination of Father and Mother at the beginning. In fact, I rather grudgingly saw it as an improvement. But at the end I deeply regretted their disappearance because the earlier ending became impossible without them, and Christopher Robin's setting off to school was so absolutely right and very moving. However, after much consideration, I think perhaps its appeal would be only to adults. Your very young audience just wouldn't see the charm of it, so perhaps the very upbeat finale of the latest draft is probably to be preferred. And using characters from the stories as narration seems somehow better without the intrusion of any other human than Christopher Robin. But I should like 'Wherever I am, there's always Pooh' to find a place...

...Whether the charm of Christopher Robin and Pooh is translatable to the stage, let alone 'arena' production, seems to be very chancy. There's a curious intimacy and quietness in the books which seems to me unlikely to survive the audience participation of 3,000 very young youngsters. But maybe Milne's 'concept' is tougher (like Barrie) than I have always felt it to be...

...Never mind all this. I'm terrified of the complex mechanics of the staging and still cannot precisely visualise it. But I can recognise that you have probably managed to translate the untranslatable – the poetry – of the original – into another and acceptable language. So I hope A.N. Other & Co rise to the occasion. Will they tour it with their own stage, revolve and all, in the way that ice shows carry their ice? And how long will they expect to stay in each venue? If 3,000 children come at any one time, how long can a run run?...

Love as ever – keep me posted with the outcome of everything!
Frank

6 May

Dear Frank,

...the Disney saga continues. They cancelled the last meeting, and now I am due to go to Los Angeles round about May 17th, just for two or three days! I wouldn't mind betting that meeting will be cancelled too! What is worrying is that it just shows how low on the list of priorities this project is! Maybe I exaggerate. But there doesn't seem to be very much urgency!

You ask if I will get my money whatever happens! The answer is that the deal is done like a film script deal. I get a little bit on signature of the contract, another on delivery of the treatment, another bit on acceptance of the treatment, etc., etc. So I am not in danger of ending up with nothing!

I agree with you about regretting the loss of Christopher Robin setting off to school. The reason for that was that they see it as very 'final', which would mean there could not be a sequel show! Also, as you intimated, the lump-in-the-throat nature of that ending is rather adult in its appeal.

The songs come from several Pooh *movies, one of which has never been seen in England. To write the treatment, I was surrounded by movie scripts, tapes and sheet music of the songs, summaries of the plots, character lists, etc. I must say they have been very efficient in that direction.*

Like you, I had never seen the first movie, or indeed any of the others! I remember at the time thinking that it would be a travesty. In all honesty, however, I have to say that I was pleasantly surprised. The movie is remarkably faithful to the book. The annoying thing, of course, is the use of the American accents. But the telling of the story is really quite truthful. Yes, there is a cartoon element, which means that characters whizz around and do impossible things, but it is really quite literate, and even literal!

You are quite right about the realisation of the characters in visual terms. Nothing beats Shepard. But the Disney versions could be a lot worse.

I read over the weekend that Pooh is, in financial terms, now bigger than Mickey Mouse or any of the other Disney characters. The merchandising sales are quite astonishing.

Whether or not this arena version will ever see the light of day, I don't know. What would be really rather exciting would be if somebody liked the treatment so much that they suggested putting it on as a theatre show! For that is really what it is!…

Yours,
David

6 *May*

Dear David,

Congratulations on the delivery of Act II of Clockwork… *it's a much better libretto than most composers are given to work on, other than Wagner and Sullivan. Indeed, I think it would stand up as a 'straight' play given the support of incidental music where you have indicated it. But are you perhaps making a rather heavy demand on p.52 for music suggesting Otto's journey to Schatzberg? Suggesting a journey I can see as possible, but such a particular journey under such remarkable circumstances seems to be rather much. Played straight, the repetitions in ensembles and elsewhere would work perfectly well because the concept as a whole is not realistic. I shouldn't expect any of the musical setting to be hummable as with an opera based on arias and recitatives. This is more the sort of music devised by Britten for* Peter Grimes *and* The Turn of the Screw. *'Through composed' I think it's called. It's the sort of music appropriate to melodrama, and melodrama is what this piece really is. I've only two suggestions for detail, both merely nit-picking on p.44. 'To always get it right' moves awkwardly. I should find 'Always to get it right', or 'To get it always right', not to avoid the split infinitive (nobody objects to that nowadays) but* simply to let the words flow, as Hamlet suggests 'trippingly on the tongue'. Similarly, the deletion of 'the' before 'attack':

The great grey beasts poured on to the track,
Maddened by hunger they sprang to attack
seems to me stronger.

I hope the composer will appreciate what a good job you've done, especially in fixing the changes of location in Act II. Act 1 presents less difficulty, doesn't it?

Having admired all this, I have to confess that Pullman doesn't really 'grab' me. … Of course, we know that time is irresistible and works like clockwork, except that so far it hasn't had to stop. And we know that human beings, as distinct from cogs in machinery, can choose between a process of good and evil. All pretty obvious. Why make such a song and dance about it? …Your re-telling is plain enough, and faithful to its original. The words should come across clearly if the composer appreciates their clarity, and the singers enunciate them efficiently – as most singers do not!

I suppose it's over to the composer now. When do you expect to hear what he does?…

Love as ever –
Frank

22 May

Dear Frank,

…I am dictating this on Sunday morning, the day before setting off for Bexhill, to try to get another few tasks completed. I have to do the so-called definitive version of James and the Giant Peach for Samuel French, which shouldn't be too taxing. Then I want to do some work on a play version of a book by Dick King-Smith called Lady Lollipop. This is the one I used when I went to Lincolnshire to work with schoolchildren. It is a gentle moral *fable featuring a pig (again!), and Walker Books want me to do it as a play for children to read and act out in schools...*

Meanwhile, Coram Boy *is knocking on the door. I have said I will deliver it by the end of the year. The way the previous few months have flown by means that I had better get a move on!*

Furthermore, I am having a problem with the Coventry folk who are presenting The Twits *again, this time in London for Christmas. They want to make all sorts of structural changes to my adaptation, which I am most reluctant to do, even though I can appreciate that some of the ideas the director has come up with are not totally inappropriate. It has been decided that the local children employed in the original production, though contributing a delightful energy and bounce to the proceedings, cannot be replicated in London, for logistical and economic reasons. I quite understand it. This means that the circus opening is hard to do without looking extremely 'mini'. The suggestion is that the company of actors arrives like an itinerant troop of performers, and decide to tell the audience the story of* The Twits. *So far, so good. But then they want to revert to the running order of the book, which I very carefully avoided, because of its, in my opinion, lack of theatricality and bittiness.*

Anyway, they are trying to steamroller these new ideas through, and I am trying to fight back. I have the final say, but it is very difficult when you know that they are going to be on the rehearsal room floor, not me. We shall see...

...Thank you for your comments on Act 2 of Clockwork. *Your suggestions are excellent and will be hopefully incorporated.*

...Rather annoyingly, the composer, who has had the text for nearly three weeks, hasn't responded at all yet. Not even an acknowledgement. I know he must have received it, because he and the director have been auditioning people for another week of workshops in August. It always makes me wonder if people don't like it when they take a long time to respond! I remember he did this before, and then surprised me by hardly changing a

word of what I had written in Act 1! I think I shall just let them get on with it. It is not worth tempting fate by getting in touch!

…I think the theme of the book is responsibility. Pullman is quite strict in his criticism of Fritz for not being a responsible storyteller – starting off his story without knowing where it is going to end up. Similarly, he disapproves of Karl, who has not done sufficient work to make his clock figure in time.

It remains to be seen whether staging the piece enhances the story or trivialises it. I suppose that will depend quite a lot on the music and the clarity of the theatrical storytelling. Again, we shall see…

The Disney saga continues. The important meeting has now been postponed till the middle of July! Apparently, everybody is so busy that that is the first date available for everybody! It is due to be held in New York. Again, we will see…

Yours,
David

31 May

Dear David,

…I wonder… might Lady Lollipop make a 'proper' play as well as a classroom book? Perhaps, if the subject is another pig, too much overshadowed by Babe. I'm sorry you're having trouble with The Twits. I should have thought local children might be available in London, though I suppose it would be difficult in a less well-defined community that one would find in the country. But why change a format that has already proved successful? You must certainly fight back and establish control of your own text…

Love to you all –
Frank

11 Jun

Dear Frank,

...I loved your memories of Harcourt Williams and Jean Sterling Mackinlay [often mentioned friends of FW]. You must indeed tell me more! I remember you telling me that Harcourt Williams used to do Old Vic matinees for children, which was very unusual at that time. [These were organised by Jean Mackinlay.]

Did you ever meet Nicholas Stuart Gray? I have always known about his children's plays, which were very successful in the '50s. I learnt the other day that he was a rather extraordinary person who, until his late teens, thought he was a girl!...

...My Bexhill sojourn went reasonably well. I finished the definitive of James and the Giant Peach, *which was posted off to Samuel French last week. And I managed to do the synopsis of* Lady Lollipop. *You ask if this might make a 'proper' play. I think not. It is specially constructed to enable a class of thirty children to take part (possibly more). The story is, frankly, too slight to become a full-length theatre piece. But it is fun. I must send you a copy of the book.*

I have now met up with the director and composer of Clockwork, *who want very few re-writes, I'm glad to say. I'm stealing (or is it steeling?) myself to get them done, but all sorts of other jobs keep on getting in the way!...*

...The other day, I went to Coventry to talk to them about The Twits, *and the various alterations they want to make to the structure and script before they do the production in London for Christmas. The meeting got quite heated at times, but we ended up, as always, compromising, and I am going to slightly reshape the play. I secretly think that it might work quite well, even though I was fighting my corner to keep the original structure! In fact, I think I won the battle, with a technical knock-out, shall we say, because I have avoided the enthusiastic director totally taking over and changing everything!...*

Yours,
David

316

17 Jun

Dear David,

…yes, Harcourt Williams put on special performances for children at the Old Vic. When he proposed the idea to an official of the LCC Education Committee, the response was "But wouldn't that be too much like a pleasure trip?" He also pioneered the idea of the plays being presented without interruptions for the shifting of scenery… [John Gielgud] was one of the stars in waiting whom Billee persuaded to join the Old Vic Company, along with Ralph Richardson, Edith Evans and Dorothy Green. Under his direction, they all established themselves on the upward ladder. Jeannie's mother, Antoinette Sterling, a famous Victorian contralto, used to appear in its old Music Hall days under Emma Cons, when the audience was made up of 'rude mechanicals' in cloth caps, smoking their stinking pipes. When Antoinette came on stage, she announced: "I can't sing unless you put those pipes away. The smoke will damage my voice." All the pipes were extinguished, so she was a pioneer of the war against 'passive smoking'…

…I'm glad there seems to be some progress with Clockwork *and that you've settled* The Twits *to your satisfaction…*

Love as ever –
Frank

14 Jul

Dear Frank,

…Much enjoyed your Harcourt Williams reminiscences. He was a pioneer indeed. As was Nicholas Stuart Gray. Which brings me to Kitty Black. I much enjoyed taking tea with her in her colourful Notting Hill garden. She has, like you, a wonderful memory for her past career, and we talked a lot about her time with Tennents,

317

as well as the Company of Five at the Lyric, Hammersmith. She showed me her gallery of posters and relevant paintings, which stretched all the way up her stairs and even into her bedroom and the inside of her wardrobe! Her book, Upper Circle, *is a very good read. Would you like me to send it to you?*

…The Director and Composer of Clockwork *seem happy with the libretto, and I fancy I won't have to think about any amendments until the autumn, following another workshop with several opera singers, some of whom have already been booked to do the opera 'for real' in the spring…*

…revamping The Twits. *Bexhill came up trumps again, and I managed to do all the work relatively quickly, although somewhat grudgingly, I must admit! The Director is very clever, but hates repeating herself. This means that every time she redirects the production – and that has now happened three or four times – she tries to rethink it all. Quite the opposite from me! I said to her once that she had no reason to fear that the actors would accuse her of a lack of new ideas – most of the actors change with each new version anyway!*

The latest incarnation will take place in the autumn, on a short tour followed by a season at the Bloomsbury Theatre in London. Fingers crossed!

…Initial preparations for The Witches *have started, although things aren't moving quite as fast as I would like them to. The aim now is to rehearse in late January and to open the tour in Birmingham. More meetings this coming week.*

…We have been busy getting ready for our New York trip. This is for the American Alliance of Theatre and Education Conference, at which I will be giving a seminar entitled THE THEATRICALITY OF ROALD DAHL. So various video clips are being assembled, and I am making copious notes on how to fill one and a half hours with this topic!

Then news came through that the same AATE had, in their great wisdom, decided to award me a Distinguished Playwriting

Award for Spot's Birthday Party. *Considering the play has never been seen in the United States, this is something of a miracle! But it has happily galvanised Samuel French Inc. into feverish activity. First, they have bought the rights of* Spot's Birthday Party, *which they had studiously ignored before! Second, they agreed to help fund a booth at the Conference, from which copies of my plays could be sold. They have also taken the US stock and amateur rights of* James And The Giant Peach *and* Fantastic Mr Fox. *All this is good news.*

…The latest in the Disney saga is that I am not going to America, as originally envisaged. The top executive, Tom Schumacher, is going to be in London in a couple of weeks' time, and is taking me to lunch. Quite what this is for, I don't know, but I have decided to enjoy it no matter what! From what I can gather, they are still very happy with my treatment, and will hopefully ask me to write the script quite soon. And there was I thinking I could have a little breather!

Having said that, I still have Coram Boy *to write for Unicorn, although they now say this will not be produced until 2005, when the new theatre is due to open. I have seen the plans, which look very splendid. It is in an excellent position on the South Bank, quite near the Globe…*

Yours,
David

19 Jul

Dear David,

…Before I get on to anything else, I must respond to your exciting – but modestly voiced – announcement on your page three. A 'Distinguished Playwright' award can surely never have been better deserved. Somebody on this side of the water ought to take notice of it and match it here… Congratulations,

congratulations, congratulations! And if the honour gingers up sales in the US, so much the better…

…I'm glad the Clockwork *people seem content with their lot and will hopefully cease from troubling, unlike the Twitters. Oh dear! 2005 seems a long way off before* Coram Boy *is staged. Still, at the rate Tempus fugits, it won't really be long. Are the Unicorn people quite happy with it? The site of the new theatre on the South Bank should be a great bonus… I don't suppose you are sorry not to have to go to America for consultations with Disney. I hope you get a good lunch…*

…I remember going round to see Sybil Thorndike after a matinée [at Wimbledon Theatre] of a very light-hearted piece called Yes, my Darling Daughter *through which she romped with her usual aplomb. We had a delightful chat, during which she remarked, "Of course, that's all very well if you're a genius, but for people like you and me, my dear – !" This was typical of her gift for life enhancement, and I've never forgotten it.*

My next meeting with this great woman was in 1946 at Ellen Terry's cottage at Smallhythe, near Tenterden, when her daughter, Edith Craig, was still living there. This was at the annual Birthday Party which E.C. used to organise with a gathering of leading stage folk. She had converted a barn into a theatre with a very small stage and seating for some sixty or more people. Some sort of performance was given there, to be followed by a tea party. I had just returned from Tehran where I had spent the last three years working for the British Council, and was staying with Jean and Billee – the Harcourt Williamses – in their cottage at nearby Ebony. There we used to play 'Can you Go', a precursor of Scrabble, sitting round a beautiful oak table which E.T. had given them as a wedding present. They were, of course, invited to 'The Birthday' and took me with them. The performance in the Barn was a reading of Macbeth, *with Gielgud as Macbeth, Dame Sybil as his Lady, and Lewis Casson and Billee being everybody else. It was the most exciting experience of the play which I ever* enjoyed. Breath-taking in its immediacy. Afterwards, we gathered in the open for Tea. I was toying with a cup between Jeannie and Sybil, when Sybil suddenly nudged Jeannie and stage-whispered, "Jeannie – does your tea taste of soap?" Jeannie took a sip and whispered back, "Yes, it does!" "Never mind!" exclaimed Sybil. "It's rationed. We must drink it!" And she downed the cupful in one tremendous gulp.

...Edith Craig was a dominating personality, clad in some shapeless over-all garment. She used to bully the inhabitants of Tenterden and the surrounding villages into performing elaborate pageants in aid of this and that. The cottage is now a museum of E.T.'s possessions and quite fascinating, regularly open to the public. I have since visited it with my friends Janet and Harry Jolly when I have been staying with them in Lewes. Ebony Cottage is now occupied by Donald Sinden and enjoys every necessary modern convenience – mains water and electricity – and sanitation!

Have I told you all this before? I hope not. ... If you really enjoy these reminiscences, I'll regale you from time to time with my goings-on in Iran and Mexico. But right now you'll have had enough, so I'll just sign off with love...

Ever,
Frank

30 Jul

Dear Frank,

...I'm dictating this into my little machine the afternoon before Jacqui and I leave for New York.

...We are looking forward to the trip. We will be meeting up with several old friends, and the conference itself should be quite fun. I may have told you that Samuel French, on the strength of the award for Spot's Birthday Party, suddenly offered to pay

321

for a booth in the Exhibition Hall. This is very flattering, but involves us in rather a lot of work, because the booth is going to be mine, rather than Samuel French's!

…Since my last letter, quite a lot seems to have happened. It always does! Perhaps the most significant is that the powers that be at Disney have decided that my services are no longer required! I have been paid for the treatment I did, so I have no complaints, and in fact I am really rather relieved that I will no longer be at the mercy of so many cooks! The poor woman who thought of me for this project a year ago is deeply embarrassed and, indeed, cross with her employers. She is even threatening to leave the company.

It turns out that Disney do not produce the show themselves. They hand it over to the company that produces their ice shows. These people have looked at it, obviously decided it is far too expensive, and told Disney that the whole thing is too sophisticated for such young children – apparently, they don't need stories, just a big hug! So there we are. I still think it would make a good stage adaptation, but I don't think Disney are interested in that!

…A couple of weeks ago, I went to a school in Hammersmith to see Tony Pedley giving his Dahl performance. …He is very successfully playing it in schools now, and has bookings into March or April of next year! He loves the challenge, and the fact that the audience is so close. He also enjoys the question and answer session. I'm delighted for him, because it has really given him something to get his teeth into. And, of course, being a good actor, he does it very well! The children listen intently, laugh quite a lot, and go very quiet indeed towards the end, when he does part of the story called The Swan, *which is a remarkable piece of writing, I think. It is partly about bullying.*

*…*James and the Giant Peach *will be published by the end of the year. I delivered the 'definitive' a few weeks ago.*

I wish I had a video of the Coventry production of Fantastic Mr Fox. *Unfortunately, nobody thought to take one. It was a very good production, but, I have to admit that the director didn't use my idea of a revolving tabletop, possibly for the reasons you came up with at the time. It probably is totally impracticable! However, there was a revolve, which did exactly what I suggested. It just wasn't used as the tabletop!*

Furthermore, the audience were firmly on the side of the Fox family. [And] some puppet chickens, which were done beautifully at Coventry. They were very stupid and very funny. But we never got time to 'know' them well enough to feel sympathy when they were snatched. And we never saw them killed!…

…I much enjoyed your Sybil Thorndike stories and all the reminiscences of the goings-on at Ellen Terry's cottage. More please!

And have I ever been told how you came to work for the British Council? What happened to you immediately after Oxford?…

…I will suspend my narration until our return, so the second instalment of this letter will be all about our American trip!

See you then…!

6 Aug

We have had a very pleasant 5 days in New York. The Conference went well and my seminar attracted nearly 50 people…

We sold quite a lot of playscripts, and the Samuel French representative from the New York office turned out to be a splendidly enthusiastic young man, who will hopefully promote my plays more!

The award ceremony was on Saturday. It seemed to go on for ever! My award was the last but one, and so by the time they got to me, quite a few people had left, in order to attend other sessions. Part of the problem was that everybody, like at the Oscars, gave overlong thank-you speeches! As the time wore on, I kept cutting back my own speech, sentence by sentence in my head! In the end, I probably said everything in about 40 seconds! But I got a couple of laughs, so I can't complain! They presented me with a very heavy engraved plaque, which will probably end up looking very nice in the downstairs loo!...

...I have decided not to attempt to do anything on Coram Boy *yet. The production has been postponed to 2005, when they hope the new Unicorn Theatre will open on the South Bank...*

Yours,
David x

12 Aug

Dear David,

...I'm sorry the Disney project has been washed out, though I'm glad you've been paid for your trouble. Who owns the work now? Are you at liberty to make a traditional stage show of it? Not, I think, that this would be a very good idea. As with Wodehouse, the charm of the Pooh *books is as much in the telling as in the stories that are told, and dramatisations, though retaining dialogue, must necessarily lose all that...*

...When war broke out, I was teaching at Clayesmore School in Dorset. After Dunkirk, I decided I should do well to anticipate my call-up by enlisting first. I did this for RAF in Salisbury and was immediately put in charge of half a dozen rustic recruits, none of whom had ever been to London and across which I had to steer them en route for a training centre at Blackpool. I did this so successfully that I was eventually commissioned P/O and posted overseas with an RDF unit (radar to detect enemy aircraft) and found myself in the centre of the Anglo-Persian oilfield as it then was, as an Admin Officer. There I was smitten with rheumatic fever which, after it had been fixed by Dr. Pill at the Oil Company's splendid hospital, led to my being invalided

324

to the permanent RAF station at Habbaniya – a few miles from Baghdad – for light duties.

These became rather boring and when I read in DRO's (Daily Routine Orders) that the British Council, then a mere ten years established, had been granted leave to recruit from military personnel in the M.E. for work in Teheran, with a fellow officer called John Maclean, I decided to apply and duly presented myself before the Air Officer Commanding. The advertisement said that the Council was looking for persons with an interest in artistic and academic matters. The A.O.C. had no more idea than we had about the fledgling Council but supposed it must be some sort of cloak-and-dagger enterprise. So he slapped us on the back with "Good luck, lads!" and off we went, providing my first experience of being airborne in an antique aircraft crowded with displaced persons being returned to store as it were. I was to take charge of a rest camp for airmen stationed in the Gulf to relieve them from the effects of a very trying climate. I had a sergeant, an NCO and a paramedic with three or four airmen to assist me, and we set to work to set a camp in the grounds of the British Summer Embassy just above Teheran at the foot of the mountains by means of which, if one walked long enough, one could set foot on Everest.

We set up a beautiful camp. Unfortunately, the poor airmen in the Gulf, in addition to the heat, developed measles and were unable to come and enjoy our splendid facilities, so me and my lads had the place to ourselves and amused ourselves by exploring the foothills and swimming in the rather basic swimming pool in the Embassy grounds after we had put in a lot of hard work to clean it up.

The AOC's idea for posting to Teheran was that I should be all ready to work there for the BC after I had been demilitarised. This didn't quite work out. I had to go to Cairo (my second flight) for this, aided and abetted by a special Act of Parliament. Now that's enough for now. If you're still interested, I will regale you with reminiscences of my adventures in Teheran in my next instalment.

Love as ever to you all – from Mary too, Frank

11 Sep

Dear Frank,

...I'm glad to say that I managed to finish Lady Lollipop *in Cornwall. ...You will see how I have dealt with the desire to use thirty children. Quite honestly, some of the parts are very big, but the story demands it. Maybe I can do a bit of pruning. But we will see what the publishers say first!*

...You ask whether I could make a traditional stage show out of the Pooh *script. Not without permission from Disney, which would be extremely unlikely, I fancy!*

It now looks as though The Witches *will NOT take place, because it is financially prohibitive. Australia have gone rather quiet!*

We are now thinking about Fantastic Mr Fox *again. I would direct a new production, which would not necessarily be based on the Coventry one. Maybe you will be able to come along and root for the chickens!...*

...I much enjoyed your stories of theatre-going in the thirties, and also your enjoyable account of how you came to be working for the British Council. Many thanks for that. Please continue with reminiscences of your adventures in Teheran!

Things here seem to be busy as ever. I may have told you that I have been asked to do another Dahl adaptation. This time, it is to be Danny, Champion of the World. *It will be written for the Sherman Theatre, Cardiff, and will be presented in 2005 as part of Cardiff's centenary celebrations. The book is not an easy one to adapt! Mind you, I always say that!*

Coram Boy is really the next one I should get my teeth into. However, the director has changed! It is now to be Tony Graham, who directed Tom's Midnight Garden *so well. I am rather pleased that he is on board, but as he has not even read the novel yet, I feel it would be unwise to put pen to paper. All the discussions I had with the original director might not mean a thing now! The reason the original director has withdrawn is that she has been offered a new job running a company in Glasgow, which is certainly promotion for her. However, she is terribly sad to give up directing* Coram Boy, *which was her idea in the first place.*

There is also more discussion going on of my possible adaptation of Hartley's The Go-Between. *Not a children's project, of course. This would be a musical, with music written by a clever young composer called Richard Taylor. There is a possibility that it might be commissioned by the Library Theatre, Manchester…*

As ever,
David

22 Sep

Dear David,

Your Lady Lollipop *is quite, quite brilliant! The ingenuity with which you have overcome the problem of providing occupation for a class of thirty is simply staggering. I would love to see it done as a school play, though I suppose this might somewhat defeat the object of the exercise since, for such a performance, the actors would be selected from the whole school, not just one class.*

You've kept the original dialogue of the book, quite rightly, because it's very good. This is an advantage not always practical. It's the imaginative ingenuity exercised in providing an adequate supply of supporting parts with the invention of Palace staff, pigs and roses which is so surprising. I particularly like the roses with the instruction to use their facial expression since they are root-bound. I don't see any need for 'a bit of pruning' which you hint at. It's superb!…

I presume that you won't get the usual fee for the performances and will only receive a royalty on the sale of scripts. It's to be hoped teachers, cash strapped though the schools are, will play fair and buy the necessary thirty copies and not resort to cheating by involving the school copier. Is there any way of guarding against this? I know it's often done with sheet music for choirs.

It's a pity that Disney have such a hold on Pooh *without making use of it, and I'm sorry that Australia has 'gone quiet' on* The Witches, *but a new production of* Fantastic Mr Fox *is something to look forward to. Would it be planned to tour? And there's* Danny *to look forward to as well, as far ahead as 2005 in Cardiff. That's the date for* Coram Boy, *isn't it? I'm sorry that you're losing the director, but Tony Graham should be reliable if* Tom's Midnight Garden *is anything to go by.*

But perhaps the most exciting prospect is an adult play of The Go-Between. *I think I should prefer this to be done straight, not as a musical, even with a 'clever young composer'. This tribe are chancy…*

Love to you, Jacqui and the girls, from self and Mary,
F

27 Oct

Dear Frank,

It is over a month since your last splendid letter. I should have replied to it by now, but things have been fairly frantic here!

But first of all, many thanks indeed for your kind comments about Lady Lollipop. *I'm glad to say that Dick King-Smith and also the publisher seem very pleased with it, and, so far, haven't asked for any changes!*

Royalties will be asked for, via Samuel French, even though the book is to be published by Walker. I'm sure there will be a lot of pirate productions, but that always happens, I'm afraid! Hopefully, the schools will buy several copies, although I'm sure that the photocopier will be much in use! Just one of the hazards of the job!

Continuing some themes from your letter… The Witches *has been put on hold for a year…*

It has now been decided that Danny, Champion of the World, *the next Dahl adaptation, will open for Christmas 2004/5 at the Sherman, Cardiff. It will then tour. This is slightly earlier than originally planned, but works well now, following the news of* The Witches *delay.*

Coram Boy *should open during 2005, assuming that the new building is ready in time. So these two epics have to be written within the next 12 months.*

Lovely news came through the other day. Tom's Midnight Garden *(the Manchester production) won the Best Children's Show in the Theatre Management Association Awards a couple of weeks ago. This is the same award that the same play won only 2 years ago, in the Unicorn production! We are all delighted.*

It has also been agreed that the Library, Manchester will commission The Go-Between. *Having said that, between you and me, I am beginning to feel (as you do, I think) that a musical is not such a good idea! This may be a problem, because it was the composer who brought me the idea! I really have to sit down and read the book a few more times and come up with a few honest, if harsh, decisions!…*

…Tony Hatch and I are seriously thinking of working on another project. One that has come up was suggested to me by the current Children's Laureate, Michael Morpurgo. He wrote a lovely story called The Dancing Bear. *I must send you a copy.*

So you will see that possible projects are stacking up somewhat!

*…*The Twits *has happily opened… The new version seems to be working well, and they have a very clever company of actors/musicians who are displaying tremendous skill and versatility. Some of them are even acrobatic! We got a very good review in the Manchester Evening News, which I hope to*

send you. The tour has been progressing well, and will arrive at the Bloomsbury for Christmas. Meanwhile, it seems that any professional productions of the play will have to be kept on ice for many years to come, because, as I may have told you, John Cleese wants to play Mr Twit in a major Disney movie. Disney naturally insist that they have all the rights, including the stage rights, and it seems that the Dahls are reluctantly agreeing to their demands. This is a big problem with adapting well-known books, particularly when they become fashionable. A similar thing has happened to Clockwork. *Now Philip Pullman is the bee's knees, film producers are snapping up every title he has written in the last 25 years! Including* Clockwork. *It looks as though the opera will not be allowed to be produced abroad until the movie comes out. Very frustrating. I am hoping that the production next year will be so good that they will relent, in the knowledge that it will be no threat whatsoever to a movie for other companies to produce the opera…*

… But in many ways, the main activity of the last four weeks has been preparing for the Whirligig 25th anniversary party… John Gould, with whom I started the company, and who goes right back to Oxford, as you will remember, and Barry Sheppard, who became our administrator, both see themselves as semi-retired now! And, over the last ten years, Whirligig has not done very much, apart from enjoyable one-off productions of The Gingerbread Man *in upstate New York and Maidenhead. The truth is that the provision of children's theatre has undoubtedly improved since we began our pioneering work a quarter of a century ago, and we all felt that it was time to gracefully withdraw. There had been no financial crisis. The company was still well regarded. So why not have a celebration and go out with a bang rather than a whimper!*

…all our labours were richly rewarded by the party itself, which was a very warm and sometimes quite moving event. So many faces returned after many, many years. Some of them are

no longer working in the theatre. Some of them have progressed to great heights. Many of them had their very first job with Whirligig. And, I'm glad to say, the entertainment went well. Waves of warmth spread through the auditorium of Polka Theatre, here in Wimbledon, where the event was held. It was the perfect location, with enough room for caterers to provide food, coats to be safely stowed, and a perfect-sized auditorium and stage.

My main three co-conspirators throughout the entire Whirligig era were there – Sheila Falconer, choreographer; Peter Pontzen, musical supervisor; and Susie Caulcutt, designer; and cast and crew from every show. All sorts of memories came flooding back, as you can imagine!...

Yours,
David x

10 Nov

Dear David,

...Enough of this preamble. What I really want to say is how pleased I am that The Twits has had such a successful launch. Have you managed to fix up the necessary children for the Bloomsbury season? I'm surprised that it is such a favourite with the children, because I like it least, I think, of all the stories. But children certainly do relish the unpleasant, don't they?

The news of the Wimbledon Theatre is very heart-warming, though I'm sorry The Witches is on hold. Maybe with so much else going on, perhaps this is no bad thing. I hope there'll be no hold-up for Coram Boy, and I'm sorry for the delays to Clockwork. I still think The Go-Between would be better as a straight play than as a musical. Is the composer the originator of the idea? I like the possibility of your combining with Tony Hatch again on The Dancing Bear.

Congratulations on the award for Tom's Midnight Garden. *Richly deserved. And more congratulations on the Whirligig party...*

F

29 Nov

Dear Frank,

...The Birmingham production of Tom's Midnight Garden *has opened well. Will enclose a review. They do a remarkable ten or more weeks at the Old Rep, followed by a year-long tour! I think they replace the cast every six months or so. The* Twits *continues on its way to London, and apparently business and reviews have been excellent. I may not have explained that the latest version has dispensed with the use of children in the cast, which was against my better judgement at first, but I must admit the show works fine without them. The production feels less like a circus extravaganza than some sort of East European storytelling theatre piece. But the new young company are remarkably versatile, playing musical instruments, doing circus-style physical tricks and acting the parts well too! The tour has now been extended and will run for five or six weeks after Christmas, including a week at the White Rock, Hastings! I hope they do well there, although I rather fancy they won't. Having said that, they did a week earlier this month in Torquay, a notoriously difficult theatre venue, and managed to take £50,000 in the week. This is remarkable in itself, but even more remarkable when one considers the low seat price offered to school parties. I suppose it just reflects the popularity of the book, which is still in the top ten children's book list...*

...Now to the American trip...

Within 8 hours of leaving these shores, I was in an office of the Kennedy Center in Washington DC, trying to flog the idea of them bringing Spot's Birthday Party *over as part of their children's program (note the American spelling!). It may work* out, although I think, as always, they were worried about the financial implications.

I stayed in Washington for two nights, at the home of a former Samuel French employee, now long-since returned to the States, where she is Artistic Director of a children's theatre company. They have just managed to build a brand-new theatre for themselves called Imagination Stage, and a splendid building it is. They opened it with The BFG, which is why I was invited to help host a Benefit Night, which was fun. Unfortunately, The BFG had closed a week or two earlier, but it seems to have gone down very well. They are now talking of doing another one, possibly James and the Giant Peach.

…[I then flew] to Seattle, where I saw The Gingerbread Man in its songless version! It has received very good reviews and is sold out, but I have to say I missed the songs and also missed the audience participation, which the director seemed intent on stamping out. The Gingerbread Man depends, in my opinion, on audience participation. If you don't have an audience that joins in, the play grinds to an embarrassing halt! In Seattle, they just kept going, never encouraging the audience to join in, and, even when the full house of schoolchildren were desperate to warn Cuckoo about the poison, they carried on quickly and efficiently to the blackout, taking no notice whatsoever. A great shame! Having said that, the children obviously enjoyed the show, and listened intently throughout. It is just the different culture, I suppose. But I know that if they had seen the production performed in the way we would do it, they would have enjoyed it more. Never mind. The Seattle Children's Theatre people are delightful, and maybe one day I might get invited to direct something there. Unlikely, again because of the finance, but meanwhile, I suppose, I must be pleased they are doing my plays anyway!…

Yours,
David

2004

The usual rapid reply was not forthcoming from FW due to illness affecting his sister and himself, so that it was January before he was able to respond; but the letters then came rapidly, each replying to the other within days.

5 Jan

Dear David,

…I am delighted that The Twits *has been doing so well and has survived the amputation of children from the cast list. The success at toffee-nosed Torquay is rather surprising, but I suppose, even there, there are children who know what they like.*

…It was a relief to learn on p. 4 that you were safely back in UK without in-flight incidents, and to know that Bexhill did its stuff for the synopsis of Danny, Champion of the World. *It's not a very promising title, but I don't suppose Dahl's fans will be deterred by it…*

Ever, Frank

7 Jan

Dear Frank,

*…*The Twits *seems to be going well at the Bloomsbury. It is a very lively, noisy production, which Jacqui and the girls disliked immensely! But the general consensus seems to be favourable… It continues its tour into March.*

Bexhill went well, and I produced a synopsis of Danny, Champion Of The World. *Since then, I have had a meeting with the director, in Cardiff, and am making some revisions. You will be sent the second draft! It is quite an interesting story, in that there is really no fantasy content whatsoever.*

334

Whether or not this will be a disadvantage, I'm not sure yet.

The situation on The Witches *has taken a rather frustrating twist. The Ambassador Theatre Group still want me to do it, but say that the only way to make it work financially is to do a co-production with Birmingham Rep, who would present it as a Christmas show, 2004. That is fine, except that Birmingham want to have some sort of 'ownership' on their own Christmas show, and have decided that they want me to employ a different designer. Susie, who has designed for me since* The Owl and the Pussycat Went to See… *in 1968, is occasionally a little temperamental! But she is also very clever, and loyalty makes it very difficult for me to accept that I have to drop her services. Her original designs for* The Witches *worked extremely well, mainly because she worked closely with the illusionist. In fact, we all three worked closely together, and to have to start again seems crazy. Susie doesn't know the situation yet, but I am meeting her on January 6th. Quite what will happen, I don't know. If I decide to pull out of the whole thing, I have the feeling that ATG will cancel the three-year contract. I'm very much in two minds about the whole thing anyway! A tricky situation!…*

…Am enclosing a selection of reviews and other bits and pieces, which I hope might be of interest. Do you fancy coming to see Clockwork *at Poole? A matinee? Let me know how you feel about that, so we can organise something, if it seems a good idea!*

Very Happy New Year and much love to you and Mary from all the Woods – Jacqui, Katherine and Rebecca are all fine, I'm glad to say.

Take care,
David

7 Jan

Dear Frank,

…Many thanks indeed for your January 5th letter, as well as the postcard you sent a short while before. Nothing much exciting has happened since the last letter! But I have decided that I cannot go ahead with The Witches *using a new designer, partly because I feel it will be very unfair on Susie, but also because I can't bear to once again go through the complicated process of working it all out, including all the provisions for magic and illusion, puppetry, etc. Changing the designs just for the sake of giving Birmingham 'ownership' seems wrong to me. So I have suggested that they find another director as well as a new designer, and I will act as some kind of consultant. Whether or not they will agree, I don't know yet.*

…The reason why Seattle wanted no songs was, so they told me, because they couldn't afford to pay a musician! Quite why they wanted to cut the audience participation, I don't know. But it is true that the whole idea of audience participation is anathema to some directors, who hate children shouting out! You won't often hear it at a Unicorn show, or in the last few years, at a Polka production. But, funnily enough, the new artistic director at Polka, my namesake Annie Wood, has directed a play this Christmas, in which the children do have the opportunity to participate, and take it vociferously!

Yours,
David

8 Jan

Dear David,

Your splendid package arrived this morning, presumably having crossed mine on the way. I'm rushing this for Pat to post tomorrow after she has collected Mary and self from the hair shop, when she will be able to confirm, I hope, that she will be free to ferry us to Poole for the matinee of Clockwork *on Saturday, 6th March at 2 pm. If she can't make it, we'll charter a taxi so we shall be a party of TWO, come what may, and hopefully THREE. Watch the space above!…*

…I'm glad to hear that The Twits *has been going well in Bloomsbury, even if Jacqui and the Girls didn't care for the production. What was your reaction?*

I'm sorry to hear of the 'frustrating twist' (anagram of TWITS?) with Ambassador Group and Birmingham. Why on earth can't they see how splendidly Susie has provided for all your shows? But of course you can't risk losing that contract. Oh dear! How very awkward for you.

…Now I'll sign off but leave this open so that I can let you know about Pat's ability to come to that matinee. Is the 'Lighthouse' the Leisure Centre which we've been to before?

And a Happy New Year to all the Woods with love from F & M, Frank

P.S. How will the US new passport regulations affect you?
I look forward to draft of Danny. *It still seems to me an unalluring title.*

    F

P.P.S. Have you heard the music [for Clockwork*] at all?*
Is it tuneful and memorable, or does it favour the Kellogg school of composition, i.e., 'snap-crackle-pop', leaving one always waiting for a melody to begin?
I hope it's atmospheric and spooky!

    F

9 Jan

Alas! No, Pat cannot make it. But we'll be there! F

13 Jan

Dear David,

Oh, I say, I say! Your noble offer to chauffeur us to Poole on 6th March is accepted with alacrity and thanks and thanks. Mary will arm you with her blue 'disabled' badge which will allow you to park immediately outside the main door of the Leisure Centre. We found this out when Pat took us to Spot's Birthday Party *in pouring rain.*

And here's an idea. If you can spare the extra time, how would it be if we aimed at reaching Poole in time for us to stand you lunch in the restaurant at the Centre? This would put some gilt on the very substantial gingerbread.

Your splendid further instalment of the David Wood story arrived with your noble suggestion for transport. I think you're quite right to leave the new management to its own devices for The Witches. *They evidently want to put their own stamp on the production, so it will be as well to let them get on with it, magic, illusion, puppetry and all. I suppose it might be as well for you to be on stand-by as a consultant in case they become too entwined and require to be sorted out…*

… Directors who can't appreciate the value of children's participation shouldn't be directing children's theatre. I'm glad your namesake isn't among them…

Love as ever to you all –
Frank

Dear Frank,

Thanks for yours!

Fine – We'll aim for 11.00, Francis Gdns – 12.30 arrival for lunch. Row E 1,2,3,4! Much looking forward to it –

Stop press. Jonathan Church, exciting young director of Birmingham Rep, will direct The Witches *under my hopefully helpful eye. Jonathan endeared himself to me by saying his career was due to me! – he was taken to see* Plotters *when he was 8!!!*

Am dashing off to Bexhill today for more time on Danny, the Champion of the World *– yes, the title is unwieldy – but I guess the publicity folk will bill it as*

DANNY
the champion of the world

– or some such!

Clockwork *started rehearsing yesterday – they had a read-through followed by a sing-through!!*

In haste –
Take care –

Love to both –
David x

Dear Frank,

…[Here is] the Danny *synopsis for your perusal. I don't know whether you have ever read the book. Maybe it is better for you to read the synopsis WITHOUT reading the book, at least in the first instance!*

Delighted our Poole plans for Clockwork *have materialised. Rehearsals have started. I am keeping away for the first two weeks! Too many cooks! Hopefully, things are going well.*

Looking back over your last two letters, here are some responses. First, I'm glad to say my tooth problem has settled down!

The Twits *finished its run at the Bloomsbury, and is now on the road again. I think I sent you a nice review in* The Times.

The situation regarding The Witches *has been resolved, hopefully, in a reasonable compromise, although it means that my own production will not be revived. A brand-new production will be mounted by Birmingham Rep, directed by their talented young Artistic Director, Jonathan Church… I have agreed to be a consultant on the production, and have told them often how complicated it is. Fingers crossed they will listen…*

…Bexhill went fine, although I think I am slowing down a little. I didn't get as much done as I had hoped! Also, I arrived in the familiar surroundings of room 208, where I have worked for seven or eight years now, only to find that they had rearranged all the furniture in a totally unsuitable design! I ended up moving it all back again to the way it always was! I like the desk by the window overlooking the sea. I don't really know why they changed it round. They told me it was because of water coming in through the window when people left it open. Quite what that has to do with it, I don't know!

I've been invited to work in the British School in Brussels for four days in the autumn. Am trying to work out whether I should be here during the build-up towards The Witches *and also* Danny. *Maybe I would be better off escaping to Belgium instead! Nice to be asked, anyway. I suppose I would do the stuff I would normally do in schools, using my own books for storytellings and trying to get over the message that 'books are fun'…*

Yours,
David

As ever, the response arrived within days.

Dear David,

…this reply may be only patchily coherent. Mary and self are both under the weather, and what weather! How did you fare?…

…I'm sorry that the compromise over The Witches *means that your own production won't be revived, but a brand-new production by Birmingham Rep should be something to look forward to where you should be able to put your oar in. And maybe with* Clockwork *you'll be able to insist on clear enunciation so that your words won't be wasted. The invitation to Brussels should be an interesting new departure, but perhaps you should concentrate on* The Witches *and* Danny.

I notice that the draft you have sent me is the Third. Does that mean that you've been having problems (apart from, of course, with the furniture in Room 208)?

Danny *strikes me as being quite a bit different from Dahl's usual work – and none the worse for that, though it does seem very complicated and I shouldn't like to be an ASM for it. I find it has a lot going for it if the scene changes can be smoothly managed. The main difference, I think, is in the absence of fantasy. It's absolutely realistic, even though the device for drugging the pheasants may seem a bit far-fetched. It's all plausible, nevertheless, and the characters of Dad and Danny come across vividly even from the draft, and all the others are surprisingly real. This makes me wish that enough actors could be involved to obviate doubling so that there might be a larger shooting party. It's not only the Baby Austin that needs to be three-dimensional. The Rolls will need to be likewise, as well as the caravan and the filling station, and Hazel's Wood. This doesn't mean that the cars should be real vintage models but they'll need to be convincing mock-ups, especially when the Austin is eventually driven away. And if the gamekeepers are to be seen walking in the woods, those trees will need to be three-dimensional too. The relationship of Dad and Danny is very touching, more so, I think, than that between Grandma and grandchild, largely because of the restrained imagination in* The Witches. *The quiet ending is beautiful. The participation of the audience as beaters will not destroy the illusion that all is 'for real'.*

I find myself wondering will an audience of town children in the 21st century have any conception of gamekeeping and poaching? You'll have to prompt them in the dialogue. What does Dahl do about it in the book?

The ending of Act One is also very 'piano', not creating any great suspense. And here again the reality of the situation for Dad and Danny must be 100% real. It makes me recall the ending of The Cherry Orchard. *Oh, this is a very different Dahl! It's a very moving play, a comedy with an underlying sadness, like* Twelfth Night.

Enough of these lucubrations! Am I reading too much into a mere scenario?…

…Love to you all and congratulations on the website as well as the overcoming of the difficulties of Danny,

Frank

16 Feb

Dear Frank,

…We go to Cornwall today, staying just under a week. It is Jacqui's half-term. Hopefully, I will get a bit of work done on Danny *while we are there.*

Since I last wrote, we have seen His Dark Materials *at the National. This is based on the famous Pullman trilogy. I have*

always believed it virtually impossible to stage successfully. I have to say that I was impressed with what the National had done, but by no means overwhelmed! Lots of things about it worked fine, but an equal number were really unsatisfactory, and unable to match the scale of the books. But it was good to see the National doing something for young people (although most of the people around us were certainly not young), and to see them do it with all the resources and skills at their disposal…

…Have recently been to several rehearsals of Clockwork, which opens this Wednesday in Bury St Edmunds. It all seems to be going ok, although I still worry about the clarity (or lack of it) problem. Fingers crossed. Opera singers are a different breed from actors. Tony, the director, was pulling his hair out last time I saw him!…

…Thank you for your thoughts about Danny. You are absolutely right. It is completely lacking in fantasy, and will probably be a relatively serious play. The reason you had what I have called the Third Draft is that I have been working quite closely with Phil Clark, the Director at the Sherman Theatre, Cardiff, who will be doing his stuff when the play has its premiere in December. We decided to bat it around in the early stages, so I actually did slightly less detailed work until the Third Draft.

The surprising thing is that the book is incredibly popular, particularly in America, I have found. Many people say it is their favourite Dahl. I agree with you about the doubling problem. I have kept it to an absolute minimum, but they won't be able to afford to pay more than half a dozen! And you are right about the cars. All three will need to be three-dimensional, I think.

We are hoping to use a certain amount of video, which will be something new. We think that we will use it behind Danny's drive to the wood, and also to show the pheasants falling. There are a few other problems to solve, but the main thing, I think, is just to write it.

I agree about the splendid relationship between Dad and

Danny. This is what I will be working on most, I think. We have made the decision to increase the whole area of responsibility. Danny feels he is left out of quite a lot of major decisions and is even unaware of the problem that Hazell poses. Hopefully, seeing Dad and Danny develop as a team will be at least as interesting as seeing Grandmother and Boy develop in The Witches...

Yours,
David

2004 Clockwork –

Theatre Royal, Bury St Edmunds – 18ᵗʰ February 2004
An opera in which Fritz begins the story of Dr Kalmenius, whose mechanical figures seem to take on a life of their own. But Fritz is horrified when halfway through the story, the fictional Dr Kalmenius appears.

25 Feb

Dear David,

...We ...continue to be impressed with your ability to do so many things at once, even on holiday. I hope you managed to put in some work on Danny. *It's remarkable that that particular book should be one of Dahl's most successful. I think that this probably indicates that quite young children are given to speculation about many aspects of life usually thought of as concerning only the teens and above. Using video seems a very good wheeze to iron out some of the difficulties of representation. Certainly, there is a parallel with the relationship between Grandmother and Boy in* The Witches, *though that was less central – or seemed less central, being taken for granted as it were during most of the action so full of suspense. All really successful comedy incorporates a shadow. One of my favourite*

instances is in Twelfth Night *when Sir Toby confesses, "I would we were rid of this knavery"…*

…Mary and I have both been rather under the weather throughout Feb. Which is usually one of my favourite months because daylight begins to lengthen and daffodils to show their heads, all anticipating spring and the flowers that bloom, tra-la! …So here I am, well wrapped up, fixing my own lunch and scribbling this indecipherable script to you. But don't worry. We shall both be fighting fit for 6th March. Now that's really something to 'stiffen the sinews and summon up the blood'! Meanwhile, Mary joins me in sending love to you all – and adds, "Don't overdo the exercises."

Frank, as ever

The joint visit to *Clockwork* at Poole took place as planned, and the first draft of *Danny* was ready soon after that.

17 Mar

Dear Frank,

Here is the first draft of Danny *for your perusal.*

Bexhill was good to me, as usual, and I managed to complete the second act within the three days I had put aside. Now the script has gone to Cardiff, where, next week, there will be a rehearsed reading with a group of actors and an invited audience. I just hope they don't all pull it to pieces too much! I will be there and will try to stand firm if I disagree!

Last night was the first night of Clockwork *at the Linbury. Am enclosing our first review from the* Evening Standard. *Not a rave, but not bad either. In fact, the performance went very well and everybody was very happy afterwards. Jacqui thought it was much sharper than the performance we saw with you. Maybe the singers knew that there were critics out there!…*

...It was lovely seeing you and Mary. I hope you are feeling a little stronger now. I'm delighted that you were able to see Clockwork *– it's a little bit different, anyway!*

Thank you for your recent letter in which you rightly say that many of the children in the audience will have read the book, so won't be totally confused if they cannot hear every word. Certainly, this will be the case with school parties, I'm sure...

Love,
David

24 Mar

Dear David,

Oh, what an exciting package! Huge thanks for it. I've enjoyed the Danny *script enormously. Indeed, I will go so far as to say that it is a Magnificent Multi-media Show – but I shouldn't like to have to stage it because technically it is so very demanding. The dialogue comes over beautifully and the contrast between the quiet exchanges between Dad and Danny and the other action is beautiful, but all the characterisation is good, and the holding back of audience participation until it slips naturally into the action is very effective and will probably allow the children to release a lot of pent-up energy. The use of Danny as narrator, slipping easily in and out of the action, is masterly. He must be played by a real boy as near the right age as possible, a sort of Billy Elliot with amplified voice for addressing the audience, because it seems to me that a very large stage is required to accommodate the many acting areas. The scene shifting from one to another will, I think, help the action to move swiftly and smoothly and provide interest in the continuity. The spectators will be as interested in the mechanics as in the plot. I suppose every theatre of any size has a trap for Dad in the pit, or he could be in an orchestra pit where there is one. The revolve will need to be extensive, won't it, to accommodate the filling station and interior and exterior caravan?*

Ideally, the cars should be real, though that wouldn't be really practical, but they must look real. In 1933, my brother had an open two-seater Baby Austin which would interfere less with sight lines than a saloon and could carry a bicycle fairly easily strapped across the 'boot'.

I particularly like the wordless opening sequence. Might this be choreographed in slow motion (without strobe), and might it be even more effective without any sound? I note that Dahl has taken care of my concern that today's town children would know nothing about poaching or gamekeeping by having Dad explain it to Danny. The whole is delightfully subversive! I like the quiet ending to Act One in the realisation that Dad and Danny are about to lose their home. I'm a little concerned for the pheasants and the hens. Puppetry will conveniently take care of the one Danny handles, but what about the others as they tumble from the trees and land on the roof of the Rolls? Perhaps showing them on the screen will help, but some will actually have to land to be swept up. Giving the Headteacher, doctor and Council Official a sex change shouldn't matter at all, even to those who have read the book. I shall be eager to hear the outcome of the rehearsed reading in Cardiff. Is it intended to tour the production in due course? If so, the need for a very large stage may limit the choice of venue. How about Chichester?

Bexhill did you wonderfully well this time. Did you have to rearrange the furniture before you could set to work?

The Standard *review is interesting, and fair enough, though the 'wizened operaphile' seems to have been overly fascinated by the puppet Callum. Perhaps, like me, he doesn't really go for Pullman's complex plotting! Though he seems to have been able to follow it well enough.*

…I won't detain you any longer, because I'm not really with it

just now. …I …find concentration on the printed word extremely difficult, but I have managed to take real pleasure in Danny *and should love to see how it works out on stage. I'm glad you'll be at the reading to fight your corner because I'm sure it will work if the mechanics of mounting it can be properly organised…*

P.S. If Jacqui thought the Linbury performance sharper than that in Poole, this may have been because the singers have become more confident in their singing and can act a little more forcefully.

F

29 Mar

Dear Frank,

…Yes, the workshop and rehearsed reading of Danny *went very well. One or two useful things came out of it, a few nips and tucks, and the realisation that to attempt to do it with only six actors is probably pushing it somewhat! Seven is more realistic…*

The actors all seemed to enjoy reading the play. Not all of them were chosen as ideal for the roles they played. One of them was particularly inept, in my view. But, typically, he was the one with the most criticism and "wouldn't it be better if…?" I decided I wouldn't listen too hard to his criticisms!

The audience was small but bright, including several teachers. They all seemed to think it was lovely! We also did a session with sixty children from a local primary school. The first half was read to them, and then they were asked various questions, dividing into groups to talk about the pros and cons of poaching! All the moral questions of the piece! Quite interesting! Most of them saw little wrong with poaching, as long as no guns were used, and as long as the pheasants were being caught for food, rather than killed for sport. Some of the boys, however, saw absolutely nothing wrong with blasting the pheasants from the sky with a shotgun! Nearly all of them were anti-fox hunting, which perhaps is not particularly surprising. We were not in hunting country!

I'm glad you enjoyed the script. Yes, technically, it will be a nightmare. I think the director is intending to use quite a lot of video backgrounds for the Woods and for the pheasants. But puppets will be used too in certain scenes. I know he is hoping to have three-dimensional cars, although there may well be traffic problems in the wings!

One idea we were all hoping to employ was to have a revolve. However, touring a revolve is notoriously difficult, particularly when you arrive at a theatre with a raked stage! So we will see. I'm quite relieved that I am not directing this one!

Your idea for the first scene – to be performed silently, in slow motion, is an interesting one, which I will pass on. The idea of Danny *being done at Chichester is very appealing. However, the licence given to Cardiff was for a middle-scale tour. So theatres like your own in Winchester are more likely to take it – and of course, the size of stage may well prove a problem! But at least all the problems can be sorted out in advance, and the designer already knows most of the theatres the show will visit.

Yes, indeed, I had to rearrange the furniture in Bexhill, before I could set to work! Not too much of a problem. And, as you say, my three days there were well spent – Bexhill and room 208 did me proud, as ever!

Now to* Clockwork. *There have been several more reviews, some of which I will send you. Very good ones, I'm glad to say, although some of them omit to mention the chap who slaved over the words! All they are interested in is the music! Stuff the storyline and the structure! Never mind, at least they are all positive, and* The Times *gave it four stars!

The tickets have become like gold dust, particularly for the public performances. Considering the business on the tour was really dreadful, mainly because, I think, the word 'opera' put schools and parents off (!), the reception in London is* *particularly gratifying. Possibly the use of the Unicorn mailing list, augmented by the Royal Opera House mailing list, led to both Unicorn regulars and also opera devotees deciding to book...*

...Last Friday, I went to Birmingham for a preliminary meeting re. The Witches. I met the new designer, who seems very nice. In fact, I know his work quite well, and in the past he has designed several of my shows for the Leeds Playhouse – rather well, I seem to remember. Hopefully, this Birmingham production will be ok...

Love and best wishes,
David

19 Apr

Dear David,

...My sickness has now been identified as

POLYMYALGIARHEUMATICA

...the principal function of which is to subject me to hot and cold flushes and insuperable disposition to sleep. I'm trying to dash this off in a fairly lucid interval to tell you how pleased I am that Clockwork *has been so well reviewed except for the omission of the skill of the librettist. I suppose opera critics have come to ignore librettists and libretti because most opera plots are so silly. Your deft handling of a very unusual plot should have attracted exceptional attention.*

Never mind. It's good that the reading of Danny *went so well. I suppose some reader took on the stage directions. The director seems to be prepared to cope with the problems with which they present him. It would be splendid if our Theatre Royal could take it in. It would find a receptive musically minded public here. The stage area might just about accommodate the action but there is virtually no wing space to accept units to be trundled on and off...*

...Now I'm just about to nod off again so I'll sign off with

renewed thanks, apologies for the delay in sending them, and with love to all from self and M.

Frank.

10 May

Dear Frank,

…The positive reaction to Clockwork *has led to an invitation from the Berlin Festival to take it there, it seems. However, they want it sung in German! I think I will leave them to it!*

No more news on the Danny *tour. I will certainly mention the Theatre Royal, Winchester to them…*

…I had another meeting about The Go-Between. *There is now interest from two theatres to present this proposed musical version. I still have a very strong feeling that it would be better as a play, but as it was the composer who brought the idea to me, I suppose I had better do a little bit of work on it! But it will have to wait until I can get my head round* Coram Boy.

We went to Cornwall at the beginning of April, and I managed to do absolutely no work at all …But I made up for it somewhat by going to Bexhill a week or so later. Progress, however, is very slow on Coram Boy. *I have done 34 pages, which represents probably only one-fifth of the play! Tony Graham, the Unicorn Director, is taking these thirty-four pages to a drama school, where he has been asked to do some workshops. He will play around with my work, and hopefully make sense of it! But* Coram Boy *is so sprawling a novel, it is proving difficult to keep the clarity! I suppose I will press on, in the hope that all will be well in the end.*

There are moves afoot to revive Spot's Birthday Party *next year, plus interest in the idea of it going to Australia. Could be interesting!*

Polka Theatre, the children's theatre in Wimbledon on the board of which I have sat for twenty-seven years, have just announced they are to present my adaptation of James *and the*

Giant Peach *for Christmas. In all this time, they have never done one of my plays before!…*

…I may have told you that I have been given permission to adapt Goodnight Mister Tom, *the novel by Michelle Magorian. I have wanted to do this for many years. There was a very popular television version starring John Thaw. The book is about an evacuee. ATG are interested in this becoming one of my productions for them, to follow* The Witches. *Birmingham Rep, are, as you know, staging* The Witches. *We had one meeting, at which I met the director and designer, who seem competent. Fingers crossed!…*

Love and best wishes,
David

27 May

Dear David,

…This will probably not be a very coherent return because my Polymialgia Rheumatic does not permit of coherence. I have been surprised to learn that it is not at all unusual not only among geriatrics (like me) but also among the young. I find this very disappointing because I had thought I was afflicted with something rather special if not quite unique. Never mind. The general verdict is that it takes ages to get rid of. Indeed, one does not get rid of it; it is merely reduced to quiescence. I'm not sure about the spelling of that last word but I shall let it stand…

…I'm not surprised that Coram Boy *is proving a difficult nut to crack. I still cannot understand why the Arts Theatre should want that particular book for their reopening. Have they offered any explanation? I've been wondering whether there is any way in which you might simplify the very complicated plot.* The Go-Between *should serve better, though as I remember it, the idea of its being presented as a musical seems mistaken.*

It may work, of course, but I can't see it being so suitable as Clockwork. *I wonder why the Germans want to do it, though I suppose it has resonances (now that's a good word) which are Germanic.*

The possibility of a revival of Spot's Birthday Party *surfacing down under is quite exciting. Have your plays been taken up there to any satisfactory extent?…*

Ever –
Frank

By July, FW had become more unwell and was in hospital.

7 Jul

Dear Frank,

We have all been thinking of you and hoping that things are progressing well…

…After dictating this, I shall be driving to a school in a village near Bath, where the first performance of Lady Lollipop *will be taking place. Dick King-Smith is due to be there too. Indeed, the school performing the play is the very school where Dick used to teach! They asked if they could do performances in advance of publication, and everybody agreed.*

The head teacher is very enthusiastic. However, when I went down to the school last week to have a look and 'give a hand', it was plain that the production was in a fairly chaotic state! She didn't seem to have much support from other teachers, and was doing it all herself with more enthusiasm than expertise! You know the sort of thing!

…Yesterday, I had a meeting about an event we are trying to organise at the Duke of York's Theatre to celebrate the centenary of Peter Pan. *We are thinking of having a reading of* An Afterthought, *the extra act Barrie wrote in 1908, the one where*

Wendy is grown up and her daughter is, as it were, the next in line for Peter to fly off with! We are hoping to have the event on the actual day the play opened, which was December 28th, several days later than planned, because of technical problems! Apparently, this date is very difficult for the theatre because it is a bank holiday, and there may be nothing actually playing in the theatre at the time. If so, just to open the doors of the theatre would cost £4,000, believe it or not!

We are also working with the Theatre Museum, who will put on a display to coincide with the event. They have various interesting items, including the original poster and the original flying harness.

We are all well, and send you and Mary every good wish. Another letter very soon!

Lots of Love,
David

2004 Lady Lollipop –

Farmborough Primary School, Bath, 7ᵗʰ July 2004
Princess Penelope is a right royal brat. What would she like for her birthday? "I wanna pig!" she yells. And she gets one. But Lollipop is no ordinary pig. When people look into Lollipop's bright, intelligent eyes, it seems to change them. For the better…

By the end of the following month, *Coram Boy* was ready to be sent to FW.

2 Sep

Dear Frank,

…By now, you may have received the Coram Boy *script, the size of which might have given you a nasty shock! Don't feel you have to plough through it! But, as you know, I always send you the first copy, and much value your thoughts…*

...Danny, the Champion of the World *and* The Witches *are in pre-production. It feels quite strange, because I am hardly involved in this process! I am letting the directors of the Sherman, Cardiff and the Birmingham Rep. get on with it! Occasionally, they ring me to pick my brain, which is fine, but the casting, organisation of the design, and everything else is down to them! Fingers crossed both productions go well. They will both be embarking on tours after their home run.*

Meanwhile, the tour of Tom's Midnight Garden *goes on and on, and seems to be going extremely well. They are having a short rest at the moment, then, with a new cast, setting off for the autumn, and touring well into 2005. I'm not complaining!*

...I may have told you that with Action for Children's Arts, I am organising an event at the Duke of York's to celebrate the centenary of Peter Pan. *The event is coming together well. We are working in conjunction with the Theatre Museum, as well as ATG, who own the theatre, and Great Ormond Street have now become involved. I am asking Sir Donald Sinden (a distinguished Hook in his day) to host the event, which will take place on the morning of December 18th. ...I will keep you informed!...*

...Please don't bother to reply to this letter. But maybe we can have a chat on the phone.

Lots of love to you both, and all good wishes from us all,
Yours,
David

5 Sep

Dear David,

I had intended to acknowledge the safe and very welcome arrival of Coram Boy *long before this, but Mary and I are both 'under the weather' as the saying is, she particularly so and suffering all manner of aches and pains and disabilities. I'm recovering well from the surgery on my hip but am not exactly a picture of health in other ways...*

I'm very much enjoying Coram Boy. *It was bound to come out at length because the plot is so extremely complicated. At the moment, my feeling is that when the action shifts to Ashford it goes very well, but the earlier episodes are difficult to grasp without having the Stage Directions to clarify the action. I had been hoping it might be possible to cut some of the complications. The time switch is ingenious but I feel an audience might not be able to keep up with it. However, I will let you have a revised reaction to this when I have had time for a second reading.*

...I'm glad the centenary of Peter Pan *is to be fittingly celebrated. I'm a great admirer of Donald Sinden. I always remember him as the most effective Malvolio I've ever seen. I think he acquired the Harcourt Williamses' cottage at Ebony, near Tenterden in Kent.*

...Love to you all – from Mary too,
F

10 Sep

Dear David,

I am sorry to have been so long in sending you my reactions to your version of Coram Boy. *I have enjoyed reading it and am delighted by how clearly the characters are realised as the story quietly unfolds. But I am wondering whether you have not been too faithful to your original in following its development so exactly. It seems to me a not-well-constructed book. It offers two stories – one of Gardiner's evil world and the other of Ashford, with Mrs Lynch (not sufficiently explained, I feel – how does she slip away from her housekeeping duties to hobnob with the riffraff in the Black Dog, for instance?). The two plots should have been more closely integrated. If Aaron is the Coram Boy of the title, he should dominate the whole action and not just creep in at half-time. I would like him to be narrator of the whole, even for the years before his advent.*

As you say, it's very long. But there seems to be quite a bit that could be cut – the scene with the stable lads, for instance, and the Coram children in the fields. And Mother Catbrain is by no means necessary. Some of Meshak's speeches could be pruned, too.

The 'fluid' production you stipulate, a kind of cinematic technique, should work well, though, as I think I mentioned the other day, the rather rapid toing and froing of time in the early scenes might lead to some bewilderment among the audience. The action throughout is inclined to be similarly paced, with limited confrontation of the kind of which Sir William's attitude to his heir is the strongest example. However, it moves to a splendid swashbuckling climax, a little more of which might quicken the pulse of earlier scenes. The transformation of Gardiner into Gaddarn is signalled by the former's declaration that he is not always going to be a tinker of pots and pans, but it would help to have a little more detail of this development.

In spite of these strictures, I feel that because the characters are so vividly realised, the story – stories – grip the attention and are sufficiently satisfying. Nevertheless, I still find myself wondering why the Arts Theatre chose this particular novel to be dramatised for its reopening. Is it perhaps located anywhere near the hospital, thus establishing a raison d'être?…

Love to all…
Frank

2004 Danny, the Champion of the World –

Sherman Theatre, Cardiff – 19th November 2004

9 Dec

Dear Frank,

Am enclosing reviews of Danny, the Champion of the World, *which has opened successfully in Cardiff. Business is very good. Very clever actors/musicians, who act the story as well as playing all the music! I am encouraging the ATG folk to go and see it because I think it could be a touring proposition for the end of next year, going into 2006.*

James and the Giant Peach *has opened at Polka here in Wimbledon, and apparently it is breaking box office records, which is good. They have done a nice production, with a very ingenious set, part of which is inflatable, believe it or not! In the second Act, the whole of the forestage inflates to become the top of the peach! The actors are able to lie on it and walk on it!*

In Birmingham, The Witches *has opened too. I think the production is ok, although I have to say I don't think it is better than our original one! There are some very nice performances, however, and we will just have to hope that the tour is successful. We now know that it will be going into the West End for Easter, playing at Wyndham's. The powers that be (ATG) have insisted that we have a name in the cast, and so a lady called Ruby Wax is coming into the show just for the West End. She is an American, who was an actress until she started doing other strange television shows, interviewing people and generally being rather unpleasant! I hope to heaven she can do it. We have had very little proof of that. Luckily, I won't have to rehearse her into the show!*

I seem to be spending most of my time at the moment organising the Peter Pan Centenary Celebration *at the Duke of York's. I am enclosing some information. We are very pleased that there will be ten celebrity guests. Hayley Mills is the latest addition – she played Peter back in 1969! My greatest achievement is in reuniting the Peter and Captain Hook from 1956! John McCallum and Janette Scott will meet up once again! Julia Lockwood is flying in especially from Spain. Hopefully, it will be a nice event…*

…As you know, our visit to Buckingham Palace on October 29th went well! [DW was there to receive his OBE.] *Looking back, it was a very pleasant day. Everything at the Palace is brilliantly organised. And our lunch was very splendid indeed!*

I went to Bexhill to try to get a bit of work done. Have done a synopsis for a possible musical called The Dancing Bear, *based on a book by the Children's Laureate, Michael Morpurgo. This is the one I hope to write with Tony Hatch. I will send you a copy of the synopsis.*

Have virtually decided not to go ahead with the adaptation of The Go-Between. *I have done some work on it now, and honestly feel that it would be better as a play, rather than as a musical. The problem is that it was the composer who approached me, so it really does have to be a musical! I think I will throw in the towel on this one!* [In fact, the production went ahead in 2016.]

Tony Graham of Unicorn is worried about Coram Boy. *He is of the same opinion as you – he feels that the book is flawed, and never really makes up its mind who the story is about. I can see what he means. While I was laid up with my bad back, they did a reading of the play at RADA. They kindly made a tape of it for me. Listening to it, I can see that the protagonist seems to change regularly, and the play is obviously too long. I think it is a real problem, and I am not sure that we will resolve it. Maybe it won't open the new Unicorn Theatre next year after all!…*

Yours,
David

The two men managed to meet up in Winchester for lunch, although FW was by then very unwell.

22 Dec

Dear David,

…I hope the Arts Theatre will opt for Tom's Midnight Garden *for its reopening production. Or perhaps it might go for* Clockwork, *though I suppose a new piece is really preferable if they can find something very special. By DW for choice!*

Which brings me to your Dancing Bear. *I'm not happy with it on the same grounds as I criticised the* Coram Boy. *The story is flawed in much the same way. The Bear should be the mainspring of the story which sidelines him almost as soon as it has begun. The 'Purple Hat' might be more apt, but that is also lost sight of after a brief appearance. No doubt the film-making could be interesting if not too much of a muddle. I don't see the lyrics being really essential to it, though no doubt you will make a good work of them. Did Tony choose the story? It's broken backed, an example of what goes wrong when unity, that classical benchmark, is abandoned. I can visualise a plot in which the Bear is a telling protest against the cruelty of making, or trying to make, animals perform like humans. He could refuse to co-operate with his tormentors, until either they give up or he collapses – making possible a happy or unhappy resolution. Will your lyrics provide narrative links to push the action along, or will they aim to express the emotions of the characters? They must be seen to be structural, active and not merely ornamental or diversionary.*

I'm sorry to be so destructive, but I do think you'll be seriously handicapped by the central flaw.

Ruby Wax is just a name to me. She occurs not infrequently in the Radio Times, *but her line of business seems not to be suited to a straight play. Will she take on the leading witch?*

She can hardly be just one of the ordinary witches. And I don't suppose she'd think Grandma a starring role.

It's great to know that the Dahl adaptations are doing so well. His stories are all very classically planned and Morpurgo should take a leaf out of his book.

…Love to you all, as ever, and thank you yet again for the splendid packets. Keep them coming through 2005!

Frank

23 Dec

Dear Frank,

Many thanks for your letter of December 22nd. It is amazing how, although I know you are not feeling that great, you manage to retain your interest and enthusiasm and, indeed, your sharp, laser-like critical faculty! More about that, in a moment…

The Peter Pan Centenary Celebration *went remarkably smoothly, and was enjoyable, informative and, at times, extremely moving. I felt that all my efforts organising the event had been really worthwhile. The stalls and circle were virtually full, and the audience were very enthusiastic. You will find the programme and a photo from the* Stage. *They will give you an idea of what happened.*

But it is worth saying that the Theatre Museum lady did a very good twenty-minute speech, accompanied by some wonderful slides, talking about Barrie's early career and the genesis of the play. Stephen Reynolds then did a delightful section on the build-up to the first night, the technical problems, etc. He also talked about some of the equipment still under the stage of the Duke of York's, thought to have been used to hoist the house up to the treetops.

Sheila Hancock proved to be a wonderful host. Very warm and enthusiastic, witty and suitably celebratory. Maybe I should send you a copy of the script I prepared for her. She embellished it very skilfully, but, in the main used what I had suggested. One or two factual errors were discovered. Apparently, Wendy Craig was the last Peter Pan at the Scala, not Hayley Mills as the Theatre Museum had erroneously informed me!

The Parade of past Pans and Hooks was quite wonderful. Some lovely anecdotes, and some moving reunions. There were several stories about the flying going wrong. Donald Sinden spoke of drunken pirates getting cross with each other for pinching each other's lines! Julia Lockwood spoke of the mother who, very confusingly, pointed out to her child in a loud voice, during a performance in which Margaret Lockwood was playing Peter, and Julia Lockwood was playing Wendy – "You see, Peter is really Wendy's mother!" Then Unicorn gave a beautiful reading of An Afterthought, *which brought a lump to the throats of most of the audience, I think. Susan Wooldridge (you may remember her from* The Jewel in the Crown) *proved to be a wonderful grown-up Wendy. Her anguish as she cried out, "Can I come too?" was heart-stopping.*

…I was very pleased that Action for Children's Arts had agreed to work on this, and honestly feel that unless I had pressed everybody into action and service, a proper celebration of the centenary in the theatre where it first all happened, would not have taken place. A memorable day…

…Now on to The Dancing Bear. *Many thanks for your thoughts on this, which I will take very seriously indeed, before we take the project any further.*

Last week, Tony Hatch and I had a meeting, at which we were both saying the Bear is the most important character. We both agreed that he needed to be made more of. But you have put your finger on it when you point out that, in the story, he is far from central, which does indeed make life extremely difficult. The original Morpurgo story is a very short one, and reads well in my view. Morpurgo himself suggested it to me for adaptation, and I rather liked the idea of doing it as a musical, because of the musical situations in the story – both folk music played and sung by the locals, and contemporary pop music brought to the village by the pop singer and film crew.

…You were absolutely correct about Coram Boy. *And I am sure you are equally astute about* The Dancing Bear. *Thank you for waving the red flag so eloquently!*

On to The Witches. *Ruby Wax is a kind of actress, but she has become more of a television presenter/celebrity in recent years. I have never met her, but she apparently impressed Jonathan, the Director, enough to accept ATG's suggestion that she play the Grand High Witch, in the West End only. I must say I am relieved that I am not directing, and having to put her into the show!*

The Grandmother is played by Dilys Laye, who is a splendid actress. She is, I think, 70 years old. I first met her back in 1964 or 5, when I nearly left Oxford to take part in a revue in the West End. Dilys Laye was to be in the cast, and we all had lunch in a posh restaurant! Laurier Lister was putting it on. Unfortunately, it all fell through and I had to plead with Lord Franks, the Provost of Worcester College, to let me go back! Looking back, I am very glad things turned out that way!…

Love,
David

26 Dec

Dear David,

Oh! What a splendid bundle! The script provided me with a very illuminating picture of how the Peter Pan Centenary *shaped up to expectations. What a time you must have had in getting in touch with all those participants. Tell me… was the whole centenary your original idea? The response was wonderful and justly restored Barrie to the recognition of which there has not* been much evidence of late. …How sad was the neglect which buried him so hastily before his time…

I hope you've found time to be festive at this overemphasised and exploited celebration, which becomes more and more commercialised and adrift from its original purpose…

I'm glad that you find my critical comments useful and shall look forward to progress with Tony Hatch. What audience are you aiming at with The Bear Dances?

Now I'll waste no more of your time in trying to decode this scribble except to thank you again for that latest exciting packet of reviews and another extended letter. How do you manage it all?

Love to you all – Mary takes her eyes from the TV to say remember to add her love if I'm writing to you. So here it is.

Frank

30 Dec

Dear Frank,

…My mother did pretty well on Christmas Day. …On Tuesday morning, I took her to see James and the Giant Peach at Polka, which she seemed to enjoy.

…I am enclosing a photocopy of An Afterthought. I am sure you have read it at some point, but you may not have a copy. I had thought that my copy was, in fact, from my Frank Whitbourn shelves, but I now find I bought it in a shop in Cecil Court a few years ago. So maybe you haven't seen it in this edition.

Sadly, no recording was made of the Peter Pan event. I had tried several television companies, to see if they would be interested in making some sort of documentary… Really, I should have arranged for a sound recording of the event to be made. Stupid, really. But it foolishly escaped my mind. The reminiscences of our celebrity guests would have been so well worthwhile recording… Never mind.

On Radio 4 over the holiday period, there seemed to be a lot of Barrie interest, including Alan Bennett reading from the book version of Peter Pan *and a nice programme about Barrie's early life. On Radio 3, there was a reading of part of the play, including the original John Crook music, recorded in New York, featuring Rosemary Harris as the narrator and Hayley Mills as Wendy! It was nicely done.*

The Dancing Bear will be, I think, aimed at family audiences rather than just children. However, there is another thought that we might make it a musical play that schools and youth drama groups can perform. Until we get going, it is impossible to say how it will turn out. Tom, my agent, seems to think it is a potential winner, but we will see. I am taking your cautionary comments very much to heart!

Love and best wishes from us all to you and Mary, and here's hoping 2005 will be a peaceful and happy one.

Yours,
David

2005

2 Jan

Dear David,

Oh, I say! Yet another splendid bundle! Hugissimus thanks for it. I'm especially glad to have the photostat of An Afterthought. *I know I once had a copy of it, but I can't find it now. What I may have done with it I just don't know. I thought perhaps I had passed it to you, but you managed to pick it up in Cecil Court. Oh, what jolly excursions that territory conjures up! I've just noticed in the* Radio Times *that there is a celebration of the centenary of* Peter Pan *on BBC1 at 5 something this evening. I must make sure that I catch that...*

...I've just looked at my copy of Peter Pan. *It didn't get into print until 1928, when four editions followed rapidly. I suppose JMB was reluctant to publish the text while the play was still running. Other plays came out after their initial run was terminated, though revivals were frequent and amateurs took them up. It appears in the Definitive Edition of 1928 which however does not include* An Afterthought.

Yes, certainly, The Dancing Bear *would be right for Family Viewing, but what impresario would put it on? Hopefully, it could be taken on in the classroom, providing 'extras' for all those members not given the named roles. Teachers do seem now prepared to take themselves out of the stranglehold of Government targets. But even with your 'book' and lyrics, I feel it would need more action – which the book would have to provide...*

...So I'll detain you no further. Oh yes, I will. Did you know that about 1928 or '29, The Times *published a long story by JMB – Farewell, Miss Julie Logan – occupying the whole front page? It was added subsequently to the uniform edition.*

So, all the best for 2005 and lots of productions of the Works of DW, OBE!

Love to you all and thanks again for such a splendid bundle,
Frank

12 Jan
Huge thanks for that splendid packet and Congratulations on those reviews of James and the Giant Peach. *I'm doubly delighted because I've never thought of it as one of Dahl's better efforts. But you've really made something of it.*

We suffer indifferent health just now, but soldier on.

Love to all –
Lucky you to be in Oxford!

One more postcard was received from FW. He wrote it eighteen days before he died.

6 Feb

Oh, I say, what a splendid bundle! Huge thanks as ever. But you mustn't attempt too much, what with your bad back and all. This does seem to be the Year of David Wood OBE! Mary is managing very well. I'm pretty poorly, thank you, but we keep on keeping on.

> *Love to all as ever,*
> *Frank*

FW died peacefully in his armchair. His sister, Mary, rang DW with the sad news, and asked him to give the eulogy at the funeral. For DW this was a privilege. It seemed like the end of an era. But life and work continued, and DW, much missing his mentor after nearly fifty years, was busy as ever.

2006 Fimbles Live! –
Bloomsbury Theatre, London – 5th April 2006
Based on the TV characters, with a children's TV presenter as the human guide.

2006 The Queen's Handbag –
Buckingham Palace Gardens – 25th June 2006
The plot involved the baddies, who had not been invited to the party, trying to sabotage the events by stealing the Queen's handbag in which were her spectacles and her speech, to be given after the show. Harry Potter and many other characters help retrieve the handbag and save the day.

2008 The Tiger Who Came to Tea –

Bloomsbury Theatre, London – 27ᵗʰ August 2008

The play faithfully follows the delightfully surreal story of the Tiger coming to tea with Mummy and Sophie, and is introduced by a back story as Daddy goes to work and the Milkman and the Postman visit before the arrival of the Tiger. The Tiger having devoured all the food and the drink in the house, the family set off for supper in a café – sausages, chips and ice cream.

2009 George's Marvellous Medicine –

Capitol Theatre, Horsham – 28ᵗʰ October 2009

Put-upon George tries to 'make better' his demanding and vindictive grandmother by concocting an extraordinary medicine, which magically makes her grow and grow and then shrink until she disappears forever. DW created a brief back story to make George's behaviour easily understood and accepted by the audience, who help him mix the medicine.

2010 Guess How Much I Love You –

Rose Theatre, Kingston – 19ᵗʰ May 2010

The affectionate relationship of Big Nutbrown Hare and Little Nutbrown Hare.

2011 Goodnight Mister Tom –

Chichester Festival Theatre - 2ⁿᵈ February 2011

Young William Beech is evacuated from London to escape the air raids of World War Two. He is put into the care of Tom Oakley, an elderly recluse. The withdrawn William blossoms, and Tom, who has never recovered from the early death of his wife, blossoms too. And when William has to return to his disturbed and cruelly strict mother, it is Tom who eventually rescues him.

2013 The Magic Finger –

Imagination Stage, Bethesda, Washington DC – 3ʳᵈ April 2013

The last of eight Roald Dahl adaptations.

2022 Coming to England –

Birmingham Rep. – 31ˢᵗ March 2022

Floella Benjamin's memoir telling the story of how, as a child, she left Trinidad to live with her family in London.

Eulogy spoken by DW at FW's funeral

Today we celebrate Frank's life – much as we miss him, much as we are sad to lose him – let's celebrate the happiness we shared with him, as a brother, an uncle, or a great uncle, or an ex-pupil, or friend. He was such a special man, and I am honoured to be asked to speak about him.

Frank taught me so much – not at school, though I envy anyone in his class at school – rather as a fellow theatre enthusiast who was lucky enough to attend a residential drama course run by him. It was 1958. I was fourteen, theatre-mad in a world where such an interest was looked on as somewhat odd. Thanks to Frank (he insisted on being called Frank, not Mr Whitbourn, which made him immediately approachable), that week was the best week of my life, where I found I wasn't alone – it shaped my life. Helping him learn his lines as a revivalist preacher, I laughed a lot and learnt a lot and found an adult who understood. He became my mentor, and for nearly forty years, was the first person to read all my plays, to enthuse, to make spot-on critical judgements, to advise, to encourage. I can't tell you how much I valued and how much I will miss such an acute sounding-board. I treasure the three overflowing box-files of his wise and witty letters written in that unique, exquisite copperplate hand.

I want to share with you some gems from these letters. They reveal his amazing memory, his humour and the richness of his experiences. And his enthusiasm! Having received a package of press reviews or a new manuscript from me, he would start:

"I say, I say! What a splendid plop on the doormat! Hugissimus thanks!"

He came to see a play of mine and wrote about a child in the row behind complaining, "There's a VERY LARGE GROWN-UP in front of me, whereupon I tried to curl up into obscurity!"

He wrote of his love of books: "I was obsessed by books before I could read them. At about five I was given a book called The Wallypug of Why *and I can still see myself sitting in a little chair pretending to read and chuckling over it. I read to my mother when she was ill. She enjoyed the sound of her little Frankie's voice – and so of course did he!"*

"Whenever any kind uncle pressed a half-crown into my expectant little hand I was off to our local bookseller, William Pile – in Sutton High Street - to buy another volume."

And of course he later wrote plays and books including the splendid history of Lock's, the hatters, a branch of the family who made hats for the gentry and indeed for Nelson and Jane Austen's brother.

Not to mention those wonderful Christmas poems he sent us.

He took his writing seriously:

"I shudder to think how many Scandinavian trees I may have used up in the course of my long and not especially productively poetical – or do I mean 'poetically productive'? – life! I wake up in the night with a sudden flash – or quirk – of illumination, and up I have to get and jot it down for fear it will have fled by morning, like the ghost of Hamlet's father. And how often by daylight it doesn't seem so marvellous and necessary after all!"

Typically modest.

Later, theatre became his great passion. He wrote:

"That was a time when Mary and I did a lot of theatre-going. We used to take a return 'cheap-day ticket' (eighteen pence) from Sutton to Victoria (train every twenty minutes) and head for one of the major cinemas where admission was one shilling before noon. After the movie (we just called it a 'film' in those days before the American invasion) we queued at a theatre for pit or gallery for not more than three shillings which included sixpence for hire of a camp stool which stood in to keep our place for us while we snatched a bite at Lyons – 'brunch' for 1/3d – whither we returned after the play for a second snack which exhausted our cashflow."

He loved Shakespeare, of course, and J.M. Barrie, whom I admire hugely too. Barrie wrote Peter Pan, *and sometimes I think of Frank as*

Peter Pan, not that he didn't grow up, rather that his mind stayed ever young.

He, like me went to Oxford. He, like me, got a 'gentleman's third class degree'! And we were proud of it! His tutor at Merton was the famous poet Edmund Blunden, whom he much admired.

Teaching became Frank's vocation, first at Clayesmore, where he inspired later-to-become actors, Michael Balfour, Michael Ingham, and Stephen Joseph, who became the great pioneer of theatre-in-the-round. One day the young Stephen said, "Please sir, could you write a play for my puppet theatre?" – Frank did. It was called Ask a Policeman and was published – for 8 guineas!

Thanks to a fellow teacher he met the famous actor-manager Harcourt Williams, and stage-managed for him, and even acted what Frank called "the inferior end of a cow". He stayed often with the Williamses and met John Gielgud and Sybil Thorndike.

When war broke out, Frank joined the Airforce, but The British Council were looking for military personnel "with an interest in artistic and academic matters". Frank ended up in Teheran and had a wonderful time.

"I put on The Tempest and A Midsummer's Night Dream in a superb setting and knew that the weather would co-operate. We also did Flecker's Hassan translated into Persian with real camels en route to Samarkand! These were my glory days!"

After his long teaching career, mainly at Collyer's, Horsham, directing plays and writing them, Frank retired to Winchester with Mary. As he got older, his wit never diminished. He loved gardening – most of the time.

"There's no notable news except that 'the rain it raineth every day', but at least I don't have to stagger forth of an evening with my watering-can".

He still wrote his wonderful letters –

"I note that my penmanship is even more obscure than usual. I think this must be because Mary and I have had a visit from our chiropodist *this morning, and though I don't write with my feet (even if it looks like it!), I suspect it's a side effect."*

He didn't like the work of Andrew Lloyd Webber! "The only moment I enjoyed in Phantom *was when the candelabra got stuck and wouldn't go up or down and we sat in the dark for twenty minutes or so while sweating stage hands tried to fix it. That interlude was almost worth the exorbitant price for admission. It was rewarded with the largest hand of the afternoon".*

We all loved Frank. We all, family and friends, are grateful for his love. Above all, hundreds and hundreds of us will forever be grateful to him for opening the door to the joys of drama and literature. Some years ago I was to speak at the funeral of my headmaster's wife, who also opened doors for us. I asked Frank if he knew a suitable poem with which to close. He didn't - but wrote one especially.

It is appropriate that I end with his poem, to thank HIM.

".... One who loosened
Windows opened onto far horizons, lit
Candles of courage for doubting youth to climb
Dark midnight stairways, or illuminate
Blind corners in the corridor of Time."

Frank, hugissimus thanks!

David Wood – 9 March 2004

Afterword

Although the correspondence inevitably ceases with FW's death in 2005, there are many tantalising mentions of projects which then seem to disappear, as DW explains.

Perhaps it is inevitable that over the years many potential projects bite the dust. For every seed of an idea that flowers and grows to fruition, there are many that fall on stony ground. Some progress to small plants that show promise but then are nipped in the bud. In my case, some of the most likely winners, to change metaphors, fell at the first fence, some of them at the last hurdle. But they all created a glint of excitement at the time.

For television, I worked on animation ideas for Enid Blyton's Mary Mouse, *Annette Mills'* Muffin the Mule, *and Kathleen Hale's* Orlando the Marmalade Cat. *Enid Blyton and Annette Mills were long dead, but the extraordinary Kathleen Hale was very much alive. Her books had been iconic in my childhood. This was in 1986. Kathleen was eighty-eight. I remembered* Orlando *from childhood but knew nothing of his creator. I suppose I was expecting a granny in a shawl and slippers in a picturesque cottage. I was right about the cottage, but Kathleen was wearing denim and dangly earrings, and was reading the autobiography of Bob Geldof. Later, rereading her books, I realised she wasn't an elderly version of motherly cat Grace. She was the young kitten Tinkle, alive, alert, witty, gleeful – with an undiminished rebellious streak. Like all classic children's books, hers can be read on many levels, appealing to the child in all of us, at any age. In real life, she displayed the same humour, observation, wordplay – she told me about 'Big Mick, the mowing postman', who did her lawn, and the rotund lady with drooping lip she secretly called 'the burst plum'. She complained about 'cabbage the colour of army uniform'.*

Working on the proposed Orlando *film script, I was somewhat daunted, wanting to create a faithful adaptation. But a reassuring moment came when Kathleen laughed at a line, looked up and said, "I like that – is that you or me? If it was you, I wish I'd thought of it!" In fact, I think it was her line, not mine, but from then on I think she trusted me.*

Kathleen taught me about the importance of quality in children's writing – "They have no taste," she said. "They'll accept anything because they know no better – why should they? It's our responsibility to give them the very best we can."

She rather disapproved when I adapted Noddy *for the stage. Enid Blyton, or 'the Pied Blighter' as she called her, once in public to her face, I believe, was twee and sentimental. She preferred Roald Dahl. She wrote to me, 'He is so deliciously subversive about parents, etc.' I took her to see my adaptation of Dahl's* The BFG *at the Oxford Apollo Theatre, and afterwards she entranced the acting company and crew backstage, going up the line like a royal visitor.*

This is from one of her letters, all of which I treasure:

'I ought to have written to thank you before but I fell ankle-deep into correspondence requiring immediate replies to several demands etc... I really only want to sit quietly snoozing in my Ingle Nook wearing a mob cap and with a warm old cat on my lap, and clay pipe. I've got the Ingle Nook and a lap, but no cat or cap or clay pipe...'

She did see Orlando move, alas only in a two-minute animation trial, but she loved it. The proposed TV film or series was never made. But it was a privilege to know Kathleen. When she died, aged 101, I was honoured to speak at her funeral.

Television and film scripts that were never made included adaptations of Andrew Taylor's *The Coal House* and Ian Strachan's *The Flawed Glass*. Theatre Projects, who had filmed DW's screenplay of Arthur Ransome's *Swallows and Amazons* for Anglo-EMI, asked him to work on further Ransome stories, including *Pigeon Post, We Didn't Mean to Go to Sea* and *Great Northern?*

Other aborted film projects include *Sparky's Magic Piano*, a proposed version of the best-selling children's record; *The Crowstarver*, the poignant book by Dick King-Smith; and *The Selfish Giant*, a musical animation film based on Oscar Wilde's magical story with Don Black, the lyricist, and Barrington Pheloung as composer. Other projects with Don Black included *Sherlock and Santa*, with music by Charles Strouse, and *The Lady in Red*.

DW went to New York to discuss a stage adaptation of *Octonauts*, a children's television series. His Roald Dahl adaptations were very successfully produced on tour, notably *James and the Giant Peach*; *Danny, the Champion of the World*; and *George's Marvellous Medicine*. His adaptation of Philippa Pearce's *Tom's Midnight Garden* also toured to great acclaim. But, along with *Octonauts*, proposed collaborations on a stage version of *M.I. High* and of the book *Dinosaur Roar* failed to take off. Another trip, this time to Tokyo, involved one of Japan's largest producing houses and a family show called *Kureomon* about an elephant. The proposed London version never happened.

A Don Black collaboration did make it to the stage, however.

We first worked together on Abbacadabra, *a musical that didn't exactly 'get away', but arguably never attained its potential.*

Cameron Mackintosh noticed in his Paris office an LP record, a fairy tale album using songs by ABBA with new French lyrics. Intrigued, Cameron listened to it, liked it, and invited me to create a theatre production. Don contributed English lyrics to the familiar ABBA tunes, and the show opened for a Christmas season at the Lyric, Hammersmith. A starry cast included Elaine Paige as the evil witch Carabosse; Finola Hughes, fresh from Cats as Cinderella; Michael Praed as Aladdin; Sylvester McCoy as Pinocchio and Phil Daniels as a robot. At the time, the story had a contemporary feel. A group of schoolchildren managed to enter a computer game and rescue the fairy tale characters from a terrible fate. The three main children were played by young actors who all achieved major success as adults – Jenna Russell, Dexter Fletcher and Nigel Harman. The show proved a major success. Tickets were like gold dust, thanks partly to the excited response of ABBA fans, and partly thanks to a clutch of enthusiastic press reviews. During the run, Cameron invited Don and me to his office and told us that, with a few rewrites, Abbacadabra could within two years be a hit all over the world. I honestly thought that my meal ticket had arrived! Cameron had reinforced my hopes from the jubilant press night, at which I was sitting next to Andrew Lloyd Webber. During the tumultuous curtain call, Andrew whispered to me, "I think you've written another Joseph." Nevertheless, Abbacadabra was never seen again! Because the show included familiar British pantomime characters, I think Cameron felt it was too much linked to the Christmas season, and might not work all year round. Whether or not that was the reason, Abbacadabra became, for me, 'one that got away'.

In 1976, DW was approached by the producer Peter Bridge to work on a stage adaptation of *The Wombles*, the highly successful books and TV animation series about the furry creatures who recycle unwanted things found on Wimbledon Common. The idea was that he would work alongside Elisabeth Beresford, the creator of *The Wombles*, to deliver a fairly large-scale production. The script was duly delivered to Peter Bridge. Unfortunately, he responded by saying that the whole thing was ridiculously overblown and expensive and he couldn't possibly produce it. And so the show remains on the shelf, unproduced.

DW's family had all enjoyed *Mr Benn*, the television animation series about the ordinary man who regularly visited the fancy-dress shop and, having tried on a costume, set off on an extraordinary adventure. So he was intrigued when Clive Juster, of King Rollo Films, suggested he might meet the composer of the music for the series, with a view to creating a children's musical, based on a book by David McKee, *Mr Benn*'s creator. Don Warren lived nearby.

> *We had a couple of good conversations. The idea was that a private school in Oxshott, at which his son taught music, would present the musical, performed by a large number of their children. Having visited the school and met the teacher who would direct the show, I wrote the play and was pleased with it. I sent it to Don but never had a reply. Perhaps because I was busy with other things, I never chased it up. But a year or so later, I was invited to the school to see the production. It was certainly not the one I had written! Nothing like it! It turned out that Don said he had never received my play and it was thought I was not interested, so they did their own version. Just one of those things, I suppose.*

Rather more frustrating was the *Coram Boy* saga. When Unicorn Theatre for Children were in the process of building a brand-new theatre near Tower Bridge, DW was thrilled to be invited to write the opening production. This was to be an adaptation of Jamila Gavin's superb novel, *Coram Boy*, set at the time when Thomas Coram set up his celebrated Foundling Hospital. Hogarth and Handel featured in the moving story. Emily Gray, the Associate Director at Unicorn, was to direct.

We had meetings, and I discussed my adaptation with Jamila Gavin herself. Writing the synopsis of the play took some time, because Unicorn could not afford a large cast. This meant finding a way of actors doubling, and making sure that the two characters an actor played were never on stage at the same time. The synopsis was approved. Then, throughout the summer, I worked on the play. Everyone seemed pleased with the result, including Jamila. RADA students held a play reading. Plans were in place for a children's choir to take part. Meanwhile, the building work was progressing and the theatre was going to open on time.

Suddenly it was announced that Emily, the director, was leaving Unicorn to take up the artistic directorship of Trestle Theatre. I was told that she would no longer be able to direct the production. Tony Graham, Unicorn's Artistic Director, who had very successfully directed my adaptation of Philippa Pearce's Tom's Midnight Garden, *considered taking on the mantle of* Coram Boy *director, but eventually decided against. Quite rightly, he felt that he was going to be so busy coping with all the teething problems of the new building, as well as the razzamatazz of its opening celebrations, he wouldn't be able to concentrate on directing a new play. Reluctantly, Unicorn decided to abandon plans to produce* Coram Boy, *but gave me a very kind consolation prize by reviving* Tom's Midnight Garden *as the opening production.*

Meanwhile, Jamila Gavin was upset that the play was no longer happening. We met and discussed possibilities. As a result, I suggested to my agent that the National Theatre might be approached. They had already produced Christmas productions of several children's book adaptations, including The Wind In The Willows *and* His Dark Materials. *I wondered whether* Coram Boy *might be suitable for this slot. Within hours, the National, said Tom Erhardt, my agent, not only wanted to read the play, they wanted it biked over immediately. The script was delivered, but we heard nothing for several weeks. Alas, eventually, the news came through that the National loved* Coram Boy, *the book, but not my play. They discovered that Unicorn had given up the adaptation rights, had quickly secured them for themselves, and had asked Helen Edmondson, a playwright I much admire, to work on a new adaptation. Disappointing is too weak a word to describe my feelings. I could understand that the National would need a larger-scale production than the play I had written, but they obviously didn't feel I should be asked to revise my play for a larger cast. Not only that, they didn't even ask me to go in for a cup of coffee to talk about it! I was pleased that Helen's play became a great success for the National. I felt that Jamila deserved this. The book is a very special one and deserved to be given a wider audience. But I still look back ruefully on all the wasted hours I spent! That one really did get away...*

Another major near-miss was *Matilda*. In 1993, Cameron Mackintosh suggested that DW should work on a musical adaptation of Roald Dahl's novel.

I had already adapted The BFG *and* The Witches, *both of which had received critical acclaim, toured the UK and played in the West End. Cameron put me together with Anthony (Ants) Drewe, the lyricist, and George Stiles, the composer, whose musical version of Kipling's* Just So *I had seen and admired at the Tricycle Theatre. Ants endeared himself to me by telling me that the first theatre show he had seen as a child was my production of* The Owl and the Pussycat Went to See... *at Chichester. George and Ants had, I think, chosen* Matilda *from other Dahl titles, and I was very happy to work with them. One reason why Cameron had got involved was that Dahl's widow, Felicity, or Liccy, as she was generally known, had asked me to set up a meeting with*

Cameron, in order to ask him for his advice on finding an agent to look after forthcoming Dahl theatrical ventures. The three of us had lunch together, and Cameron suggested some agents, one of whom was my own agent, Tom Erhardt, who was eventually chosen by Liccy to look after Dahl too. This arrangement proved happy and profitable for many years, during which I adapted eight of Dahl's classic children's books.

Although Liccy was unwilling to give us the musical theatre rights of Matilda, *she said she was happy for us to come up with a proposal. So George, Ants and I started work. I came up with my usual detailed synopsis, showing how the story might be told, and suggesting places where songs might be incorporated. George and Ants came up with some excellent songs. I wrote several scenes, until we felt we had enough material to do a presentation to our agents, other interested parties and, of course, Liccy and other representatives of the Dahl Estate. We decided to introduce our work ourselves. I read from the synopsis, George accompanied himself and Ants singing the songs, and we all played characters in the sample scenes. The reception was warm, but no decisions were made immediately, which seemed very reasonable. Unfortunately for us, Liccy eventually decided that she did not want to give us the rights to proceed. I heard that she felt she had not heard 'a hit song', which seemed a little harsh, having only heard the numbers once. But maybe there were other factors, even though I had hoped that my track record with* The BFG *and* The Witches *would stand us in good stead. As the years went by, we regularly approached Liccy and the Estate, asking if they might change their minds. But it was not to be. Many other writers were itching to get their hands on* Matilda. *And suddenly we heard that the Royal Shakespeare Company had bought the musical theatre rights. It took many years for their project to come to fruition, and they worked with several different writers, composers and lyricists. Eventually, Dennis Kelly was hired to write the book, and Tim Minchin the songs. The rest is history.* Matilda *became one of the biggest ever musical theatre hits. So maybe Liccy's judgment was completely justified, and the Stiles/Drewe/Wood version of* Matilda *was never seen.*

The producers at Clarion, with whom he had worked on *The BFG* and *The Witches*, plus two *Noddy* plays, invited DW to think about a possible *Pingu* stage show, based on the popular TV series.

We thought the perfect way of presenting Pingu *might be to do it on ice, but we wanted a theatre rather than an arena-sized production. I was dispatched to the Birmingham Hippodrome during their Christmas pantomime season. Robin Cousins, the celebrated Olympic ice skater, was appearing in the show, which incorporated an ice ballet. I saw the show and was impressed by the speed with which, apparently, an ice rink had been created on the stage. Afterwards, I went backstage to meet Mr Cousins, who explained that in fact he and the other skaters had not been dancing on ice, rather on plastic! A clever material had been developed, creating a surface on which skates could travel with almost the same facility as ice. Mr Cousins agreed, in principle, to be a consultant on* Pingu. *Unfortunately, the project never went any further.*

After directing adaptations of *Babe, the Sheep-Pig* and *Fantastic Mr Fox* at the Open Air Theatre, Regent's Park, DW suggested to the theatre directors that he might adapt Nick Butterworth's *Percy the Park Keeper* for the following summer. Nick and DW had had positive discussions about coming up with a show that used inventive puppetry to portray Percy's animal friends. It seemed perfect for an open air production, but the project never got the go-ahead, and never went any further.

DW feels that another category of 'ones that got away' refers to shows like *Abbacadabra*, that actually did happen, but never achieved their full potential. There are three more in particular that spring to mind for him.

First, Guess How Much I Love You, *the hugely successful book by Sam McBratney. I was sitting in the back row of the Shaw Theatre, about to watch a Birmingham Stage Company production, when the young lady sitting next to me introduced herself. Sally said she was a producer, and asked if I would be interested in adapting and directing* Guess, *the rights of which she was negotiating with Walker Books. Plans moved swiftly ahead. I enjoyed working on the script and songs. My regular team reassembled. Designer Susie Caulcutt, choreographer Emma Clayton and musical supervisor Peter Pontzen all came on board. Auditions took place and rehearsals began at the Rose Theatre, Kingston, where we opened successfully three weeks later. Sally then took the show on tour and produced a rather splendid DVD of the production. I shall never forget the enthusiastic reaction of the primary schoolchildren who had been invited to the first preview, which was really a dress rehearsal. I suppose they were aged from six to eight, and joined in the audience participation happily and noisily. Interestingly, audiences, as the Rose run and the tour progressed, seemed to be younger, and not many primary school parties came. It became clear that the show was perceived by the public as being for the under-fives. It was absolutely fine for the very young ones, but worked even better with the early-years primary audience, many of whom missed out, either because the teachers felt the show would be too young for them, or because they felt that they had no time to bring the children to the theatre, thanks to the impending tests.*

Nevertheless, we hoped very much that the show would return. Sally had worked extremely hard and imaginatively to get things going, and I was sure that she would want it to continue. But fate took a hand. Sally fell in love with a Rolling Stone. She married Ronnie Wood and before very long had two beautiful girl twins. Furthermore, the Rolling Stones went on tour several times and Sally accompanied them. Nobody realised, including Sally herself, that as time went by, her stage rights on Guess How Much I Love You *expired. Suddenly news came through that another company had acquired the rights, and another version was imminent. As I write, the production is touring in the Middle East and I think is having considerable success. A shame, but just one of those things.*

Shaun's Big Show *got off to a great start. Ed O'Driscoll of Calibre Productions had successfully produced several stage tours and asked me if I would be interested in adapting* Shaun the Sheep, *the sparkling animation series by Aardman, as a show that would introduce the world of dance to primary school children, as well as entertaining the public. The idea was to incorporate as many dance forms as possible into a continuous narrative, with no dialogue, but an orchestral score featuring well-known tunes, both classical and pop. I loved the idea, and immediately asked if Bill Deamer could join the team. Bill had choreographed superbly a production of* The Boy Friend *at the Open Air Theatre, Regent's Park. His ability to create pastiche choreography of different dance styles and eras was, I thought, unparalleled. He waxed enthusiastic about the idea. I started work by watching every single Shaun animation film, learning about the characters and the humour. With Ed, I visited the Aardman Studios in Bristol and met the creative team working on the series. Simon Townley came on board as musical arranger and supervisor. For years, he had been a major player in the celebrated Pasadena Roof Orchestra. It turned out he had studied at Worcester College, Oxford, my alma mater, some years after me. He delivered brilliant musical tracks. Bill, his assistant Kylie, and I auditioned a considerable number of* dancers, and assembled a very talented cast. Rehearsals were an absolute delight, and we opened at the Gordon Craig Theatre, Stevenage to a wonderfully responsive audience and some ecstatic newspaper reviews. Julius Green, who was working with Bill Kenwright's organisation, came up to me afterwards and seriously told me we had created 'a work of genius'. I really thought we had a big hit on our hands.

But on tour, despite more enthusiastic reviews and online comments, the show didn't attract large audiences. The schools didn't support it sufficiently, and the public only came in limited numbers, even though those that came clearly loved it. The conclusion we came to was that the perception of the show, thanks to the fact that the television series was aimed at small children, would only appeal to very young children. In fact, the production had a very wide appeal. Adults loved the somewhat camp spectacle of sheep dancing together like cygnets in Swan Lake and dancing a spoof of the famous Dirty Dancing 'lift'. But the business just wasn't good enough, and any future life for Shaun's Big Show was doomed.

Another short-lived success was Clockwork, the opera for which I wrote a libretto, based on Philip Pullman's remarkable novel. Tony Graham of Unicorn Theatre secured the rights, and I was teamed with the composer Stephen McNeff. At first, I wondered if I would feel out of my depth trying to create an opera, but the intricate story proved to be an exciting challenge, and Stephen wrote an electrifying score to accompany my words, very seldom asking for rewrites. The whole enterprise developed rewardingly smoothly, as did the rehearsals, with a very fine cast of experienced opera singers. We opened in the Linbury Studio, the smaller auditorium of the Royal Opera House, Covent Garden. The reception was more than encouraging, as were the reviews.

However, the whole enterprise was clouded by the fact that when I was midway through writing, word came through that a major film studio had bought the film rights of Clockwork. *Part of the deal was that our opera could only be performed by Unicorn Theatre, and could not be exploited further. Although this news was very depressing, I was happy to carry on writing, because I was so enjoying the exercise. But it was obviously frustrating to know that the opera had little chance of a future life. As years have passed, I understand that the film was never made and the rights expired. Now I believe the opera has been published, but we are still waiting for another company to revive the opera.*

DW is philosophical, however, about the realities of life as a writer for children's theatre, and the uncertainties of theatre in general. Despite all the unrealised projects, as well as the complexities of managing rights to the literary works he has so often adapted, DW continues to develop innovative work for children's theatre. For so many years associated with his adaptations of the stories of Roald Dahl, he has had to accept the decision of the Dahl Estate to no longer permit these versions to be produced professionally in the UK, as they investigate other ways of bringing the stories to new audiences in different genres. At the time of writing, his adaptation of Floella Benjamin's memoir *Coming to England* has just opened in Birmingham, and no doubt there are many more projects just around the corner.

Although at the time it rankles when a promising project hits the buffers, I have tried never to dwell too long on the feeling of waste or resentment that, although perhaps justified, never actually helps. Remaining positive and grateful for the many projects during my career that have actually landed successfully has proved a much healthier reaction. You can't win them all! And life is always full of surprises. Some of the least promising ideas come to fruition. The absolute certainties are never guaranteed.

My experience co-creating children's books echoes the ups and downs in my theatre, film and television work. Richard Fowler and I have produced about twenty children's books, many of them successful, but still lurking unpublished in the drawer lie titles such as The Adventure Playground, Santa Paws, The Story Tree, The Dolls' House, Bad Bears, The Dressing-Up Chest, Owl's Birthday Party *and the somewhat implausible* Hungry Hoover…

All part of the wonderful world of fantasy and creativity in which I have been lucky enough to wander all my professional life.

Person List

Jean Anderson 1907–2001
Actress

K D Anderson 1911–1998
Head of Chichester High School for Boys from 1954 to 1972

David Armitage
Artist and illustrator of *The Lighthouse Keeper's Lunch*

Ronda Armitage
Author of *The Lighthouse Keeper's Lunch*

Daisy Ashford 1881–1972
Writer of a novella when only nine years old

Cynthia Asquith 1887–1960
Writer and socialite who was also secretary to JM Barrie

Alan Ayckbourn b 1939
Playwright and director

Peter Baldwin 1933–2015
Actor and toy theatre enthusiast. Attended Chichester High School before DW

Michael Balfour 1918–1997
Actor and artist. Taught by FW

John Barber 1912-2005
Drama critic for the *Daily Express* and the *Daily Telegraph*

Harley Granville Barker 1877–1946
Actor, director, writer and playwright

Katharine Barker b 1941
Actress. Played Grandmother in a revival of *The Witches*

Gillian Baverstock 1931–2007
Author and daughter of Enid Blyton

Lilian Baylis 1874–1937
Theatrical producer and manager associated with the Old Vic and Sadler's Wells

Alan Bennett b 1934
Actor, author, playwright and screenwriter

Leonard Bernstein 1918–1990
Conductor, composer and author

Don Black b 1938
Lyricist for musicals, film and television. Worked with DW on *Abbacadabra*

Enid Blyton 1897–1968
Children's writer

Edmund Blunden 1896–1974
Poet, author and critic

Michael Bogdanov 1938–2017
Theatre director

Howard Brenton b 1942
Playwright and author. Attended Chichester High School for Boys, as did DW

Karen Briffett
Actress who created the roles of Noddy and Babe, in *Babe, the Sheep-Pig*

Benjamin Britten 1913–1976
Composer, conductor and pianist

Charles Boyer 1899–1978
French-American actor. The production of *Man and Boy* went to New York but was not well received

Lance Burton b 1960
American stage magician

Richard Burton 1925–1984
Welsh stage and film actor

Barbara Cartland 1901–2000
Best-selling romantic novelist

Susie Caulcutt b 1944
Set and costume designer, particularly associated with plays by DW

Jonathan Church b 1967
Stage director and artistic director of several theatres

Emma Clayton
Choreographer and Assistant Director of many DW productions

Stephanie Cole b 1941
Stage, TV and film actress

Fay Compton 1894–1978
Actress

Gladys Cooper 1888–1971
Actress, theatrical manager and producer

Rowena Cooper b 1935
Actress

Bert Coote 1867–1938
Stage and film actor

Tom Courtenay b 1937
Actor

Edith Craig 1869–1947
Theatre director, costume designer and activist for women's suffrage

Wendy Craig b 1934
Actress

Nick Curtis
Theatre critic of the *Evening Standard*

Felicity (Liccy) Dahl b 1938
Married Roald Dahl in 1983

Roald Dahl 1916–1990
Novelist, screenwriter and author of children's books

Michael Denison 1915–1998
Theatre and film actor

Roy Dotrice 1923–2017
Stage, television and film actor

Anthony Drewe
Writer of musicals with George Stiles

Janet Dunbar
Author of *J M Barrie: The Man behind the Image* (1970)

Peter Duncan b 1954
Actor, television presenter and director

Richard Edwards
Author of picture books and poetry for children, including *The Forest Child*

Tom Erhardt 1928–2019
American literary agent who worked in British theatre for fifty years

David Essex b 1947
Singer, songwriter and actor

Edith Evans 1888–1976
Stage and film actress

Ruby Evans
Actress. Played Sophie in a revival of *The BFG*

Sheila Falconer
Choreographer. Worked with DW on most Whirligig productions

Andrew Fell b 1957
Theatrical producer and manager

James Elroy Flecker 1884–1915
Novelist, playwright and poet, author of *Hassan, the Golden Journey to Samarkand*

Dexter Fletcher b 1966
Film director and actor. As a child, he appeared in *Abbacadabra*

Michael Foreman b 1938
Author and illustrator of children's books

Richard Fowler b 1944
Illustrator and author known for paper engineering

Jamila Gavin b 1941
Writer of children's books, including *Coram Boy*

John Gielgud 1904–2000
The production of *Ides of March* was based on Thornton Wilder's novel, with Gielgud as Caesar

Pearl Goodman 1920–2018
Actress, writer and artist. Worked with Joan Littlewood in the original Theatre Workshop

Dorothy Ann Gould
South African actress. Created the role of the Grand High Witch in *The Witches*

John Gould 1940-2012
Pianist, songwriter, composer and performer. DW's Whirligig co-producer

Tony Graham
Theatre director and former artistic director of the Unicorn

Claud Gurney 1897–1946
Writer and director. Taught FW

Kathleen Hale 1898–2000
Artist, illustrator and children's author known for the marmalade cat Orlando

Sheila Hancock b 1933
Actress

Aurand Harris 1915–1996
American teacher who became a leading children's playwright

Linda Hartzell
Theatre director associated with Seattle Children's Theatre

Tony Hatch b 1939
English composer for musical theatre, pop and television. Co-wrote *Rock Nativity* with DW

Jeanne Hepple b 1936
Actress

Eric Hill 1927–2014
Author and illustrator of children's books, including *Spot*

Seymour Hicks 1871–1949
Actor, playwright and producer

C. Walter Hodges 1909–2004
Artist, writer and illustrator of children's books

Peter Hollindale b 1936
Educationalist and literary critic

Ian Holm 1931–2020
Actor in stage, film and television

David Horlock 1942–1990
Director of the Redgrave Theatre, Farnham and Salisbury Playhouse before his untimely death in a road accident. Attended Chichester High School for Boys, as did DW

Tony Husband b 1950
Cartoonist, writer and illustrator. Co-creator with DW of *Save the Human*

Michael Ingham
Acting name of Peter Worrall Thompson

Barry Jackson 1879–1961
Theatre director and founder of the Birmingham Repertory Theatre

Derek Jacobi b 1938
Actor

Barbara Jefford 1930–2020
Stage and film actress

Terry Jones 1942–2020
Author, director and writer, member of the *Monty Python* team

Melody Kaye b 1952
Actor who was a founder member of Whirligig Theatre Company and also worked for Joan Littlewood and Ken Hill at Stratford East

Mike Kenny
Writer specialising in young people's theatre

Dick King-Smith 1922–2011
Author of over one hundred books for children

Jeremy Kingston
Theatre critic for *The Times*

John Kirkpatrick
Folk song and dance musician. Composed music for *Fantastic Mr Fox*

Olga Knipper 1868–1959
Actress who was married to Anton Chekhov

Bernard Kops b 1926
Dramatist, poet and novelist

Robert Lang 1934–2004
Actor

Charles Laughton 1899–1962
Stage and film actor

Dilys Laye 1934–2009
Actress. Played Grandmother in a revival of *The Witches*

Maureen Lipman b 1946
Film, TV and stage actress, and writer. Created the role of Meg in *Meg and Mog Show*

Julia Lockwood 1941–2019
Film, television and theatre actress

Margaret Lockwood 1916–1990
Stage and film actress

Cameron Mackintosh b 1946
Theatrical producer and theatre owner, particularly associated with musical theatre

Jean Sterling Mackinlay 1882–1958
Singer and actress married to Harcourt Williams. Proponent of theatre for children

Michelle Magorian b 1947
Actress and author of children's books, including *Goodnight Mister Tom*

John McCallum 1918–2010
Australian theatre and film actor

Hayley Mills b 1946
Actress

John Mortimer 1923–2009
Barrister, dramatist and author

Adrian Noble b 1950
Theatre director and ran the RSC from 1990 to 2003

Trevor Nunn b 1940
Director and Artistic Director of the RSC and the NT

Una O'Connor 1880–1959
Irish-American character actress

Laurence Olivier 1907–1989
Actor, theatre manager and director

Elaine Paige b 1943
Singer and actress best known for her work in musical theatre, starred in *Abbacadabra*

Chris Parr b 1943
Theatre director and television producer and executive. Attended Chichester High School for Boys, as did DW.

Philippa Pearce 1920–2006
Author of children's books, including *Tom's Midnight Garden*

Anthony Pedley b 1944
Actor especially known for playing the BFG

Barrington Pheloung 1954–2019
Australian composer who was based in the UK

Peter Pontzen b 1944
Musician, accompanist, composer and musical arranger/director. Long-time musical associate of DW

Eric Porter 1928–1995
Actor

Eric Potts b 1965
Actor, writer and director and noted pantomime Dame. Also created the role of Big Ears in *Noddy*

Philip Pullman b 1946
Author of books for adults and young people

Simon Rattle b 1955
Conductor and music director

Michael Redgrave 1908–1985
Actor, director and author. DW played his son in *A Voyage Round My Father*

Ralph Richardson 1902–1983
Actor

Christopher Ricks b 1933
Literary critic and scholar, and was Professor of Poetry at Oxford from 2004 to 2009. DW's tutor at Worcester College

Patricia Routledge b 1929
Actress and singer

Jenna Russell b 1967
Actress and singer. As a young actress, played in *Abbacadabra*

Jeremy Sams b 1957
Director, writer and composer

Dorothy L. Sayers 1893–1957
Crime writer and poet

Bob Scott b 1944
Actor and businessman. At Oxford with DW. Co-director of WSG Productions, of which Whirligig Theatre was a part

Janette Scott b 1938
Actress

Aubrey de Sélincourt 1894–1962
Writer, classical scholar and teacher

Lesley de Sélincourt b 1925
First cousin and later wife of Christopher Robin Milne

Michael Seraphim b 1958
Actor. Played in many DW productions, including *Meg and Mog Show* and *The See-Saw Tree*

Barry Sheppard 1939–2022
Theatre manager associated with Oxford Playhouse and Whirligig

Ned Sherrin 1931–2007
Broadcaster, author and stage director

Donald Sinden 1923–2014
Actor

Adam Stafford
Actor and director. Played many roles for Whirligig. Created the role of Bruno in *The Witches*

Jacqueline (Jacqui) Stanbury b 1948
Actress who has been married to David Wood since 1975

Antoinette Sterling 1841–1904
American contralto associated with sentimental ballads

George Stiles
Writer of musicals with Anthony Drewe

Dale Superville
Actor who created the role of Spot in *Spot's Birthday Party*

Rosemary Sutcliff 1920–1992
Novelist known for her children's historical fiction

Lowell Swortzell 1930–2004
American playwright and academic, authority on children's theatre

Tatiana Tarasova b 1947
Russian figure-skating coach who launched the Russian All-Stars ice ballet

Richard Tate b 1943
Actor. Created the role of the Lighthouse Keeper in *The Lighthouse Keeper's Lunch*

Ellen Terry 1847–1928
Actress

John Thaw 1942–2002
Actor

Sybil Thorndike 1882–1976
Actress

Margaret Tyzack 1931–2011
Actress

Irving Wardle 1929–2023
Writer and theatre critic for *The Times* and the *Independent on Sunday*

Ruby Wax b 1953
Actress and mental health campaigner. Played the Grand High Witch in a revival of *The Witches*

Andrew Lloyd Webber b 1948
Composer and impresario of musical theatre

Timothy West b 1934
Film, stage and TV actor

Rex Whistler 1905–1944
Painter, designer and illustrator

Janet Whiteside 1932–2015
Actress. Created the role of the Grandmother in *The Witches*

John Wiles 1925–1999
South African novelist, television writer and producer, who also wrote plays for young people, which were performed at the Cockpit in London

Harcourt Williams 1880–1957
Actor and director, also Director of the Old Vic from 1929 to 1934, where he included Gielgud and Richardson in the company

Judy Wilson 1938–2006
Actress. Created the role of Mrs Hogget in *Babe, the Sheep-Pig*

Susan Wooldridge b 1950
Actress

Gerard Young 1938–1972
Sussex-based journalist and historian

Picture Credits

All images are from the author's personal collection, unless otherwise indicated.

1, 2   Mary Wright

6, 7, 8, 9   [Box WWII 111/Folder 1-4], Ralph W. Kerns Second World War photograph scrapbooks and correspondence (2016.118.w.r), Center for American War Letters Archives, Chapman University, CA.

12, 13, 14, 17, 18   © Donald Cooper/photostage

15b   © Laurence Burns/ArenaPAL

16, 19, 20   © Dee Conway/Bridgeman Images

21   Photo on front cover of *Theatre for Children*: © Alan Wood

22   © Sarah Ainslie

23   © Robert Day